TANTRIC KNOWLEDGE

THE OXFORD CENTRE FOR HINDU STUDIES
MANDALA PUBLISHING SERIES

The Oxford Centre for Hindu Studies Mandala Publishing Series offers authoritative yet accessible introductions to a wide range of subjects in Hindu Studies. Each book in the series aims to present its subject matter in a form that is engaging and readily comprehensible to persons of all backgrounds – academic or otherwise – without compromising scholarly rigor. The series thus bridges the divide between academic and popular writing by preserving and utilising the best elements of both.

TANTRIC KNOWLEDGE

Philosophy, History, Practice

Gavin Flood

MANDALA
San Rafael Los Angeles London

For my friends at the Oxford Centre for Hindu Studies.

CONTENTS

List of Illustrations

Diagrams

Figures

Preface and Acknowledgments

Tantra has become a notorious topic associated in the popular imagination with improving your love life, mostly in the North Atlantic, or with sensational magic and nefarious goings on, as we see in Bollywood movies. Both of these representations have a tenuous link with the historical reality of Tantra, its long history and traditions of practice and belief. This book is intended as a general introduction to the history of Tantric traditions: what it is, where it fits into the history of South Asia and beyond, what its links are to Hinduism and Buddhism, and how contemporary Tantra transforms the older tradition. The book is entitled *Tantric Knowledge* because Tantric traditions claim to possess knowledge about the nature of the universe, the nature of ourselves as human beings, and how we fit into the wider cosmos around us; Tantric knowledge is what the texts and traditions profess. The study of these traditions raises interesting questions of both historical and existential importance. What is the origin of Tantric traditions? Who composed the Tantras and why? Are these traditions of historical interest only or do they have anything relevant to tell us today? In this book, we will address these questions, although the application of Tantric knowledge to contemporary concerns will not be our main focus. The problems of yesteryear are not those of today, although some might argue that the Tantras provide resources for solutions to contemporary problems.

The overall structure of the book is a straightforward narrative. We begin with the wider religious, social, and political context of India, looking at the kinds of texts, traditions, practices, and ideas that the Tantric literature assumes. The Tantras themselves are texts composed in Sanskrit from around the seventh century CE (although parts of the earliest Tantra may go back to the fifth) which have their own account of how they came about from a divine source. We will also offer some highly speculative thoughts or hypotheses about the origins of some themes in Tantric traditions. We will begin quite simply with an account of the central spine of the Tantric tradition focused on the god Śiva, the Śaiva Siddhānta, that came to dominance in the medieval period, and which provides the core ideas about cosmology, Tantric categories, and ritual practices. We then go on to see how antinomian traditions respond to this central tradition. We will step sideways to see how the religion of Viṣṇu adapted Tantric ideas and practices, examine the philosophies of Tantra, and finally see how Tantrism spread worldwide and has developed into the global phenomenon of Neo-Tantra.

Tantric Knowledge is essentially a descriptive book in which I present the self-representation of the Tantras – what they say about themselves – and let the texts speak through quotation. I restrict my account to 'Hindu' Tantric traditions although I do refer at times to Buddhist Tantra. The rationale for this is that, firstly, our evidence to date shows that the earliest Tantras were composed within a Śaiva milieu and, secondly, the development of Buddhist Tantra cannot be adequately dealt with in a book such as this. Buddhist Tantra integrates Tantric philosophy and practice into the Mahāyāna, becoming the Vajrayāna, and forming the core tradition of Tibetan Buddhism that has strong contemporary, institutional life. But readers who are knowledgeable about the Vajrayāna will recognise elements of its philosophy, practice, and deities in these pages. I placed the term 'Hindu' in inverted commas above because this word is of more recent origin and was not known when the early Tantras were composed, although it does identify texts that share a common worldview about the nature of the cosmos and human life within it. Unless otherwise stated I am responsible for probably about half of the translations, most of which come from untranslated (although mostly published) sources. Although I have given references in the apparatus, I have not cited the Sanskrit texts themselves, for which those interested will need to dig out the texts from elsewhere. I have made reference to secondary sources but not exhaustively. Our knowledge about the Tantric traditions has been transformed in the last thirty years by the ground-breaking work of Alexis Sanderson and his students, to which the following will make ample reference, and which I would encourage the interested reader to follow up, as well as by the work of Professor Diwakar Acharya at Oxford and Professor Harunaga Isaacson in Hamburg (on Buddhist Tantrism). I have followed Sanderson's mapping of the traditions in the pages to come.

I would like to express gratitude to my friend and colleague Dr. Lucian Wong for his encouragement in writing this book and for guiding it to production. I would also like to express thanks to other friends and colleagues at the Oxford Centre for Hindu Studies, Dr. Bjarne Wernicke-Olesen, Dr. Rembert Lutjeharms, Dr. Jessica Frazier, Shaunaka Rishi Das, and Tanja Jakobsen for their conversation on topics Tantric and for their encouragement in producing this book, along with Lal Krishna for organising the Continuing Education course on which the book is based and Surabhi Acharya for her administration. I would like to thank my friend and colleague Professor Alexis Sanderson who has provided a model of scholarship to aspire to; his work has shaped our understanding of Tantrism and he has re-written the history of religion in medieval India more widely. Without his research, a work of synthesis such as this could not have been undertaken. I would also like to offer thanks to Prema Goet for conversation about these topics, to the anonymous readers whose recommendations I have adopted, to Professor Jim Mallinson and Dr. Christopher Wallis for their careful reading of the text, and to Dr. Valters Negribs and Steve Turrington for their excellent comments on the script.

Introduction: Remarks on Meaning and History

Tantra has been notorious in the history of Indian religions and in its global, Western form is virtually identical with methods of enhancing one's love life. This identification of Tantra with sex is partly true in its historical origin in ancient India, but only partly. If we can make a distinction between Tantra and Neo-Tantra, where Tantra refers to the historical tradition as it arose in the early medieval period and which has Hindu, Buddhist, and Jain expression, and Neo-Tantra which refers to the modern identification of Tantra with a form of sex, then this book is about the former. We will explore the development of Tantric knowledge as it arose within the history of Indian religions, looking at its central features, its claims, and its practices. We will see how Tantra must be seen within the history of Indian religions if we wish to seriously understand it and how it changed in new cultural contexts – as we see today with Neo-Tantra, which is a transformation (and some would say distortion) of the ancient tradition, mostly through the medium of English and other European languages.

The purpose of this book is not to make claims about the value of Tantric knowledge nor its truth, although I will touch upon philosophical issues, but to present a historically and textually accurate account of its main developments, practices, and philosophies. It is then, essentially a book of historical description rather than philosophical evaluation. It assumes that the truth of traditions needs to be seen in the *longue durée* and that although as scholars we are always writing within the horizon of our age, this presentation nonetheless aims at being an accurate historical narrative. We will begin in this introduction with a brief reflection on what Tantra is, as we need some pre-understanding of what it is we are chasing after, and secondly, we will present a brief sketch of its history as I see it. Much of what follows may be open to alternative ways of reading the material, but this is my way, and I will support it with textual and other evidence. The reader, however, should not be alarmed as the book is intended to be easily read and will not present a heavy-duty apparatus supporting all its claims. Nevertheless, I will present sufficient textual support for the main points I wish to make about the meaning and history of Tantra, and I intend to alert the reader at times when my interpretation of the religion is speculative.

What is Tantra?

A good place to begin is the word itself. Tantra comes from the Sanskrit verbal root *tan*, which means 'to extend', 'to stretch', and 'to weave'. The noun can refer to the stretching of a loom or the warp threads of a loom. By extension it comes to mean a general conceptual framework as well as a text written on birch bark or palm leaf pages strung together with a thread. In this sense of 'the thread that strings a document together' it is akin to *sūtra*, an aphorism, related to the English word 'suture'. Not all Tantric texts are called Tantra, many are called Āgama or Saṃhitā, and sometimes '*tantra*' refers to non-Tantric texts such as the animal stories of the *Pañcatantra*, so it can simply mean 'book'. But the vast body of texts known as Tantra designate what was believed to be a new revelation, superseding the Veda. Thus, we can speak of followers of the Veda – the traditional ancient scriptures of Hinduism – known as the Vaidikas, and followers of the Tantras, known as the Tāntrikas. The followers of the Veda were the Brahmins, the highest caste, who maintained (and still do) Vedic ritual purity rules, and who were keen to maintain the social status quo. The Tāntrikas followed the teachings of the Tantras, some of which radically advocated going against Vedic ritual purity in order to gain an enlightenment that transcended the old rules. But not all Tāntrikas were rebels. Much of Tantra is mainstream, Brahmanical religion; today in Kerala a Tantri is simply a Nambudiri Brahmin priest who installs images in temples: a very traditional role. Beyond its complicated history in Hinduism, tantrism was adopted by Buddhism, and particularly Tibetan Buddhism, and also by Jainism.

But what then is Tantra? It is not enough simply to say that it is a type of text and tradition that developed within Indian religions, we need to specify something of the kind of thing it is.[1] On the one hand there has been a tendency to vilify Tantra, that it is crude or primitive magic or nefarious immorality, as we see in many nineteenth-century scholars such as Monier Monier-Williams, the Boden Professor of Sanskrit at Oxford, who thought the Tantras to contain 'the worst superstitious ideas that have ever disgraced and degraded the human race',[2] while on the other hand there is a tendency to romanticise

1 André Padoux has an excellent discussion of the terms '*tantra*' and '*tantrism*' along with the history of their use. See *The Hindu Tantric World: An Overview* (Chicago: University of Chicago Press, 2017), 4–17.

2 Monier Monier-Williams, *Hinduism* (London: Society for the Promotion of Christian Knowledge, 1880), 129, cited in my *The Tantric Body* (London: Tauris Press, 2006), 3. For references to other similarly negative statements, see Hugh B. Urban, *The Power of Tantra: Religion, Sexuality and the Politics of South Asian Studies* (London: Tauris Press, 2010), 7.

Tantra, as we see with some modern teachers such as Osho (a.k.a. Bhagwan Shree Rajneesh) who claims that Tantra is not an intellectual proposition but an experience[3] and other Tantric groups that claim that the essence of Tantra is enhancing sexual pleasure.[4] These two tendencies have militated against a more balanced study of Tantra, promoting either a rationalisation that sees Tantra in terms of corruption or an anti-intellectualism that sees Tantra as transcending reason and thought. While it is true that many Tantric traditions are interested in 'experience' of the teachings, it is not the case that these traditions have been anti-intellectual or anti-reason, as we see in the robust philosophical discussions between Śaiva nondualists, dualists, and Buddhists. Perhaps one approach at the beginning in response to the question 'what is Tantra?' would be to ask practitioners themselves. Hugh Urban did this and among the answers he received from two priests at the very important Tantric goddess shrine in Assam, the Kāmākhya temple, were that Tantra is essentially *mantra*, the power of sacred sound, while a second priest claimed it to be the body (*tan*) and mind (*man*) together in a spiritual practice.[5]

These responses to Urban are interesting because they emphasise the importance of practice when we discuss Tantra. Tantra is concerned with the repetition of *mantras*, with the production and use of ritual diagrams (*yantra*, *maṇḍala*), with daily ritual, and with *yoga* that emphasises the body. While some Tantric traditions were transgressive in their advocacy of caste-free sexual congress for a spiritual end, most were focused on practices that are not that far from the orthodox Brahmanical

3 Bhagwan Shree Rajneesh, *The Book of the Secrets 1: Discourses on the Vigyan Bhairav Tantra* (Poona: Rejneesh Foundation, 1974), 3–4.

4 Urban, *The Power of Tantra*, 6.

5 Ibid., 5.

world, such as the repetition of *mantras*, visualisation, and making offerings into the sacred fire. David White has argued that the original forms of Tantra were transgressive, in particular the production of sexual fluids to offer to ferocious deities,[6] and that this 'hard-core' Tantrism became stripped of transgression and adapted to more mainstream traditions.

We will visit these debates later in the book, but it is important for the reader to be aware of these issues, especially as what we can call Neo-Tantra, which identifies Tantra with enhanced sexual practice, has such dominance in global modernity. Neo-Tantra is focused not so much on salvation as the enhancement of bodily, sexual experience and the developing of Tantric *yoga* focused on a subtle body system and centres of power in the body called 'wheels' or 'circles' (*cakra*). Indeed, 'chakra', like 'yoga', 'karma', and 'nirvana', has become an English word. In identifying Tantra with the enhancement of somatic pleasure, Neo-Tantra identifies and elides the tradition with that of *kāma*, the pursuit of pleasure as an end in itself that we find in Kāma literature such as the *Kāma Sūtra*. In this literature, *kāma* is a legitimate goal of life for the householder, as we will see, but is concerned with pleasure and not with salvation. Traditional Tantra, on the other hand, has not been concerned with pleasure for its own sake but with salvation – liberation (*mokṣa*) and power (*siddhi*). These are distinct from the traditional goals of life (*puruṣārtha*) of the Brahmin householder of duty (*dharma*), wealth or success (*artha*), and pleasure (*kāma*), so from a traditional perspective, it could be argued that Neo-Tantra is a 'mispractice', in eliding *tantra* with *kāma*, for its traditional goal is not pleasure but salvation and power.

6 David Gordon White, *The Kiss of the Yoginī: Sex in its South Asian Contexts* (Chicago: Chicago University Press, 2003), 17.

It is worth saying at this stage that the earliest Tantra we currently possess, the *Niḥśvāsatattva Saṃhitā*, contains no transgression, although this does not necessarily mean that there were not transgressive, orgiastic practices taking place that were not recorded but which infiltrate into mainstream Tantric tradition at a later date. The 'Tantric orgy' or *melaka*, for example, is a form of collective worship involving group sex that has no earlier literary precedent, as Alexis Sanderson observes.[7] Perhaps this collective worship is coming from tribal regions, although there is no explicit evidence, but it may suggest much older forms of shamanistic religion focused on fertility and sacrifice, although such a view must remain speculative.

While it might not be possible or desirable to come up with a precise definition of Tantra as a system of belief and practice, there are prototypical features that we can identify, some of which are not exclusive to Tantra, but which nevertheless are of central importance. I think we can identify the following four features as prototypical of Tantric traditions.

1. Tantra entails initiation (*dīkṣā*), that is the transmission of tradition, or specifically of the *mantra* or set of *mantras*, from teacher to student and is a pattern that ensures the salvation of the disciple. Initiation is a necessary condition for liberation. Part of the success of Tantric religion is that it guarantees success through the *mantra* or *mantras* conveyed at initiation. While initiation into the adult community is important for Brahmanical tradition, with Tantra, initiation comes to be the guarantor of salvation; through initi-

7 Alexis Sanderson, 'The Śaiva Exegesis of Kashmir', in *Mélanges tantriques à la mémoire d'Hélène Brunner / Tantric Studies in Memory of Hélène Brunner*, Collection Indologie 106, ed. D. Goodall and A. Padoux, 231–444 (Pondicherry: IFI / EFEO, 2007), 282.

ation the teacher can take on the sins of the disciple who will be liberated at death or within a specified chain of reincarnations in which he uses up remaining karmic residues (the *Mālinī-vijayottara Tantra* claims liberation is achieved within seven lifetimes following initiation). Initiation shows the centrality of the transmission of tradition through a lineage of masters or gurus, an idea common to Tantric traditions. Correct transmission is essential to preserve the authenticity and truth of Tantric religion and essential for the success of attaining liberation and power.

2. Tantra is characterised by a shared ritual process in which there is symbolic identification with a deity and the identification of the cosmos with the body. This ritual process follows a pattern of (a) the purification of the physical body through the symbolic destruction of its elements (*bhūta-śuddhi*); (b) the creation of a divine body through imposing *mantras* upon it (*nyāsa*), for only a god can worship a god; (c) inner or mental worship (*antara/mānasa-yāga*) which is visualisation of the deity within or brought into the body; and (d) outer worship (*bāhya-yāga*) which is making offerings to the god in an external image or diagram. This is a common pattern of ritual shared by Tantric traditions. It could be argued that this ritual pattern is in fact definitional of Tantra, for even transgressive practices are usually set within it. A further element that could be classified within outer worship is making offerings into the sacred fire, which thereby aligns Tantric religion with the Vedic.

3. Tantric worship entails the use of *mantra*, or sound-formulas, that are understood as the sound-body of the deity used with the purpose of attaining liberation,

power, or bringing about a specific outcome such as curing a child of sickness. Orthodox Brahmanism uses *mantras* too – such as the famous Gāyatrī – but Tantric *mantras* are characterised as containing 'seeds' (*bījas*) of a single syllable, in themselves meaningless, such as *huṃ*, or *phaṭ*. It also entails the use of ritual diagrams (*yantra, maṇḍala*) that are integral to external worship. Behind this is a whole hierarchical cosmology that we shall examine in later chapters.

4. Tantra involves sacrifice. The ritual slaughter of animals – goats, cows, and even wild animals – is prescribed in Tantric texts. It is arguably the case that sacrifice was the central, external ritual tradition of the medieval Tantric kingdoms that ended with their demise and with the rise of the Delhi Sultanate, and later the Mughal then British empires. This tradition of sacrifice to the Goddess in one of her forms survived in the Tantric kingdom of Nepal and in places on the margins of central India that still retain an echo of this older form of religion, in Kerala and Bali. The relationship between Vedic and Tantric sacrifice is not clear, but both kinds of sacrifice were practised in the medieval kingdoms.

Arguably then, if not definitional, these four features of (1) initiation, (2) shared ritual pattern, (3) use of *mantras, yantras,* and *maṇḍalas*, and (4) sacrifice are prototypical features of Tantra and show how Tantra is mostly about practice rather than theology or philosophy.

A Sketch of the History of Tantra

The earliest Tantric texts can be dated to around the seventh century CE, although elements within the *Niḥśvāsa-tattva*

Saṃhitā, as I said above, may go back to the fifth. This is very old indeed. Tantric religion emerged within Brahmanical traditions that we retrospectively name 'Hindu', although we need to be very aware that that term was not in use in the early period. Nevertheless, it is a useful shorthand to distinguish the form of religion that claims the Veda is its revelation from other kinds of religion, notably the *śramaṇa* traditions of Buddhism and Jainism that possibly, or even probably, have an origin outside of the Vedic realm (as Bronkhorst has argued).[8] Tantra arose within the non-*śramaṇa* tradition but came to impact upon those traditions that quickly and easily adopted it; there are strong textual arguments for this, as we will see.

However, I want to begin with two speculative but arguably valid hypotheses. The first is that sacrifice was the central ritual act of the state-supported religion of the medieval kingdoms; the second is that the transgressive, sexual dimension of Tantra – that became known as 'left-hand' Tantra – originated in non-literate, shamanic practices that are rooted in the deep, prehistoric past. Let us look at both hypotheses in turn.

The fact that sacrificial religion is still strongly present in some areas of South and Southeast Asia, especially Nepal, Kerala, and Bali, suggests that these regions preserve an earlier form of religion or are a remnant of a pan-South Asian form of religion centred on sacrifice. Tantric religion in the medieval period, by which I mean the post-Gupta era after about 620 CE, was supported by royalty and became the main, state religion until the thirteenth century. During this time, sacrifice – the immolation of animals – was arguably the central, state-supported ritual practice, so we might even speculate that vegetarian ritual offering (*pūjā*) is modelled on blood

8 See Johannes Bronkhorst, *Greater Magadha: Studies in the Culture of Early India* (Leiden: Brill, 2007).

offerings (*yajña/bali*). This is supported by the fact that the kings of Nepal, with a link to the Tantric Goddess Taleju, practised sacrifice throughout the history of the Mallas, as we will see. Sacrifice provides the central image in the Hindu imaginaire from an early period, being found within the *Mahābhārata* where the internecine war is regarded as a sacrifice, and especially in the *Bhagavad-gītā* which is deeply concerned with the sacrifice/renunciation dynamic. Here gods and humans owe life to sacrifice, and the gods give pleasure nourished by sacrifice (3.9–13). We also have the proximity of renunciation to sacrifice, in the sense that renunciation and asceticism are the internalisation of sacrifice and the denial of death, or symbolic control of death.[9] Sacrifice is the central ritual practice for worshipping the Goddess. Durgā and her forms in Nepal are still offered sacrifice and have been throughout her history, as is the Goddess in the Kāmākhya temple in Assam, the most important Tantric pilgrimage site. In the *teyyam* dance possession rites of Kerala each performance culminates with a sacrifice, and we might speculate that the name of Bali might be from *bali*, blood offering. Thus, we have the Tantric affirmation of sacrifice in Nepal where Tantra was a state supported religion until recent times and blood sacrifice relegated to the margins of Brahmanical influence in Kerala and Bali.

With the demise of the Indian Tantric kingdoms in the thirteenth century, Tantra becomes more esoteric, concerned with the correspondences between the macrocosm and the microcosm, and the external religion becomes more internalised with meditative or yogic practice among renouncer traditions. The centrality of sacrifice to state religion is also supported by the concern of Tantra to transcend death, understood perhaps

9 On this theme, see Gavin Flood, *Religion and the Philosophy of Life* (Oxford: Oxford University Press, 2019), 139–140.

Figure 0.1. The Kāmākhya temple in Assam during Durgā Pūjā festivities.

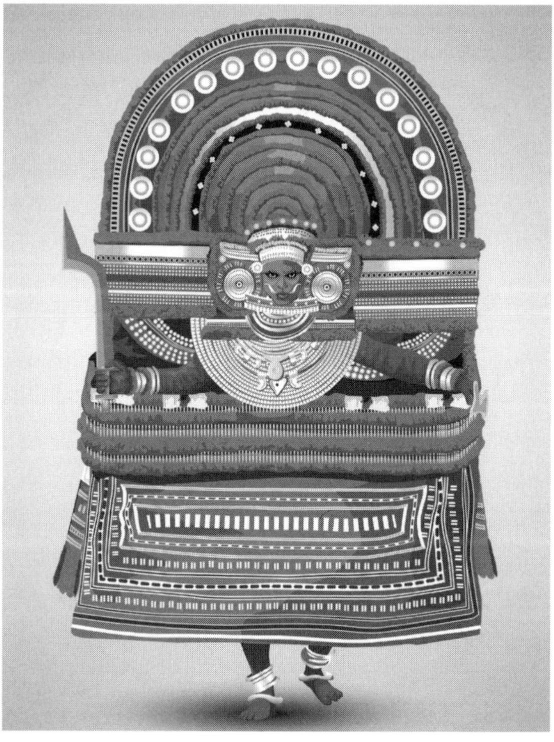

Figure 0.2. A teyyam *dancer.*

literally as cultivating the nectar of immortality within the body (as later *haṭha-yoga* taught), or as achieving immortality through a subtle body that transcends the physical.[10] There is a correspondence between literal sacrifice and the transcending of death and repeated dying through Tantric practice.

The second speculative hypothesis I would like to propose is that the symbolism of Tantra, as well as some of the practices focused on the body, may derive from ancient roots. In what came to be called Shamanism, the main form of religion across northern Eurasia possibly for millennia, one of the main concerns was healing the sick, healing the present through connecting with the ancestors, and transcending death. The shaman would enter a trance state and there are suggestive parallels between the shaman's journey to the other world and the Yogi's journey up through the body. The sexual orgy of Tantrism could come from this ancient tradition that celebrates the proliferation of life through sexual union, which is linked to the transcendence of death – symbolised, for example, by drinking out of skull bowls.[11] This must remain speculative, although Sanderson has speculated that the *melaka* may have tribal origins, although there is no evidence for this. There are then elements of Tantra that could be very ancient:

---

10 For Danish readers, see Bjarne Wernicke-Olsen and Silje Lyngar Einarsen, eds., *Hovedvaeket om Haṭhayoga Svātmarāmas Haṭhapradīpikā* (Holberg: Narayana Press, 2022).

11 Some of these links were observed by Mircea Eliade. See his *Shamanism: Archaic Techniques of Ecstasy*, trans. Willard. R. Trask (Princeton: Princeton University Press, 1964), 234–235. On prehistoric drinking from skulls, see Weston La Barre, *The Ghost Dance: Origins of Religion* (London: Allen and Unwin, 1972), 404–406, and references in Eliade, *Shamanism*, 234, note 29. Also see Andrea Acri and Paolo E. Rosati (eds.), *Tantra, Magic, and Vernacular Religions in Monsoon Asia* (London: Routledge, 2023).

Figure 0.3. A modern day Aghori practitioner in the Kāmākhya Temple in Assam.

sacrifice, the symbolism of death, especially worship with skulls as in modern day Aghori practice,[12] and the transcendence of death. This cluster of symbols and practices may also have involved deities with animal heads or theriomorphic deities, especially goddesses called Yoginīs, such as we find in Śākta Tantric texts.[13] But let us move from the speculative to the more certain, for which we have textual evidence.

12 Prema Goet, *Against the Grain* (London: Utkranti Press, n.d.).

13 For further reflection on this that brings in the anthropology of cultures, see Geoffrey Samuels, *The Origins of Yoga and Tantra: Indic Religions to the Thirteenth Century* (Cambridge: Cambridge University Press, 2008), 229–235.

As stated previously, the earliest Tantra to date is the *Niḥśvāsa-tattva Saṃhitā* (mostly seventh century CE) that we will examine more closely in Chapter 3, although there were precursors to the Tantric tradition in ascetic groups and the tradition was already developing before the earliest textual evidence. I will simply sketch a general picture at this stage of the history, without textual backup, that will be documented in the coming chapters. During the first millennium around the seventh century CE the religious picture of India is something as follows:

1. There is a strong Vedic tradition of ritual sacrifice of the Śrauta Brahmins whose tradition is derived from *śruti*, Vedic revelation, along with its philosophical justification in the school of Vedic exegesis or Mīmāṃsā, which defended sacrifice against Buddhist objectors. This tradition is supported by kings in varying degrees throughout the period down to the demise of the Hindu kingdoms in the north with the rise of the Delhi Sultanate.

2. There is Brahmanical, theistic worship of different deities as reflected in the 'ancient texts' or Purāṇas, and in the epic literature, the *Mahābhārata* and *Rāmāyaṇa*. These bear witness to the rise of theism in India, as does the *Bhagavad-gītā* and, following it, the *Śvetāśvatara Upaniṣad*.[14] In particular we see the rise of the gods Viṣṇu and his 'incarnation' (*avatāra*) Kṛṣṇa, Śiva, and the Goddess (Devī). These theistic traditions were articulated by the Smārta Brahmins who derived their tradition from the *smṛti*, the secondary

14 I document the development of Hindu monotheism in *Hindu Monotheism* (Cambridge: Cambridge University Press, 2020), 15–32.

revelation (which included the law books, the epics, and the Purāṇas). These theistic traditions often emphasised devotion (*bhakti*).

3. Apart from the Mīmāṃsā there are the philosophical schools of Vedānta (the tradition that begins with the end of the Veda) or Uttara Mīmāṃsā (the later exegesis); Sāṃkhya, the dualist tradition, and Yoga.

4. During the early first millennium we have the religion of Śiva emerging articulated in ascetic groups called the 'higher' or 'outer' path (*ati-mārga*) that claimed to transcend the Vedic revelation, and the path of *mantra* (*mantra-mārga*). The key ascetic sect of the Ati Mārga worships Śiva and is known as the Pāśupata. Tantra is the Mantra Mārga in its earliest period as we will see. The schools of philosophy known as Vaiśeṣika (atomist school) and Nyāya (school of logic) might be linked with or coming out of the early Śaiva Pāśupata sect. The textual origins of Tantra are in the worship of Śiva found in the Mantra Mārga and the worship of the Goddess in the Kula Mārga.

5. Buddhist impersonalism is intellectually and culturally important too and the theistic traditions react against it; Buddhism in turn responds to the success of the Śaiva traditions. The other heterodox tradition is Jainism, which adopted Tantric religion and produced its own Tantras.

In presenting a list in this way I am attempting to simplify a complex picture, but a simplification that is nevertheless accurate. Many of these traditions vied with each other for royal patronage and we know that kings and queens supported several different traditions. Buddhism adopted and adapted the Śaiva Tantric model in its more esoteric forms, and later postural yoga (*haṭha-yoga*) in turn seems to have originated in Buddhism during the eleventh century, as Mallinson shows.[15]

By the thirteenth century the Tantric kingdoms except for Nepal have declined and there has been the rise of devotion focused on Viṣṇu and his forms, particularly Kṛṣṇa. On the eve of modernity around the sixteenth century, we therefore have a picture of Muslim rule in the north, the development of new ways of thinking about God, the human person, and reason – especially in Bengal – with the remaining Hindu kingdoms in the South. Tantra has gone underground in Bengal, in the sense that it is no longer supported by the state and exists in the context of the rise of devotion (*bhakti*) to Viṣṇu (as we find in the religion begun by Caitanya (1486–1533)). An older contemporary of Caitanya in the Panjab, Guru Nānak (1469–1530), within the Sant tradition, is also advocating devotion, but to a formless (*nir-guṇa*) deity and founding a community that was to develop into Sikhism. Tantra in the south becomes orthodox with the Śrī Vidyā tradition of the Smārta Brahmins, associated with the Śaṅkara monastic orders, and in Kerala becomes orthodox, Nambudiri Brahmanism. Tantrism travels to Southeast Asia – the Khmer kingdom supports Tantric Śaivism – and it goes further south to Java and Bali. Buddhism by the thirteenth century has disappeared from India but flourishes in Tibet where Tantric Buddhism or the Vajrayāna becomes the main, state religion. By the nineteenth century Tantra has become divorced from its state association. In Kerala it is simply normative Hinduism; it begins to be translated into the West

15 James Mallinson and Péter-Daniel Szántó, *The Amṛtasiddhi and Amṛtasiddhimūla: The Earliest Texts of the Haṭhayoga Tradition* (Pondichéry: Institut Français de Pondichéry, 2021).

in the late nineteenth and early twentieth century. Sir John Woodroffe (also known as Arthur Avalon) is instrumental in its transference to the West through his translation work and scholarship. Tantra also resonates with the Theosophical Society and, moving forward through interesting mediations such as Alistair Crowley, to the 1960s, begins to influence culture in Europe and America through gurus such as Rajneesh and later Western gurus up to the present day. We can call this new development Neo-Tantra in order to differentiate it from its older origins. It is within this general outline that we need to locate Tantra, beginning with its Brahmanical context.

I
The Tantric Revelation in Context

The Tantras did not develop in a vacuum, but within the history of Indian religions and with other textual genres composed in Sanskrit during the first millennium CE. The Tantric textual corpus is vast. The Tantras claim to be revelation from a divine source and so are akin to the claims made about the Veda. In this first chapter we need to present the general background within which Tantric literature arose and to which it responded and quoted from.

The Vedic Revelation

The earliest religious poetry in India is a large group of texts collectively known as the Veda. These texts are revered by the Hindu tradition as revelation, or that which has been heard (*śruti*) by the ancient sages, the *ṛṣis*, and passed to the human community. These texts, the oldest of which is the *Ṛg Veda*, are hymns to a variety of deities, mostly gods of natural forces, who live at three levels of the cosmos, in the sky, in the atmosphere, and on the earth. The origin of many Hindu deities such as Viṣṇu and Śiva (as Rudra) can be traced back to here. The Veda is also about ritual sacrifice and the symbolic meaning of sacrifice. Later texts, the Upaniṣads, were more metaphysical, emphasising the knowledge of an absolute reality (Brahman) in order to escape from the never-ending cycle of reincarnation (*saṃsāra*). But later texts still, such as the *Bhagavad-gītā*, stressed devotion (*bhakti*) to a transcendent God. The priestly class, the Brahmins, were the maintainers of this tradition and remain so today. It was passed down from teacher to student, the texts being learned by heart by countless generations. The Nambudiri Brahmins of Kerala still maintain these traditions of Vedic learning. These Brahmins who followed the Vedic revelation (*śruti*) were known as Śrautas.

So, by the time of the early medieval period, after the Gupta empire around 600 CE, the tradition of Brahmanical learning was flourishing, with the different schools of philosophy emerging and clarifying their doctrines against each other. There were traditions of law (*dharma*) that defined the good Brahmin's duties and obligations, such as the *Laws of Manu* (*Manu Smṛti*); these were regarded not as revelation but as

Figure 1.1. Nambudiri Brahmins in modern-day Kerala performing a śrauta *ritual.*

having inspired, human authorship and were thus classified as 'those scriptures that are remembered' (*smṛti*). Because of this we might refer to this literature more accurately as a secondary revelation. At this time, following from the *Bhagavad-gītā* and *Śvetāśvatara Upaniṣad*, we see the development of theism, the belief in a single God of whom all the others are aspects or manifestations. This theism developed in the great epics the *Mahābhārata* and *Rāmāyaṇa*, as well as in the large body of texts called Purāṇas, the ancient scriptures, that contain stories of the gods, and stories of the kings and their dynasties. By the early years of the present millennium, many people were tired of the Veda and were keen to develop more demagogic sources of knowledge. So, while the Vedic scriptures are the primary source material for ancient Hinduism,[1] there are other important scriptures within the *smṛti* category, particularly the law books, but also the 'ancient narratives' called the Purāṇas (the epics too are part of the *smṛti* classification).

---

1 The term 'Hinduism' is, of course, of recent origin; I use it simply as a shorthand to denote a range of traditions rooted in the Veda which distinguished themselves from Buddhism, Jainism, and the Materialists. The Persian word 'Hindu', denoting those who live around the Indus, is quite late, appearing as a self-designation in Kashmir in the fifteenth century where the Sanskritised *hindukaḥ* is used by the historian Śrīvara, as Sanderson shows, and in Bengal in the sixteenth century, denoting those who were not 'Yavanas' or Muslims. In these regions the term probably refers to people who shared common cultural practices such as marriage customs and cremation of the dead. See Alexis Sanderson, 'Tolerance, Exclusivity, Inclusivity, and Persecution in Indian Religion during the Early Mediaeval Period', in *Honoris Causa: Essays in Honour of Aveek Sarkar*, ed. John Makinson, 155–224 (London: Allen Lane, 2015), 156, note 2. For the use of the term in Bengal, see Joseph O'Connell and Rembert Lutjeharms, *Caitanya Vaiṣṇavism in Bengal: Social Impact and Historical Implications* (London: Routledge, 2018).

Legal Discourse

The treatises about law, the Dharmaśāstra, are of great importance for the formation of Brahmin identity and instructing the Brahmin community in how to behave. One of the earliest of the law books is the *Law Code of Manu* (*Manu Smṛti*), composed between the second century BCE and the second century CE, which, along with the *Yājñavalkya Smṛti*, are foundational to legal discourse and have many commentaries on them.[2] However, these texts – and others in the tradition – are not simply law books, but contain a wealth of information about Brahmanical practice, about how to live, what to do, what rituals to perform, about the stages of life, and the structure of society. They contain details of purity rules and expiation rites for the omission of rituals that should have been done. The morally upright Brahmin is one who performs his correct ritual duties and adheres to the Vedic worldview. We might even see the law books as the antithesis of the more extreme Tantric practices because of their concern with ritual purity, even though they directly influenced the later Tantric tradition (the *Mahānirvāṇa Tantra*, for example, contains legal material, including material derived from British law, thus dating that particular text to not earlier than the eighteenth century).[3]

The Law Books were concerned with legal matters such as inheritance, as well as purity rules. They also reflect gender expectations and patriarchal attitudes. Women, for example, according to Manu are subject to male authority, to father as

---

2 Patrick Olivelle, *The Law Code of Manu* (Oxford: Oxford University Press, 2004).

3 Duncan M. Derrett, 'A Juridical Fabrication of Early British India: The *Mahānirvāṇa Tantra*', in *Essays in Classical and Modern Hindu Law*, Vol. 2. *Consequences of the Intellectual Exchange with Foreign Powers* (Leiden: Brill, 1977), 197–242.

a daughter, to husband as a wife, and to son as a mother.[4] Woman, according to Manu, is the field (*kṣetra*) in which a man sows his seed to produce male offspring[5] and so has no inherent autonomy (*svātantrya*). Yet such attitudes are not shared by all the law treatises: Hindu legal texts may have been the first in world history to recognise women as having rights to inherit property, although there was debate about this, some arguing that a man's property should go to the closest male relative rather than to his widow. The eleventh-century Jīmūtavāhana in his legal treatise suggested a compromise, that the widow should inherit if there are no sons.[6]

We need to understand not only the religious background to the Tantric traditions but also the legal and political frameworks in which they developed. The legal treatises give us insight into social and political practices as well as attitudes and the wider structure of society to which the Tantras responded. The affirmation of women as gurus important in religious practice in what we might call the economy of salvation in more extreme Tantric groups, for example, needs to be seen in the context of wider patriarchal attitudes and the legal status of women. Whether Tantric texts represent a social impulse to greater freedom and equality for women is a moot point, but it is certainly the case that some later

---

4 Olivelle, *Law Code of Manu* 5.147–148. Also see Julia Leslie, *The Perfect Wife: The Orthodox Hindu Woman According to the Strīdharmapaddhati of Tryambakayajvan* (Oxford: Oxford University Press, 1989), 305–316.

5 *Manu* 9.33. See Wendy Doniger, 'The Body in Hindu Texts', in *Religion and the Body*, ed. Sarah Coakley (Cambridge: Cambridge University Press, 1989), 167–184.

6 Ludo Rocher, *Jīmūtavāhana's Dāyabhāga: The Hindu Law of Inheritance in Bengal* (Oxford: Oxford University Press, 2001), 177–178, 186, 195. Also see Duncan Derrett, *Studies in Hindu Law* (Turin: Indologica Taurensia, 1994), 78.

Tantric traditions held women in high esteem and there was probably more parity of observance. The earliest texts emerging from the ascetic Ati Mārga make little reference to women but Goodall notes that the *Kiraṇa Tantra* introduces a practice intended for women initiates, the *yāga* of Gaurī.[7]

Orthodox Brahmins following the *smṛtis* were known as Smārtas and were highly orthodox. Thus, by the time of the Tantric revelation there were two important groups of Brahmins: those who followed and performed the high, formal rites of Vedic revelation, the public rites and sacrifices, the Śrautas (followers of *śruti*); and those who followed the law books and Purāṇas, performed domestic rites and maintained the sacred fire at home, the Smārtas (followers of *smṛti*). The Śrautas followed Vedic texts on public ritual such as the *Rudra Kalpa*. Apart from following the law codes, by the time of the first millennium CE the Smārtas worshipped the main gods Viṣṇu, Śiva, and Devī as they were encoded in the Purāṇas; one group focused on five gods: Gaṇeśa, Sūrya, Śiva, Devī, and Viṣṇu worshipped in a single rite, the *pañcāyatana pūjā*.[8] The Vaidikas of the *smṛti* could be Śaiva Smārtas who followed texts such as the *Skanda Purāṇa* and the *Vāyu Purāṇa*. The more extreme Tantras rejected the law books while other, more conservative traditions aligned themselves with orthodox Brahmanism, as we will see.

There was also a group of texts called Śivadharma that encoded legal practices, the social and religious obligations of those who worshipped Śiva.[9] These texts were orthodox in

---

7 Dominic Goodall, 'Introduction', in *Śaiva Rites of Expiation: A First Edition and Translation of Trilocanaśiva's Twelfth-century Prāyaścittasamuccaya*, ed. R. Sathyanarayan (Pondichery: IFP, 2015), 15–63, 32.

8 Gudrun Bühnemann, *Pūjā: A Study in Smārta Ritual* (Vienna: De Nobili Research Library, 1988).

9 Peter Bisschop, *Universal Śaivism: The Appeasement of All Gods and Powers in the Śāntyadhyāya of the Śivadharmaśāstra* (Leiden: Brill, 2018).

orientation, regarding the maintenance of caste boundaries as most important, and followed laws of Brahmanical purity. But since the Śaivas who followed these texts were not initiated into a specific Śaiva sect, they were regarded as general scriptures for the edification of the wider Śaiva public of the Brahmins.

Both Śrauta and Smārta Brahmins adhered to orthodox *dharma* (duty) with regard to social class or caste and with regard to the stages on life's way. This was known as *varṇāśrama-dharma*, one's duty (*dharma*) regarding social class (*varṇa*) and stage of life (*āśrama*). They also adhered to the goals or purposes of life (*puruṣārtha*).

By the time of the Guptas, Indian society probably had a complex array of caste groups, but the model was that of the older tradition: four estates or classes (*varṇa*) arranged according to a scale of purity, with the Brahmins at the top, followed by the nobles or warriors who rule (*kṣatriya*), the commoners (*vaiśya*), and those who serve (*śūdra*). Marriage was strictly within caste group (castes are endogamous) although outside of family or clan (*kula*) (clans are exogamous). It was also important to maintain caste purity, not only by consuming food that itself is pure, but by not eating outside of one's caste group. Thus, caste is defined by rules of endogamy and commensality.

These rules are in turn governed by attitudes to purity and pollution. In Hinduism all products of the body are polluting, and the body itself is arranged in a hierarchy according to this scale: the head is the purest part of the body and the soles of the feet the most impure. When a Brahmin washes, he does so from the head downwards, so washing away impurity. Thus, tasks that concern bodily products, such as those carried out by people who sweep the villages and so have to deal with human waste, by barbers who deal with hair and nails, and by those who deal with the disposal of the dead, are polluting. Such jobs are therefore impure because what they handle is polluting in the logic of caste. Because of this, people generally knew their place in the social order. The Tantric traditions both affirmed this order and rejected it. The more orthodox traditions aligned with the Veda were keen to maintain rules of ritual purity and caste segregation, while other traditions rejected any social division based on caste or gender, consciously using the categories of purity and impurity to reject Vedic values. Living in cremation grounds, consuming impure food, and practising sexual congress outside of caste restrictions were practices of more extreme Tantric sects that challenged orthodox norms and attitudes as we will see. Indeed, living beyond the bounds of Brahmanical purity laws did give the adherents of these groups a certain freedom, even power, because they wielded the ability to pollute higher castes, having thrown off inhibition (*śaṅkā*). But it is important to remember that not all Tantric traditions rejected society and the rules of purity, marriage, and commensality; in fact, most did not.

The stages of life for the orthodox Brahmin, or technically for the twice-born (*dvija*) who had undergone an initiation (*upanayana*), were four: student, during which the young man learned the Vedic scriptures; householder, in which he married and raised a family; hermit, in which he retired to the forest and devoted his life to religious activity; and renouncer, in which he gave up all social obligation in order to seek liberation. Originally these stages may have been lifestyle choices, but they became codified into a sequential structure.[10] This is an ideal model, and most people would have simply become householders, although some did – and still do – become renouncers, and the hermit stage might be reinterpreted simply to mean

10 Patrick Olivelle, *The Āśrama System: The History and Hermeneutics of a Religious Institution* (Oxford: Oxford University Press, 1993).

retirement. Some young men become renouncers without going through the householder stage. A more complex picture of the householder's journey through life is provided by the Hindu rites of passage (*saṃskāra*) from birth to death. There are sixteen such rites, codified in the law books and handed down through tradition.[11] The Tantric traditions simply assume this social structure; some proto-Tantric sects, the Pāśupatas, regarded themselves as a fifth stage, beyond the Vedic scheme. Lastly, something needs to be said about the goals of life – the purposes of life for the orthodox Brahmin and other higher caste groups – before we tackle the Tantric revelation itself.

Goals of Life

In orthodox Brahmanism there are four goals or purposes of human life (*puruṣārtha*): duty and responsibility (*dharma*), wealth and prosperity (*artha*), pleasure (*kāma*), and liberation (*mokṣa*); each had a body of literature associated with it (everybody has heard of the *Kāma-sūtra*). The first three of these – *dharma*, *artha*, and *kāma* – were the original classification, with *mokṣa* being added later.[12] This indicates that the initial orientation of Brahmanism was towards the affirmation of worldly values. The good life is doing one's duty, gaining wealth, and having fun. Liberation or salvation, which potentially undermines or negates those values, came later. The *puruṣārtha*

11 Rajbali Pandey, *Hindu Saṃskāras: Socio-Religious Study of the Hindu Sacraments* (Delhi: Motilal Banarsidass, 1969).

12 Charles Malamoud, 'On the Rhetoric and Semantics of the Puruṣārthas', in *Way of Life: King, Householder, Renouncer*, ed. T. N. Madan (Delhi: Motilal Banarsidass, 1988); Gavin Flood, 'The Meaning and Context of the Puruṣārthas', in *The Fruits of Our Desiring, an Enquiry into the Ethics of the Bhagavadgītā for our Times*, ed. Julius Lipner (Calgary: Bayeux, 1997), 11–27.

scheme highlights a tension in the history of Hindu thought and practice between values of world affirmation, on the one hand, and world negation in favour of a transcendent goal, on the other.[13]

Some traditions are orientated towards transcending this world in the belief that salvation lies elsewhere, perhaps only attained after death, while others are orientated towards the world in the belief that the world and ordinary human transaction are inherently good in themselves, that this life here is something to be valued as an end in itself. In the history of Western religions, Gnosticism would be an example of the former, world-negating attitude, and Christianity an example of the latter, world-affirming attitude (in its belief in a good creation). In the history of Indian religions, early Buddhism or Jainism would be examples of world-renouncing traditions in the quest for liberation (the journey to Buddhism's 'further shore'), while Vedic Brahmanism would be an example of world affirmation in the belief that this life is of value, along with affirming family life and responsibility to parents, gods, and teachers. But Hinduism also contains within it a tradition of renunciation and desire for transcendence beyond the world, indeed as the negation of world. Even the Buddha in leaving his family became an example of attraction to the pull of world renunciation – some would say to the cost of his family obligations. Tantrism likewise contains these tensions. There were Tantric monks and world renouncers seeking liberation, yet there were also Tantric householders wishing to perform their duty and obligation to family and wider society.

The scheme of the *puruṣārthas* is a response to the ques-

---

13 See the essay by Louis Dumont, 'World Renunciation in Indian Religions', in *Homo Hierarchicus: The Caste System and its Implications*, 267–286 (Chicago: University of Chicago Press, 1979).

tions: what is the good life? What are life's highest values and goals? What should I do or how should I act? On the one hand we have affirmation of family values, worldly prosperity (political success as well as wealth), and pleasure, while on the other hand we have world transcendence and orientation to salvation away from the world. Of course, the two realms of value can accommodate each other, and Hinduism has integrated them with varying degrees of success. *The Bhagavad-gītā*, for example, integrates both realms in saying that one can – and should – do one's duty in the world (world-affirming values of *dharma*) while transcending the world as an inner attitude of detachment, giving up concern for the fruit of one's actions to God (world- transcending values of *mokṣa*). Arjuna can affirm his duty by fighting in the great battle while at the same time becoming detached from the results of his acts. The Tantras similarly accommodate these competing social goods: many texts claim the need to perform social function while transcending worldly life as an inner attitude; one's identity as a Tantric worshipper of the Goddess is secret and outwardly one seems to be a good Brahmanical householder.

Political Formation

Before looking at the Tantras themselves, I finally need to say something about political structures. In the history of South Asia three regions can be identified as having distinct political trajectories: the northern region from the mouth of the Indus to the mouth of the Ganges, about 2,000 miles but only 200 miles wide; the southern highlands; and the east coast, which themselves contain sub-regions.[14] Most of the Tantras were composed

14 Hermann Kulke and Dietmar Rothermund, *A History of India* (London: Routledge, 1990), 11.

in the northern region at a time of some political instability – or perhaps 'change' is a better word. The comparative political stability of the Vākāṭaka and Gupta empires (*c.* 320–550 CE) gave way to a period of some complexity, with the rise and passing away of different kingdoms and tribal lords, yet there were two important dynasties within which the Tantric traditions grew, namely the two empires in North India of the Gurjara-Pratīhāras (*c.* 727–1018 CE) and the Pālas (*c.* 750–1170 CE). The early medieval period witnessed the rise of these new kingdoms, accompanied by an ideology of divine kingship in which the ideal king was the universal ruler (*cakravartin*), an ideal that goes back to the time of the Buddha (*d. c.* 410 BCE). After the Guptas there is increasing decentralisation, with local kings rising and new feudal kingdoms emerging. Royal power came to be expressed in the new regional temples, centres expressing political power as well as spiritual aspiration.[15] New kings tended to build new capitals with new regional temples, avoiding the confluences of rivers which were sacred sites of pilgrimage and so potentially dangerous in bringing in those from outside the kingdom.[16] Gangaikondacolapuram in Tamilnadu, for example, was founded by the Cola king Rājendra I with a temple to Śiva, but soon after his demise the city was abandoned leaving only the magnificent temple standing, today surrounded by trees. Rājendra I expanded the empire and even went on a military expedition as far as the Ganges, hence the name of his city, 'the town of the Cola king who brought back the Ganges'.

These kingdoms were not centralised, as we might think of the Roman empire, but rather segmented, with lower rulers paying obeisance and revenue to higher rulers. Stein has called

15 Ronald M. Davidson, *Indian Esoteric Buddhism, A Social History of the Tantric Movement* (New York: Columbia University Press, 2002), 27.

16 Kulke and Rothermund, *A History of India*, 12.

Figure 1.2. Śiva temple in Gangaikondacolapuram, Tamilnadu.

this a 'segmentary state', as we find with the Cola kingdom.[17] This model was operative up to and including the Vijayanagara empire (1336 to sixteenth century), in which the king, on the occasion of the festival of Navarātri, would receive ritual obeisance from the kings of vassal states and he was thought to derive his power from the Goddess herself, while seated on a tower.[18] Many of these kings promoted Tantric traditions and gave patronage to different Tantric groups. Indeed, the impact of Tantrism on kingship extended from India through to South-East Asia with the Khmer kingdom, where we find Hindu gods

17 B. Stein, *Peasant, State and Society in Medieval South India* (Delhi: Oxford University Press, 2002), 340–343.

18 Sanjukta Gupta and Richard Gombrich, 'Kings, Power and the Goddess', *South Asia Research* 6, no. 2, (1986): 123–138.

in temple sculptures and inscriptions bearing witness to the royal patronage of Tantric traditions. The fundamental model here is of the ritual diagram (*maṇḍala*) in which the deity and his consort are surrounded by a retinue of gods, who are themselves regarded as emanations of the central deities. The king identified himself with one of the major deities, such as Śiva, Viṣṇu, or the Goddess, while tutelary deities – usually clans of Goddesses – were associated with particular wealthy and influential families. The Malla kings of Nepal, for example, were Tantric, and believed their power derived from, especially, three gods: Viṣṇu, Paśupati, and the esoteric Tantric goddess Taleju.[19] We know that the Malla king Abhayamalla, or possibly his son, commissioned the copying of the *Netra Tantra* in 1200 primarily for the protection of the king and his family. The kings of Vijayanagara underwent consecration as kings using Tantric *mantras*, a practice that directly paralleled the consecration of the Tantric adept;[20] and the same kind of Tantric consecration took place for the kings of Nepal[21] – a practice that continued into modernity until the abolishing of the monarchy in 2008 by the Nepalese Constituent Assembly. The kings of Khmer in Southeast Asia, Suvarṇa, the land of gold, likewise employed Tantric Brahmins to perform initiations. The Tantric texts themselves are aware of their connection with royalty. The Tantric text from the religion of Viṣṇu, called the *Jayākhya Saṃhitā*, for example, lists four kinds of initiate who are identified with four kinds of political actor: the ordinary initiate, the *samayin*, is associated with the military general; the next level up, the *putraka* or son of the deity, with the prime minister; the

---

19 G. Tofflin, *Le Palais et le Temple: La fonction royale dans la vallée du Nepal* (Paris: CNRS, 1993), 53, 94.

20 Gupta and Gombrich, 'Kings, Power and the Goddess', 123–138.

21 Tofflin, *Le Palais et le Temple*, 220–222.

Figure 1.3. The Vīrūpakṣa temple in present day Hampi, Karnataka, centre of the imperial capital of the Vijayanagara empire (1336–1565).

sādhaka or typical Tantric practitioner, with the prince; and the *ācārya* or teacher with the king.[22]

The economy of these kingdoms was feudal and based on agriculture, and there would also have been trade between different regions. There is little documentary evidence of the early period, which we know about mostly through inscriptions, but the Vijayanagara empire is well documented. Evidently it was an efficiently administered empire, a military feudalism, in which the imperial administration was run by the Nayaka, a military leader in charge of a sub-region: the emperor turned local chiefs into imperial administrators.[23] We can perhaps assume a not dissimilar picture in the earlier period. In Kashmir, for example, we know that king Śaṅkaravarman (883–902 CE),

22 *Jayākhya Saṃhitā*, 18.34–35.

23 Kulke and Rothermund, *A History of India*, 194–195.

Figure 1.4. A maṇḍala, *or ritual diagram. Tantra Foundation, New Delhi.*

in whose reign Tantric traditions developed, maintained a bureaucracy, and that the philosopher Jayanta Bhaṭṭa had a position within it.[24] We also know that Tantric or proto-Tantric institutions became highly successful. The Pāśupatas were a proto-Tantric ascetic order which became very successful, owning temples and monasteries, especially toward the East, that acquired tremendous wealth. In fact, they owned and ran the great Śiva temple of Somnāth on the

24 Csaba Dezső, *Much Ado about Religion* (New York: Clay Sanskrit Library, 2005), 15.

Gujarat coast.[25] These institutions became wealthy through royal patronage, and possibly agriculture, as the needs of the monks themselves were minimal. As a result, they became attractive for kings to exploit or even steal from.

So, it is in the context of kingship following the decline of the Gupta empire that the Tantric traditions arose. The feudal economy in these regions seems to have been successful and there was surplus wealth to support religious institutions and renouncers. The Tantric religion of Śiva in particular was highly successful in obtaining support and patronage, and this religion spread far and wide, reaching as far as Indonesia in Southeast Asia. The Tantric traditions are the voice not only of established political systems – not only for the kings and rulers – but also of social groups at the margins, lower caste groups, as we will see. The appeal of the Tantras to a wide spectrum of society accounts for their great success during the period between the fall of the Guptas and the rise of the Delhi Sultanate. Indeed, it would not be an exaggeration to call this a Tantric period in the history of Hinduism. We might even speak of 'Tantric civilisation', if we take 'civilisation' to be a broader concept than 'society', entailing a polity or structural politics that integrates with social structure and culture, geographically located over a wide spatial area. An earlier Sanskrit equivalent to 'civilisation' might be 'the homeland of the noble ones' (*āryāvarta*), to the north of the Vindhya mountains, in the land of ritual action where *dharma* is maintained, and liberation is possible.[26] This homeland of the Aryans was the Brahmanical ideal, defined in contradistinction to the land

25 Romila Thapar, *Somnath: The Many Voices of a History* (New Delhi: Viking, 2004).

26 Wilhelm Halbfass, *India and Europe: An Essay in Understanding* (Albany: SUNY Press, 1988), 177. Also, Flood, *The Tantric Body*, 72.

of the barbarians (*mleccha*) beyond. Tantric civilisation was certainly widespread and involved not only culture – the building of temples, art, especially temple sculpture, as well as being part of the Sanskrit literate, the Sanskrit knowing world of learned texts and scriptures forming a Sanskrit cosmopolis[27] – but political formation in the divine king. The Tantric tradition was connected with the political formation of states in the post-Gupta period, attracting royal patronage and supporting the aspirations of kings as well as providing magical support to them and their kingdoms. The Tantric revelation also appealed to lower social levels and even expressed the aspirations of marginalised people, as we will see.

So, given its popularity, what was this Tantric revelation that so attracted political patronage as well as popular support? What were these texts called Tantras?

The Tantric Revelation

So far, I have described the context within which the Tantras emerged. The dominant tradition was Brahmanism and during the first millennium CE we find the development of worship of the main deities of Hinduism. The Tantric revelation represents a new religious movement that became highly successful and attracted royal patronage. But what were these texts and why were they so appealing, not only to rulers but to common people too? I will here first describe the Tantric revelation, what the texts are, and how they are classified, and then speak about some general features of these texts that made them so appealing.

---

27 Sheldon Pollock, 'The Sanskrit Cosmopolis, 300–1300 CE: Transculturation, Vernacularization, and the Question of Ideology', in *Ideology and Status of Sanskrit: Contributions to the History of the Sanskrit Language*, ed. Jan E. M. Houben (Leiden: Brill, 1996), 197–247.

As with most new religious movements, there was some controversy about the Tantras as a new divine revelation. The Nyāya philosopher Jayanta Bhaṭṭa in the ninth century defended the idea of a new Tantric revelation; he could see no reason why there could not be a new revelation so long as it was accepted by learned people, but it had to conform to Vedic orthodoxy and must not contradict Brahmanical practice, it must not go against *dharma*. He was therefore opposed to those Tantric groups – such as the Blue or Black Clad sect (*nīlāmbara*) – which flouted Brahmanical purity laws. This sect, he tells us, practised group sex on festival occasions in public places simply covered in a blue blanket, behaviour to the detriment of the public good.[28] But so long as these groups did not threaten the fundamental social and cultural values that he perceived to be so central to his society, he thought a new revelation could be tolerated and adapted to. Jayanta's writing points to a tension in medieval Kashmir, between those who adhered to Vedic values and those who followed the new, emerging religion of Tantrism.

The very fact that the Tantric revelation was a textual revelation is important because the production of a text needs an accompanying tradition to propagate it through the generations. There needs to be a community that receives it, that practises it, that supports its being copied, and that passes it on. In many ways, the very fact that Tantrism is a textual tradition indicates its conservative nature, regardless of the content of some of the texts. In contrast to the Veda, that was originally oral in its formation, the Tantras were written and redacted over periods of time. They are scriptures and were revered as such; they themselves, not only the doctrines they

---

28 Jayanta Bhaṭṭa, *Nyāyamañjari of Jayanta Bhaṭṭa*, English trans V. N. Jha (Delhi: Śrī Satguru Publications, 1995), 562.

contain and the practices they prescribe, were sacred objects. The copying of a manuscript would have been an event, perhaps marked by a public procession.[29]

The Tantras themselves locate their origin from their deity. God is believed to be the source and the Tantra is thought to have been spoken by Śiva or Viṣṇu or the Goddess (or in Buddhism by the Buddha or in Jainism by Mahāvīra). Many texts have an account of how they were uttered by the deity and descended to earth and to the human community via a series of intermediaries, in the process becoming shorter and more simplified. They call this the 'descent of the Tantra' (*tantrāvatāra*).[30] Their declared purpose is liberation and/or pleasure and power in other worlds before liberation, for people lost in the cycle of reincarnation and suffering. It is interesting how the earliest Tantra presents the fundamental idea of its descent from a higher world but in a more straightforward way than in the later texts. As the tradition develops, the descent of the text becomes more complex as it goes through more intermediaries. Let us therefore first look at this decent of the Tantras from a higher world down to this one. I shall here give some examples from the Tantras of this descent.

---

29 Alexis Sanderson, 'How Public was Śaivism?' Nina Mirnig, Marion Rastelli, and Vincent Eltschinger (eds.), *Tantric Communities in Context* (Vienna: Osterreichische Akademie der Wissenshcaften, 2019), pp. 1-48.

30 For a good account of this process, particularly as regards the *Brahmayāmala Tantra*, see Shaman Hatley, *The Brahmayāmalatantra or Picumata*, Vol. 1, Chapters 1–2, 39–40, and 83, *Revelation, Ritual, and Material Culture in an Early Śaiva Tantra* (Pondichery: Institut Français de Pondichéry, 2018), 167–181.

Example 1: Niḥśvāsa-tattva Saṃhitā

The earliest Tantra is a Śaiva scripture of the core Tantric tradition called the Śaiva Siddhānta. The text calls itself the *Niḥśvāsa-tattva Saṃhitā,* that we can roughly translate as 'the scripture (*saṃhitā*) concerning the truth (*tattva*) from the breathing out (*niḥśvāsa*) of Śiva'. This text was mostly composed in the seventh century, but an early section goes back to the fifth. I will have more to say about this text in Chapter 2, but for now I just wish to note that it gives an account of its own origin from the supreme deity Śiva. The text is a dialogue between the Lord and the Goddess. The Goddess asks Śiva three questions: from where do letters of the alphabet arise? How many Tantras are there? And how many teachers? The Lord replies, telling her how in the beginning were a group of letters from which arose all the scriptures and all languages (or dialects), and how the scriptures of Śiva (*śiva-tantra*) came about. The text continues:

1.23 From the inactive Supreme Cause Śiva, of whom no body can be seen, came forth scripture in the form of sonic energy (*nāda-rūpam*), extremely difficult to grasp.

1.24–25 Now Sadāśiva understood it and he enlightened me; I redacted [this] scripture [that I had received] in the form of sonic energy into books. It was expounded for the gods in the form of metrical composition in *anuṣṭubh* [meter]. [From them] it reached the sages; and from them the tradition [came] among mortals.[31]

---

31 *Niḥśvāsatattva Saṃhitā, Uttara-sūtra* 1.23–25. Dominic Goodall, *Niḥśvāsatattva-saṃhitā: The Earliest Surviving Śaiva Tantra,* Vol. 1. *A Critical Edition and Annotated Translation of the Mūlasūtra, Uttarasūtra and Nayasūtra* (Pondichéry: Institut Français de Pondichéry, 2015).

Here we see that in the beginning the supreme cause of the universe and revealed scriptures is Śiva who is bodiless in his essence. From him the absolute sound (*nāda*) emanated, the sound of God, which came to be formed into the books of scripture. This was conveyed to a lower form of Śiva called Sadāśiva, the form of Śiva worshipped in the Śaiva Siddhānta, and he in turn told Īśvara ('the Lord'), the speaker of this text, who in turn told it to the other gods, who in turn told it to the sages, who told it to human beings. This process of transmission is typical, although in later scriptures there are more intermediaries between the source of scripture, namely God as wholly transcendent, and the human community that receives it.

Example 2: Rauravāgama

This same pattern of the descent of the Tantras is found in many texts. Another example is the *Rauravāgama*, like the *Niḥśvāsa*, a Tantra of the mainstream Tantric tradition of the Śaiva Siddhānta. It describes how it came down from on high to the human world. The text is spoken by the sage Ruru, who traditionally was one of seven famous Vedic sages. The text describes the awe of the sage in receiving the text: 'Ruru, his hair standing on end with awe, spoke this speech.'[32] And so he declares the text. The descent of the Tantra is described as follows:

3.5–6 Intelligent Ruru [the sage] explained to the lineage of masters about the highest, supreme doctrine uttered from the mouth of the Highest Lord, the form of which is sweet light emitted from the fire of Śiva, to the supreme master, the God, Lord Ananta, the cause of the universe.

32 *Rauravāgama, Vidyā-pāda,* Chapter 1.5cd: *harṣād udgataromāñcaḥ prāha vākyam idaṃ ruruḥ.*

3.7 By him it [the text] was spoken to the great, supreme Lord Śrīkaṇṭha, by [that] master to the gods and anti-gods, [and he] declared all to the Goddess.

3.8 And the Goddess told the supreme secret to Nandin and Lord Skanda. From Lord Nandin, it was obtained by Brahmā and by great Indra.

3.9 From him, the sage Ūrva obtained it, then again by Ṛcīka. From him it was obtained by Rāma and from Rāma, I [Ruru] received it.

3.10ab So, the graded lineage has been declared by me, in an abridged form, O twice born ones.[33]

Here we see the descent of the Tantra through a series of intermediaries to the human world. Ananta is a lower deity to Śiva, who actually does the work of creation. He is appointed by Śiva, or stands in for Śiva, to do the work of creation because Śiva himself is so transcendent to the world. From Ananta the scripture goes to the lower form Śrīkaṇṭha and then to the Goddess. She told the text to Nandin and Skanda. Nandin here refers to Śiva's attendant – not the later bull which was Śiva's mount – and likewise Skanda. They are often seen as protectors of the door in medieval Śaiva temples. Ūrva and Ṛcīka are the names of sages in the Veda. In this way the text came to the human world in an abridged form (*saṃkṣepa*).

Example 3: Svacchanda Tantra

The above two examples are from Tantras from the canon of scriptures of the Śaiva Siddhānta. The non-Siddhānta

33 *Rauravāgama, Vidyā-pāda,* Chapter 3.5–10ab (my translation).

Figure 1.5. A mid-nineteenth-century watercolour of Svacchandabhairava. Philadelphia Museum of Art, Stella Kramrisch Collection, 1994.

traditions (often referred to as Kashmir Śaivism) also have their own scriptures, which follow the same pattern. The *Svacchanda Tantra* ('the scripture of Śiva's freedom or own will') describes its descent and emergence among humans. Narrated by Śiva in the form of the ferocious Bhairava, this account can be roughly rendered as follows:

8.27 Now I will narrate succinctly the descent of the scriptures, coming from eight forms of Śiva, the supreme cause.

8.28 [The first emanation is] the very subtle nature of sound, very pure, very brilliant, with the supreme form that is Śiva, the supreme self.

8.29 He discerns different practices for different purposes of life, [enunciated] through the great souled five Mantras, seated on the lion throne of *mantra*.

8.30 [The scriptures] beginning with worldly teachings [for worldly purposes] and ending with [the teachings of] Śiva [for spiritual purposes] arise from the supreme to the non-supreme [aspects of the Lord] for those who are fit to receive his grace within their own sense spheres.

8.31 [These scriptures] constrained by the standard verse meter, are countless millions [of verses long], the god Sadāśiva himself having established [them] in words from master to disciple.

8.32 The scripture (*tantra*) from the first to the last words and sentences is distinguished and supported as the knowledge given to Lord Īśvara, by the will of Śiva.

8.33 First, he [Īśvara] told it to the Lords of Wisdom (Vidyeśvaras) of the *vidyā* [level of the universe], then from that level to the Rudras [at the levels] of the material substrate of the universe (*māyā*) to [the level called] constraint (*niyati*).

8.34 Then this supreme knowledge, very difficult to obtain, was received by Śrīkaṇṭha from Īśvara, then by him it was spoken to the (lower) Rudras by the will of Īśvara.

8.35–36 Having initiated them in this manner from the level of matter to the end of the Hundred Rudras, and also to me [Bhairava], Śrīkaṇṭha then gave the first initiation and then consecration, [presenting] the scripture for the practitioner of all purposes. And so, through me to you, O Goddess, the practice is established.

Figure 1.6. A mid-eighteenth-century watercolour of Bhairava and the Goddess. Victoria and Albert Museum, London.

8.37 As before, you also give [the scripture] to Skanda, the Rudras, and to the gods Brahmā, Viṣṇu, Indra, the Vasus, the Mothers, and those made divine.

8.38 Having taken to the world, O Goddess, you tell [the scripture] to the *nāgas*, the *yakṣas*, the sages and so to humans.[34]

We see here how the process has become much more complicated. The Supreme Śiva tells the scripture to the lower form Sadāśiva, whose five faces speak five *mantras* (see below), who tells it to Īśvara, who tells it to Śrīkaṇṭha and also to the Lords of Wisdom (Vidyeśvaras), and from them to the Rudras who live at the level of the material substrate of the universe. Śrīkaṇṭha passes the scripture on to the Hundred Rudras and also to Bhairava (the speaker of the scripture) who gives it to the Goddess, who gives it to further gods and supernatural beings, and finally to humankind. Of note here is that the Hindu gods Brahmā, Viṣṇu, and Indra appear so low in the hierarchy. I have left some names untranslated – the Rudras are lower forms or reflections of Śiva, the *nāgas* are supernatural snake beings, and the *yakṣas* are semi-divine beings, sometimes attendant upon Kubera (the god of wealth who governs the northern direction), who are sometimes malignant and cause possession. So, the revelation of this scripture descends through the levels of the hierarchical universe at which different grades of supernatural beings live; they receive the scripture and pass it on lower down until finally in reaches the human world, needless to say, in a greatly denuded form (even though the *Svacchanda Tantra* is fifteen very long chapters).

34 *Svacchanda Tantra*, 8.27–38 (my translation).

These texts share a fundamental idea of the importance of sound. God, the absolute reality who creates – or more accurately emanates – the world is conceptualised as sound. The pure form of sound emanates from God, and it is this that is the life force behind language and creates language – the sacred language of Sanskrit along with all the others that are not in themselves sacred. The grammatical tradition came to refer to the idea of God as sound, the sound absolute (*śabda-brahman*). This sound absolute as vibration emanates the form of the universe. The universe, and the scriptures within it, are thus regarded as vibration (*spanda*) of the sound absolute in Tantric traditions. *Mantras* are sound-formulas within Tantric scriptures that capture the essence of the text and are regarded as the sound-body of the deity. I shall have more to say about *mantras* in due course, but for now it is important to know that a *mantra* embodies the deity. So, a picture emerges of the pure sound emanating from the supreme source, which then manifests the sacred language of Sanskrit and manifests the Tantric scriptures, which themselves bear witness to the *mantras*, the sound-bodies of the gods. But the *mantras* that we hear in the world and the texts that we read are but reflections of the higher, subtle sound that can be perceived in meditation. Thus, meditation on the *mantra* from a scripture is thought to take the practitioner back to its source, its origin in the pure sound of God.

This basic idea of God emanating pure sound that becomes embodied in scriptures and *mantras* is the model that links ordinary human language with an understanding of the cosmos. Even the grammatical tradition recognised this. One language philosopher who had a big impact on Tantric traditions was Bhartṛhari (*c.* 450–510 CE). He argued that language (*vāc*) has a supreme origin and moves from a supreme condition as sound that can be directly perceived (that he called the level of 'seeing' (*paśyantī*)), to sound perceived in the mind as thought, the middle level (*madhyamā*), to spoken speech in the world (*vaikharī*).[35] On this model Tantric scriptures are expressions in speech, the gross level of the world, of the much more subtle sound that embodies the deity and ultimately derives from the highest level that is God. This is not unique to the Tantric worldview, however, for we also find it in the Vedic worldview: the Vedas are eternal and are received by the ancient sages who communicated them to the human community. We will have cause to revisit this, but I mention it here because to understand the idea of a Tantric revelation we need to understand the implicit view articulated by Bhartṛhari that language evolves from a supreme, subtle vibration of God, to spoken language and the words of scripture. In this view, our words come from a higher source and have the power to take us back to that source.[36]

While each of the Tantras might have its own distinct lineage in its descent, they all share this idea that God utters the text which is then transmitted through a series of intermediaries to the human world. They are regarded as esoteric or secret teachings (*rahasya*) for those who are initiated into the text and who have the necessary qualification (*adhikāra*). Yet while being secret, these texts were promoted very successfully by the traditions and became adopted by kings throughout the subcontinent. The content may be esoteric, but the fact that a king has this text, and has even been initiated into it, is a public event that brought prestige, as we will see.

The descent of the Tantras through the hierarchy of the universe came to be a model within which to locate the teachings of different traditions. The eleventh-century Tantric

35 André Padoux, *Vāc: The Concept of the Word in Selected Hindu Tantras*, translated by Jacques Gontier (Albany: SUNY Press, 1990).

36 Padoux, *The Hindu Tantric World*, 100–104.

philosopher Kṣemarāja who wrote commentaries on important Tantric texts, classified different traditions in accordance with the Tantric cosmological hierarchy. He places different scriptures at different levels. The Buddhists and followers of Mīmāṃsā (both completely opposed to each other!) are only at the level of the higher mind (*buddhi*), while the Tantric religion of Viṣṇu, the Pāñcarātra, is at the level of unmanifest matter (*prakṛti*). Both levels are classified within the 'impure universe'. Within the 'pure universe' Kṣemarāja puts the followers of the Vedānta tradition at the level of Īśvara (who we had as one of the recipients of the scriptures describe above), with the non-dualist teachings of Śiva, Kṣemarāja's own tradition naturally, at the top of the hierarchy, the top of the universe. This level is the understanding that consciousness is both transcendent (*viśvottīrṇa*) and immanent (*viśvātmaka*).[37] The Tantric scriptures are arranged along this hierarchical axis for Kṣemarāja. On this view, the scriptures of the Śaiva Siddhānta are lower than those of the non-Siddhānta (Kashmir) Śaivism because they are dualistic in their philosophy, as we will see. In contrast, Tantras that teach non-dualism, such as the *Mālinī-vijayottara*, emanate from the very highest level. In contrast to Kṣemarāja, Sanderson has argued that the *Mālinī* – and other Tantras – are in fact dualistic in their philosophies, as is seen in their concern with ritual and the external cult of the deity.[38]

Having described the descent of the Tantras, we might ask: what do they contain? What is in these texts and what are they about? The Tantric texts of the Śaiva Siddhānta came to

37 Kṣemarāja, *Pratyabhijñā-hṛdaya*, *sūtra* 8 and auto commentary.

38 Alexis Sanderson, 'The Doctrine of the Mālinīviyajottaratantra', in *Ritual and Speculation in Early Tantrism*, ed. T. Goudriaan (Albany: SUNY Press, 1992), 281–312.

be regarded as standing on four feet (*pāda*): sections on doctrine or knowledge (*vidyā-pāda*), behaviour (*caryā-pāda*), ritual (*kriyā-pāda*), and meditation (*yoga-pāda*). The knowledge or doctrinal section presents the fundamental philosophy and metaphysics of the text, the pre-philosophical speculation in the sense that they are presented as revealed doctrines rather than philosophical arguments. The *Mataṅga-parameśvarāgama* is a text containing all four feet. For example, the doctrinal sections present the categories of Lord (*pati*), bond (*pāśa*) which is the universe, and bound soul (*paśu*) to be freed. The section on ritual describes the daily rites to be performed, along with occasional rituals such as initiation; and the section on comportment describes the behaviour of the Tantric adept to be expected. The Tantras cover a range of topics, but not all Tantras cover all topics and some texts assume knowledge of other texts. Thus, we need to understand the Tantras in terms of a 'scale of texts' or a graded hierarchy. At least this is how the Tantras saw themselves, with Tantras such as the *Netra Tantra* simply assuming knowledge of other texts and so not giving detailed information about specific rituals, which it assumes the reader will know from other sources.

Along with the descent of the Tantra, another feature of some of these texts is that they contain lists of the many worlds (*bhuvana*) that make up the hierarchical cosmos. These worlds in time became mapped onto another hierarchical grid of ontic levels or *tattvas* (see below). As time goes on, these lists become more extensive as each text transcends the level of an earlier text, relegating the worlds enumerated in that text to a lower level. Thus, the earliest layer of the *Niḥśvāsa* lists a number of worlds beginning with that of Kālāgni, the 'Fire of Time', followed by various hell realms (*naraka*), up to the earth, atmosphere, and sky (known to Vedic cosmography), and beyond that to higher worlds, including those of various deities (Brahmā, Viṣṇu, and Śiva), to the top of this universe or the 'egg of Brahmā' (*brahmāṇḍa*), and moving upwards to the world of the pole star (*dhruva*). Then further worlds are enumerated up to the level of Sadāśiva.[39] The highest world of the earlier tradition of ascetics, called the Pāśupata tradition, went up to the world of the pole star, the *dhruva-loka*. The *Niḥśvāsa* thereby shows how it has transcended that tradition by adding further worlds that the Tantra incorporates. Later texts add more worlds, thus the *Mataṅgaparameśvarāgama* lists 364.[40] The lists of worlds in the Tantras thereby give us a kind of archaeology in which texts that incorporate further worlds will be later than those with fewer. As we will see, these extensive lists of worlds were regarded as a description of the universe but also had a ritual function in initiation: the worlds are mapped onto the body and symbolically destroyed, thereby destroying the initiate's involvement in the world of life and death and demonstrating his transcendence achieved through the act of initiation into the text.

Who composed these texts? It is difficult to identify precisely who composed them. While the Tantras themselves have a vertical account of their origin – they are from the world of God – a secular history needs to ask different questions and step outside of the framework of the texts. As we will see, the earliest Tantra cited above, the *Niḥśvāsa-tattva Saṃhitā,* deals with private ritual and meditation and is less interested in public, temple ritual, whereas later texts are very much concerned with public rites, temple ritual, daily ritual, and occasional rites such as initiation and funerals. Most of these texts are very long and were composed over an extended period of time

39 See the diagram by Goodall in *The Niḥśvāsatattva-saṃhitā*, 290–293.

40 N. R. Bhatt, 'Introduction', in *Mataṅgaparameśvarāgama* (Pondichéry: Institut Français de Pondichéry, 1977), xxxiv.

Figure 1.7. Sadāśiva worshipped by Pārvatī, c. 1690. Freer Gallery of Art, Smithsonian Institution.

until their final redaction. We shall pay more attention to this process in due course, but for now I want to describe how the Tantras see themselves and how they classify themselves.

There is within the tradition a complex way of categorising the various classes of Tantra. The revelation of the mainstream Tantric tradition, the Śaiva Siddhānta, worships Śiva in the form of Sadāśiva. He has five faces; out of each mouth flows a particular group of Tantric texts, a particular revelation. There are twenty-eight Tantras classified in the Śaiva Siddhānta revelation, although not all lists are the same. By way of example, the *Kāmika* lists the five mouths of

Sadāśiva and the corresponding Tantras, as shown in Diagram 1.1.[41] Each of these faces looks out to a particular direction, thus Sadyojāta is the Western direction, Vāmadeva, the north, Aghora faces South, Tatpuruṣa faces East and Īśāna is at the summit (looking up).[42]

Face	**Text**
Sadyojāta	*Kāmika, Yogaja, Cintya, Kāraṇa, Ajita*
Vāmadeva	*Dīpa, Sūkṣma, Sahasra, Aṃśumat, Suprabheda*
Aghora	*Vijaya, Niśvāsa, Svāyaṃbhuva, Anala, Vīra*
Tatpuruṣa	*Raurava, Makuṭa, Vimala, Candrajñāna, Bimba*
Īśāna	*Prodgīta, Lalita, Siddha, Santāna, Śarokta, Pārameśvara, Kiraṇa, Vātula*

Diagram 1.1. The Five Mouths of Sadāśiva and Their Corresponding Tantras.

Other lists present different texts associated with different faces. Along with these main texts in the Śaiva Siddhānta canon, there were secondary texts called Upāgama, some of which are given the same importance as these mainstream revealed texts, such as the *Mataṅga-parameśvara Tantra*, the scripture of the Sage called Mataṅga. Some of these texts have been edited and translated, especially at the French Institute in Pondicherry, but not all.

The famous Śaiva philosopher, Abhinavagupta (*c.* 975–1025 CE), categorised the Tantric revelation into three branches in his commentary on an important Tantra, the *Mālinīvijayottara* (which is not listed in the canon of twenty eight): the division of Śiva (*śiva-bheda*); the division of Rudra (*rudra-bheda*); and the

41 Jean Filliozat, 'Introduction', *Rauravāgama*, p. xi.

42 Hélène Brunner, 'Les Membres de Śiva', *Études Asiatiques* 40, no. 2 (1986): 89–93, 93.

division of Bhairava (*bhairava-bheda*).[43] These correspond to different philosophical positions, the first to dualism, the second to dualism-cum-non-dualism, and the third to non-dualism. The Śaiva Siddhānta, the mainstream Tantric tradition, theoretically accepts twenty-eight Tantras as authoritative, as listed in Diagram 1.1 (the Śiva and Rudra classification), but it is the Tantras of the Bhairava classification that Abhinavagupta regards as superior to the texts of the Śaiva Siddhānta. Following the Śaiva Siddhānta classification, Abhinavagupta says that the upper face of Īśāna is in turn divided into five, with five classes of text flowing from each. These are the Tantras of the Śaiva Siddhānta, the Garuḍa, the Vāma, the Bhūta, and the Bhairava. His main concern is with the Bhairava Tantras.

For Abhinavagupta, the most important Tantric philosopher, all of these scriptures are sacred, but they are in a hierarchical sequence with the higher levels intended for those who have the ability to receive their teachings. There is a general level of teaching or revelation whose rules apply to everyone (*samaya*), notably the Vedic scriptures, and there is a particular revelation (*viśeṣa*) for the initiated few. The Tantric revelation (*āgama*) should form the basis of one's life (*upajīvya*) and the revelation needs to be followed in order to reach perfection.[44] For him, the highest revelation is the Tantras of the Goddess. These texts are part of another Tantric tradition focused on the Goddess, on the female energy of Śiva called 'power' or 'energy', Śakti.

---

43 Jürgen Hanneder, *Abhinavagupta's Philosophy of Revelation: Mālinīślokavārttika I, 1--399* (Groningen: Egbert Forsten, 1998), 26–27.

44 Abhinavagupta, *Tantrāloka*, 37.7–9. Abhinavagupta, *Tantrāloka*, 12 vols., ed. M. S. Kaul (Srinagar: Kashmir Series of Texts and Studies, 1938).

The Tantras of the tradition of Śakti, the Śākta tradition focused on the Goddess, is called the Kula or Kaula school. The word *kula* means 'family' and refers to the different families or clans of female deities. In the Kaula classification of the Tantras, there are four streams or transmissions (*āmnāya*), again from four directions (see Diagram 1.2).[45]

Eastern transmission	Kula tradition of Kuleśvara and Kuleśvarī surrounded by eight mothers and ancillary deities
Northern transmission	Kālī cult (which includes traditions called Mata, Krama, and Mahānaya)
Western transmission	Cult of the hunchback Goddess Kubjikā
Southern transmission	Cult of the beautiful Goddess Tripurasundarī and love deities Kāmeśvara and Kāmeśvarī

Diagram 1.2. Kaula Classification of the Tantras.

It is generally the texts in the Goddess tradition that prescribe transgressive practices, such as sex outside of caste boundaries and making offerings of impure substances (sexual secretions) to the goddesses of the cult. This is the notorious side of the Tantric tradition. We shall examine these texts and traditions in Chapter 3.

45 Padoux, *The Hindu Tantric World*, 58–59.

Figure 1.8. A shrine to the ferocious (aghora) *Kālī in present-day Tamil Nadu..*

Although all these texts are called Tantras, and all form part of the new, Tantric revelation, they are different in nature, with the extreme, antinomian Tantras, which advocate erotic worship of deities, being anathema to the more conservative Śaiva Siddhānta, whereas the Śaiva Siddhānta texts would be regarded as being too inhibited for the Goddess followers. The Tantric revelation is therefore not a single voice but represents a variety of philosophical positions and a variety of practices. Nevertheless, these traditions and texts do overlap, and we can make general statements about them, even though they were so keen to differentiate themselves from each other. What they all share is a sense that this is a new revelation that, while it might be thought to affirm timeless teaching, is something that goes beyond the Veda and offers a new and dynamic way of living and a new and dynamic path to salvation and to success in this world through magical means.

Discussion Topic: Tantric Revelation

- How important is it to understand the historical context of Tantrism (or any historical religion for that matter)?
- What is a 'revelation'?
- Why would a 'new' revelation of the Tantras be controversial in early medieval India?
- What distinguishes the Tantric revelation from the Vedic?

Further Reading

Gavin Flood. *The Tantric Body*. London: Tauris Press, 2006, Chapter 3.

André Padoux. *Vāc, The Concept of the Word in Selected Hindu Tantras*, translated by Jacques Gontier. Albany: SUNY Press, 1990.

André Padoux. *The Hindu Tantric World: An Overview*. Chicago: University of Chicago Press, 2017.

II
The Central Tantric Tradition: The Śaiva Siddhānta

Having set the scene we can now look at the main Tantric tradition of the Śaiva Siddhānta, the tradition that follows the doctrine or teachings of Śiva. This was a householder religion that did not completely reject the orthodox Vedic Brahmanism but did add its own rites in the belief that initiation from the guru guaranteed liberation and/or pleasure and power in higher worlds. The Śaiva Siddhānta developed its own canon of sacred scriptures and followed a dualistic or pluralist philosophy of maintaining a distinction between self, God, and world. Originating in Kashmir, the tradition spread throughout India and is still present in the South, where it became deeply influenced by Tamil devotional or *bhakti* traditions. It is this tradition that provides the normative rites, cosmology, and theological categories that are prescribed in the dualist Śaiva Tantras.

The Spread of Śaivism

The religion of Śiva was highly successful in the early medieval period in attracting royal patronage, a support that partly – or perhaps mostly – accounts for its great success and popular appeal. As Alexis Sanderson has shown, in the early medieval period numerous new dynasties emerged in regional and sub-regional levels, with a multiplication of land-owning temples. This spread of religious activity was supported by the development of a rural, agricultural economy, that included the construction of water reservoirs and wells, which in turn allowed for agricultural expansion, which itself went in tandem with the expansion of the population. We also have the growth of towns, some of which were settlements planned by rulers in an expansion of territory.[1] Śaiva gurus became important as court chaplains, replacing the Vaidika chaplain[2] and Śaiva monasteries spread throughout the subcontinent with abbots appointed by kings, and kings appointing ministers to govern religious affairs, the 'superintendent of religious activities' (*dharma-rakṣādhikāra*).[3]

One example of this is found in the humorous play written by Jayanta Bhaṭṭa, a Nyāya philosopher in Kashmir, called *Much Ado About Religion* (*Āgama-ḍambara*). In this play the hero Saṃkarṣaṇa, a young Brahmin, becomes such a superintendent appointed by king Śaṅkaravarman (883-902), questioning all the various religious sects he sees around him and pointing out their hypocrisy, such as Buddhist monks partying with plenty to drink and dancing girls, Śaiva ascetics gorging themselves, and extreme Tantric sects having sex in public; 'oh what asceticism!' he dryly remarks.[4]

---

1 Alexis Sanderson, 'The Śaiva Age', pp. 252-53, in *Genesis and Development of Tantrism*, ed. Shingo Einoo, 41–250 (Tokyo: University of Tokyo, 2009).

2 For example, the *Netra Tantra* bears witness to this. See Alexis Sanderson, 'Religion and the State: Śaiva Officiants in the Territory of the King's Brahmanical Chaplain', *Indo-Iranian Journal* 47 (2004): 229–300.

3 Sanderson, 'The Śaiva Age', 103–104.

4 Jayantha Bhaṭṭa, *Āgamaḍambara*, translated by Csaba Dezső, *Much Ado About Religion* (New York: Clay Sanskrit Library, New York University Press, 2005), 3.19, p. 133.

Śaivism was popular among kings and lower-caste groups alike. There was popular worship of Śiva in particular by those grounded in texts that taught regulatory behaviour and which were about legal status. These texts are called Śivadharma – the Śaiva equivalent of the *Manu Smṛti* (see Chapter 1) – and form a distinct genre of literature that identifies lay worshippers of Śiva. The texts exhort the laity to support the Śaiva religious with a third of their wealth, and to donate to temples and monasteries. If the devotee performs such acts, he will be guaranteed at death to go to Śiva's heaven (*śiva-loka, rudra-loka*) at the top of the world egg,[5] where he will live happily for a long time until being reborn back on earth in a good human incarnation.[6] Along with the Śivadharma texts, there were the Purāṇas focused on Śiva. The latter were narrative texts associated with Brahmins who followed tradition (*smṛti*), the Smārtas, in contrast to Brahmins who follow only revelation (*śruti*), the Śrautas. This lay, non-initiatory worship of Śiva can be contrasted with teachings of Śiva for those initiated, and the Śaiva Siddhānta was such a tradition that required initiation. The Śaiva Siddhānta then might be classified as a mostly householder tradition in contrast with the extremely orthopraxic Vedic Tradition (for householders too) and contrasted with ascetic Śaivism (for renouncers). So during this time we have orthodox Brahmanism in its Śrauta and Smārta varieties; lay Śaivism whose devotees supported monastic organisations and temples; and the initiatory Śaivism of the Śaiva Siddhānta which was for both householders and ascetics.

---

5 The Brahmanical universe was conceptualised as a massive egg of God (*brahmāṇḍa*) with the human world in the centre and other worlds arranged in a hierarchical sequence to the top.

6 Alexis Sanderson, 'Śaiva Literature', *Journal of Indological Studies* 24/25 (2012/2013): 1–113, 2–4.

The highly orthodox followers of the Veda questioned the rise of Śaivism, even its more conformist expression as the Śaiva Siddhānta. Again, in Jayanta Bhaṭṭa's play we see these social tensions. In act four we read the words of a royal officiant:

> Take the Shaivas and their ilk: they are not part of the system of the four social estates, they reject the life-periods determined by the Veda and the Smritis and they set themselves apart by adopting a different doctrine. But these fellows say that 'We have been truly brahmins ever since our birth, for a long succession of ancestors', and in the same way they imitate the system of the four life-periods: this is a great torment.[7]

There was evidently resistance among the orthodox Vedic Brahmins to this new religion; the latter was keen to adapt itself and to appear to be orthodox by adopting credible lineages going back into the past, while still regarding itself as superior, because the teachings of Śiva (*śiva-śāsana*) that it presented required initiation (*dīkṣā*) that guaranteed liberation, in contrast to lay Śaivism, which did not.

For the laity, however – particularly the wealthy laity and royalty who could afford initiation – the origins of the Śaiva Siddhānta lay in ascetic groups focused on Śiva. These ascetic groups, that in particular comprised a tradition called the Pāśupatas, came to be referred to as the Higher Path or Outer Path, the Ati Mārga: 'higher' because they believed their path went beyond the Vedic four stages of life of student, householder, hermit, and renouncer (see Chapter 1). Later Śaiva literature divides Śaiva sects into two main groups: this Higher Path (*ati-mārga*) and the Path of Mantras (*mantra-*

7 Bhaṭṭa, *Āgamaḍambara*, 4.10, p. 195.

mārga). The Mantra Mārga comprises various sects, among which is the Śaiva Siddhānta. Thus, in its precise and narrow meaning, 'Tantric Śaivism' simply refers to the Path of Mantras. Let us examine this important distinction for a moment.

The Ati Mārga and the Mantra Mārga

The Ati Mārga refers to the path of Śaiva ascetics. Sanderson has shown that there were three layers of successive sects classified within this branch – the Pāśupata, Lākula, and Kāpālika – that we will need to look at more closely in Chapter 3, but for now the main sect was the Pāśupata, those devoted to Paśupati, a name of Śiva meaning the Lord of Beasts (i.e. cattle) or Cowherd.[8] This sect became well patronised and wealthy. It owned temples and monasteries throughout the subcontinent and must have been a well-organised institution. As mentioned in Chapter 1, the Pāśupatas owned the great Śiva temple in Somnāth on the Gujarat coast, sacked by Mahmud of Gazni in 1026 and its reportedly gold symbol of Śiva (*liṅga*) removed, presumably to be melted down. The Pāśupatas are the oldest Śaiva sect, mentioned in the *Mahābhārata*.[9] The only Pāśupata scripture that has come down to us is the *Pāśupata Sūtra*, from the second century CE, with a commentary by Kauṇḍinya, dated to the fourth or fifth century CE.[10]

---

8 The Sanskrit *paśu* means 'beast'; it can refer to any animal but especially to cattle, exactly as the English word 'beast' which, more narrowly, refers to cattle in rural areas.

9 *Mahābhārata*, the *Nārāyaṇīya* section of the *Śāntiparvan* 337.62.

10 Hans Bakker and Peter Bisschop, 'Pāśupatasūtras 1.7–9 with the Commentary of Kauṇḍinya', p. 2. Unpublished but submitted for publication in 2011 to Somdev Vasudeva, *The Tantric Reader*. Also, Chakraborti, *Pāśupata-sūtram with Pañcārtha-bhāṣya of Kauṇḍinya*.

This text purports to be the teaching of Śiva who became (the possibly historical) sage Lākulīśa (the Lord with the Club), who animated the corpse of a Brahmin in the cremation ground; such an incarnation of Śiva is also attested in the *Kūrma Purāṇa*.[11] While such ascetics were clearly on the edges of orthodox society, the Pāśupatas still regarded themselves as being within the Vedic fold, their practice being the fulfilment of the Vedic path rather than its rejection.

The teachings of the *Pāśupata Sūtra* are pithy aphorisms that the commentator reads through the lens of five topics (*pañcārtha*) or five categories (*padārtha*): effect (*kārya*, i.e. worldly existence); cause (*kāraṇa*, i.e. God); union (*yoga*); praxis (*vidhi*); and the end of suffering (*duḥkhānta*).[12] In the Pāśupata order, individual ascetics were supposed to follow a rigorous regime of ascetism. Indeed, as Sanderson has pointed out, we need to distinguish the administrative and pedagogical intention of the Ati Mārga institutions from the practices of the ordinary Ati Mārga monastic. The monastic Pāśupatin would be concerned with his own spiritual practice or *sādhana* in contrast to the worldly concerns of the teacher (*ācārya*). The Pāśupata ascetic had to be a high-caste (twice-born), celibate male whose practice involved not speaking to women, and seeing woman as temptress who could distract the ascetic from his path.

The Pāśupata ascetic followed a vow (*vrata*) or regime of practice involving five stages, each of which bound him by specific rules (*niyama*). As Bakker and Bisschop note, these can be arranged according to place.[13] They are:

---

11 *Kūrma Purāṇa* 1.51.10.

12 Bakker and Bisschop, 'Paśupatasūtras 1.7–9', p. 2.

13 Ibid., p. 3, note 8.

1. The sanctuary (*āyatana*) or temple where the ascetic should worship God with laughter, song, dance, bellowing, obeisance, and muttering *mantras*,[14] and cover himself with cow-dung ash (which is pure).

2. The public place (*loka*) or practising in public places, behaving in anti-social ways so that the good *karma* of those who shouted abuse would be transferred to the ascetic.

3. An empty house or cave (*śūnyāgāra, guhā*) in which the ascetic would meditate on the five *mantras* of Śiva.

4. A cremation ground (*śmaśāna*) where he would deepen his meditation and eventually die, passing into the fifth stage, which is ...

5. Rudra, the goal of practice. Here the ascetic gains union with his deity (*rudra-sāyujya*), which he conceptualised as becoming omniscient and omnipotent. On this last stage the commentator Kauṇḍinya implies that the deity is seen in inner vision in contrast to the merely external form of Rudra in the image in a temple.[15]

Later subsects of the Ati Mārga were more extreme in their asceticism and in their attitude to Brahmanical purity rules that they flouted. So, to simplify a complex historical picture, we can draw up the following list of sects.

1. Tradition of orthodox Brahmanism that is related to Śaivism in various ways, rejecting it, accommodating

---

14 Ibid., 1.8, p. 12.

15 Ibid., p. 15, note 24, on the difficulties of interpreting this passage.

it, or becoming it: (a) the Vaidikas based on revelation: the Śrauta Brahmins concerned with their own ritual practices who rejected Śaivism; (b) the Vaidikas based on *smṛti* and also associated with the Purāṇic worship of Śiva, Viṣṇu, and the Goddess, known as Smārtas; some of them accommodated worship of Śiva and adopted it; (c) related to this, we have the lay followers of Śiva who followed the Śivadharma texts. These last two groups are lay devotees (*śiva-bhaktas*) who worship Śiva in the temple and aspire to rebirth in Śiva's heaven.

2. The Mantra Mārga. This is the path of Tantric Śaivism comprising two main divisions, notably the Śaiva Siddhānta who followed the new revelation of the dualist Tantras and also the non-Siddhānta, traditions that were said to follow non-dualist Tantras (which we shall deal with in Chapter 3). The Mantra Mārga is distinct from the lay Śaivism of the Śivadharma and Purāṇa followers in that it requires initiation (*dīkṣā*). The follower of the Mantra Mārga aspired to magical power (*siddhi*) and enjoyment (*bhoga, bhukti*) in this and other worlds and eventually liberation (*mokṣa*).

3. The Ati Mārga. This is the ascetic path of worshippers of Śiva; a monastic order called the Pāśupata, that became highly successful in the early medieval period. This tradition was historically prior to the Śaiva Siddhānta and influences it. The goal of the Pāśupatas is liberation rather than power and pleasure. There were three layers to this tradition, the first of which, the Pāśupatas, sees itself as fulfilling the Vedic path, while the latter two, the Lākulas and Kāpālikas, are the precursors of more extreme Tantric sects (see Chapter 3).

Figure 2.1. The Somnāth temple in Gujarat.

Figure 2.2. The Jyotirliṅga, symbol of Śiva, worshipped at the Somnāth temple.

The Śaiva Siddhānta Scriptures

So, from the seventh to eleventh centuries CE, Śaivism spreads, gaining support from kings and influencing other religions, such as Vaiṣṇavism, Buddhism, and Jainism, such that they copied Śaiva models as Sanderson has demonstrated.[16] From the more esoteric Śaiva sects of the Ati Mārga, which were ascetic and meditative, the Mantra Mārga developed. The earliest Śaiva Tantra that has come to light, the *Niḥśvāsa-tattva Saṃhitā*, is the Tantra that has been breathed out (*niḥśvāsa*) by Śiva, focusing on inner, meditative practices rather than external, temple ritual. The earliest parts of the *Niḥśvāsa* can be dated to the fifth century although most of the text was probably formed in the seventh. But it took a few hundred years for Śaivism to become the dominant religion, a position it retained until the thirteenth century.

There are nominally twenty-eight scriptures,[17] although there is some variation in the lists. Other important scriptures

---

16 For example, the Buddhists appropriate Tantric Śaiva texts with few reservations. See Sanderson's detailed demonstration of this appropriation, 'The Śaiva World', 124–242.

17 Dominic Goodall, 'Introduction', in *Bhaṭṭa Rāmakaṇṭha's Commentary on the Kiraṇatantra*, Vol. 1, Chapters 1–6 (Pondichéry: Institut Français de Pondichéry, 1998), xxxvi–xlvii. For a list of them in the early Siddhānta Tantras, see Goodall, *Kiraṇatantra*, Appendix III, 402–417. See also the list and discussion in Goodall, 'Introduction', *Parākhya-tantra*, pp. xxiii-xxiv. Most of this literature remains unedited and untranslated into European languages. Notable editions and translations are those of the Institut Français de Pondichéry, especially by Dominic Goodall (of note being the *Niḥśvāsa-tattva Saṃhitā* (with others), the *Kiraṇa Tantra*, and the *Parākhya Tantra*); the earlier work of Hélène Brunner, translations and editions of the *Somaśambhu-paddhati*, and the *Mṛgendrāgama*; and Michel Hulin's translation of the doctrine section of the *Mṛgendra*. The nineteenth-century translation of the Tamil *Tiruvācagam* by G. U. Pope (1900) is still good and of note.

of this tradition are the *Kiraṇa Tantra*, the *Parākhya Tantra*, the *Rauravāgama*, the *Mṛgendrāgama*, and the *Mataṅga-parameśvara*, although these last two important scriptures known to the Kashmirians, as Goodall notes, are absent from the lists.[18] Also, within this category are scriptures focused on temple ritual such as the *Dīptāgama* and the *Sūkṣmāgama*. The lists of the Tantras may indeed reflect historical development, as Goodall observes, and we can establish chronology through the development of different doctrines, such as lists of the constituents of the universe, and through cross-reference of texts to each other.[19] Generally, as time goes on, the lists of the constituents of the universe, such as the hierarchy of ontic levels or *tattvas*, become longer, as likewise the lists of different worlds (*bhuvana*) that exist in the universe. So, between the seventh to the ninth and early tenth centuries, the earliest scriptures of the Śaiva Siddhānta were formed, such as the *Kiraṇa* and the *Parākhya* Tantras, which are pre-tenth century.[20]

These texts were ideally divided into four sections or resting on four 'feet' (*pāda*), namely sections on doctrine, ritual, comportment, and yoga. Not every Tantra addresses every topic, but many do. Let us briefly describe some of these. The *Kiraṇa* and *Parākhya* Tantras, both edited and translated by Dominic Goodall, are fine exemplars of this genre of literature. Their doctrinal sections present the fundamentals of Śaiva Siddhānta

18 Goodall, 'Introduction', xlvi. *Kiraṇatantra*, pp. i–cxxv.

19 Goodall 'Introduction', xlvii–lv.

20 See Dominic Goodall, *The Parākhyatantra: A Scripture of the Śaiva Siddhānta* (Pondichéry: Institut Français de Pondichéry, 2004). In Goodall's words, the *Parākhya* joins 'a very small corpus of published pre-tenth century Saiddhāntika writings: the *Rauravasūtrasaṅgraha*, the *Svāyambhuvasūtrasaṅgraha*, the *Sārdhatriśatikālottara*, the *Kiraṇa*, the *Sarvajñānottara*, the *Mataṅga*, the *Mṛgendra*, and the surviving writings of Sadyojotis' (p. lxxxvii).

theology concerning the nature of God, the soul, and the world. The remaining sections present an account of how this theology can be realised or how liberation can be achieved through initiation, a ritual regime, and ultimately the grace of Śiva. The *Parākhya Tantra*, for example, provides a discussion of the soul in the first chapter, refuting other philosophical schools, especially the Buddhists but also Advaita Vedānta. Chapters 2 and 3 discuss the nature of God, followed by the evolution of the universe in Chapters 4 and 5, and Chapter 6 is about cosmic sound. Chapters 7 to 13 have not come down to us, but Chapter 14 discusses *yoga* and Chapter 15 is about initiation and practice focused on knowledge (*jñāna*), ritual (*kriyā*), behaviour (*caryā*), and *yoga*.[21] So let us begin our exploration of the Śaiva Siddhānta by discussing its doctrine or theology.

Śaiva Siddhānta Theology

The sources of Śaiva Siddhānta theology are the revealed scriptures or Tantras themselves (also sometimes called Āgamas) and the lineages of theologians who composed learned commentaries on them and sometimes wrote independent texts. In Kashmir, among these theologians of note are Sadyojotis (*c.* 675–750 CE), Bhaṭṭa Nārāyaṇakaṇṭha (second half of tenth century CE), his son Bhaṭṭa Rāmakaṇṭha (respected older contemporary of Abhinavagupta), and then in the Deccan, King Bhojadeva (reigned *c.* 1010–1055 CE), Aghoraśiva (mid-twelfth century), Umāpatiśiva (mid–late twelfth century), Somaśambhu (mid-eleventh century), and Īśānaśivagurudeva (eleventh century).[22] When the tradition

21 Goodall, *The Parākhyatantra*, lxii–lxiii.

22 For a detailed summary, see Alexis Sanderson, 'Śaiva Literature', 14–26.

went south by the tenth or eleventh century, theologians came to the fore. At Chidambaram we have Aghoraśiva, the composer of ritual manuals, Somaśambhu in the Golagī monastery in the kingdom of Kalacuris of Tripurī, and Īśānaśivagurudeva in Kerala. Once established in Tamilnadu, the tradition became influenced by Tamil devotion; the poet saints, the Nāyanmārs, come to be absorbed by the tradition and their collections of poetry regarded as authoritative.[23]

Although doctrines did change through time – such as those concerning the relation or predominance of grace or effort in salvation – there are some fundamentals that did not. The Śaiva Siddhānta maintains that there are three ontologically distinct realities: God, souls, and world or universe. Each of these is eternal with no beginning and no end. Souls are bound within matter, tethered to matter, and the goal of life is to become free and achieve salvation from entanglement in matter, in the cycle of reincarnation. God who stands outside of matter acts upon it to evolve it and causes the eventual withdrawal of the cosmos back into its quiescent state. Hence God is called *pati*, the Lord or cowherd, the soul is called *paśu*, the beast or cow, and the world is called *pāśa*, the rope that binds the beast. Let us examine each of these categories, God, soul, and matter.

Pati/God

God in Śaiva Siddhānta, who is Śiva, is worshipped in the form of Sadāśiva, the white, five-headed deity. God creates the universe because it is his nature to do so and in order that souls can be liberated. In his essential nature God is beyond

23 For those wishing to follow this up, a list of these theologians and their main works is provided in Appendix 1.

form and beyond human knowledge, although the true nature of the soul is identical to Śiva except in so far as God has precedence in creation.

God is the creator and omnipotent Lord, but, asks the *Kiraṇa Tantra*, how is it possible for God to create if he lacks the means to do so, because he does not have a body? The answer is that he does so through his will (*icchā*) and we can infer this from the universe which is an effect.

> Although devoid of senses, a magnet is observed to draw out [iron] splinters. And even if the activity [of creation of the universe] should not be [directly] observed, the effects [are seen and from them the Lord's] will [which is His instrument] is known.[24]

In himself, God is formless but is understood in scripture to be differentiated according to the division of his activities, into subtle or formless (*niṣkala*), coarse (*sthūla*), and both coarse and subtle (*sakala-niṣkala*), which are identified with the manifestations of Śiva called Śānta, Sadāśiva, and Īśvara.[25] Sadāśiva, as the mediator between the subtle and the gross, is the form of God worshipped in the Śaiva Siddhānta. These manifestations of the supreme Lord are pure bodies but also understood as bodies of sound or *mantras*. So, says the *Parākhya Tantra*, the Lord's body comprises *mantras* (*mantrāṅga*).[26] This body (which is, in effect, the body of Sadāśiva) is 'full with his five *mantras*' called Īśāna, Sadyojāta, Vāmadeva, Aghora and Tatpuruṣa.[27] These five correspond to different parts

---

24 *Kiraṇa Tantra* 3.11cf. Cf *Parākhya Tantra* 2.25c–26b.

25 *Kiraṇa Tantra* 3.13.

26 *Parākhya Tantra* 2.1.

27 *Parākhya Tantra* 2.83.

of God's body: Īśāna for his head, Tatpuruṣa for his mouth, Aghora for his heart, Vāmadeva for his genitals, and Sadyojāta for his form.[28] The reason why the Lord has a body made like this is so that he can be worshipped by everyone; his body is fashioned out of pure *mantras* to achieve this end and so his body is a contrivance or imagination (*vikalpa*) for sake of worship (*upacāra-nimitta*).[29] Each of these parts of his body has a distinct function: so the head, Īśāna, is endowed with sovereignty that comprises the power of knowledge (*jñāna-śakti*) and the power of action (*kriyā-śakti*); his mouth, Tatpuruṣa, clears away ignorance; his essential nature (*sad-bhāva*) is his heart, the non-terrible one (*a-ghora*), because the state of liberation, which is lovely (*vāma*), is hidden (*rahasya*). His private parts are called Vāmadeva, with Sadyojāta he creates bodies (*mūrti*) for souls, and his body is the object of Yogis' perception.[30]

Although God, Śiva, is the creator of the pure creation or 'pure path', he appoints a regent, a lower deity, Ananta, to create the impure path that is the lower universe. 'Just as another man, powerful like himself, is employed by a ruler of a kingdom in this world [to do his business], so too this [Ananta] does everything [after being] awakened by Śiva's power.'[31]

Ananta exists in the pure course of the universe as one of the eight Lords of Wisdom, the Vidyeśvaras;[32] it is his job to enact the will of the Lord and create the lower order of the universe. Ananta is omniscient (*sarva-jña*), his body is pure

---

28 *Parākhya Tantra* 2.84–85b.

29 *Parākhya Tantra* 2.86–87.

30 *Parākhya Tantra* 2.88–95b.

31 *Kiraṇa Tantra* 3.27.

32 The *Parākhya Tantra* 2.118–119 names them as Ananta, Sūkṣma, Śivottama, Ekadṛk, Ekarudra, Trimūrti, Śrīkaṇṭha, and Śrīkaṇḍin.

(*śuddha-deha*), and he reveals the twenty-eight scriptures.[33] The commentator Rāmakaṇṭha adds that the Vidyeśvaras are the teachers of all the scriptures, namely the ten scriptures of Śiva (*śiva-bheda*) and the eighteen of Rudra (*rudra-bheda*).[34]

The *Kiraṇa* then asks a theologically ponderous question. If Śiva awakens Ananta to create the lower universe through his power, then why does he not also awaken others who are proximate to Ananta? And if the Lord helps only those who are 'suitable' (*yogya*) then this means that he must be partial and so possess passion (*rāgavān*).[35] No, comes the answer, because the Lord is always dispassionate, without hatred or affection, and just as the sun shines equally upon lotuses, awakening some but not others, so the Lord shines on all souls, some of which awaken and respond.[36] So Ananta is employed by the Lord to create the lower universe, having been given omniscience by the Lord and acting in a body made of pure, primal source material (*śuddha-yoni-maya*), and not born of past action (*a-karma-ja*) as other bodies are.[37]

It is through the Vidyeśvaras that God performs his five acts (*pañca-kṛtya*): the creation, maintenance, and destruction of the (lower) universe, his concealment of himself within the universe, and his revelation of himself to the soul whereby he frees the soul from the bondage of matter.[38] The Vidyeśvaras are thus office holders or officiants (*adhikārin*) who perform duties appropriate to their station (*sthānādhikāra*), subject to

---

33 *Kiraṇa Tantra* 3.27ef.

34 *Kiraṇa Tantra* com., p. 299.

35 *Kiraṇa Tantra* 4.1 com., p. 301.

36 *Kiraṇa Tantra* 4.3–5b.

37 *Kiraṇa Tantra* 4.7c–8b.

38 *Parākhya Tantra* 2.123–124.

the Lord's will.[39] There is thus a complex cosmic bureaucracy that ensures the smooth running of the cosmos.

Thus, by way of summary, on the one hand we have the transcendent Lord (Śiva) beyond the universe who is formless (*niṣkala*), on the other we have God embodied in pure creation with form (*sakala*). The formless God starts creation by acting upon pure matter and then manifesting himself within it. This manifestation is in three forms according to the *Kiraṇa*, namely Śānta, Sadāśiva, and Īśvara. To complicate things even further, Sadāśiva who is the main deity worshipped by the Śaiva Siddhānta, has a body that itself is made up of five parts, the five deities named above which are themselves *mantras*, namely Īśāna (head), Tatpuruṣa (mouth), Aghora (heart), Vāmadeva (genitals), and Sadyojāta (form), and he creates the Vidyeśvaras, named above who form the lower creation (see Diagram 2.1).

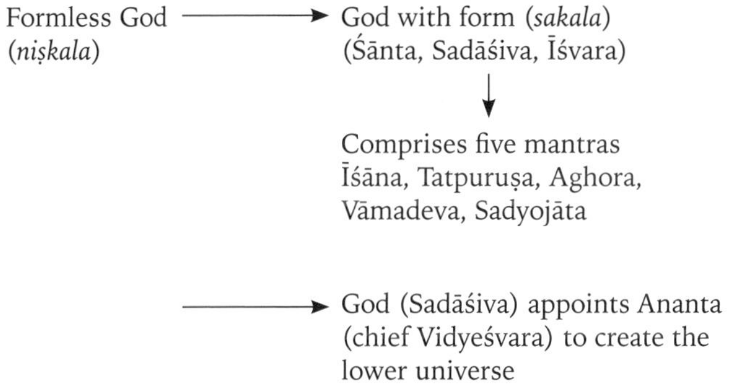

Diagram 2.1. God and Creation.

39 *Parākhya Tantra* 2.122.

Figure 2.3. Sadāśiva from West Bengal, eleventh century. Los Angeles County Museum of Art.

Paśu/Soul

Souls are innumerable. They are eternal and reincarnated over and over again in different bodies according to their action (*karma*) and controlled by other cosmological constraints. Although doctrinal details vary to some extent, all scriptural sources maintain the view that the soul is bound, entangled with material nature. There are different descriptions of this entanglement, but the basic idea is that the soul is particularised in a body, experiences a particular world through the body and senses, and this body is formed by cosmological forces as well as the soul's own actions. The soul is trapped in the cycle of reincarnation, the cycle of suffering, until such a time as its past *karma* is used up and the soul is saved through the grace of God. In the *Parākhya Tantra* we read:

> The bound soul is different from its body, indestructible, [all-]pervading, distinct [from God and from other souls], with impurity, not [innately] sentient, the experiencer of the fruits of its own actions, an agent, partially equipped with the powers of knowledge, subject to the Lord.[40]

The soul is bound and trapped within its world of experience because of its past actions but also because of cosmological constraints that bear down upon it.

As a way into this complex topic, I shall quote a somewhat concentrated passage from the *Kiraṇa Tantra* that Bhaṭṭa Rāmakaṇṭha's commentary can help us understand. The text reads:

> The bound soul's (*paśu*) consciousness is empowered by this [*kalā*], the sphere [of the operation of its senses] is made

40 Goodall, *The Parākhyatantra* 1.15.

> known by *vidyā* and it is also stained by passion. And matter (*pradhānaṃ ca*), which consists of the *guṇas* [viz. *sattva, rajas* and *tamas*] [is joined with the soul]. And the soul is bound through its connection with the organs [of sense and action] beginning with *buddhi* and with the army [of gross and subtle elements].[41]

This passage indicates how the soul is covered or constrained by cosmological forces, including the power of different levels (*kalā*) and the qualities (*guṇa*) that control the lower manifestation. *Kalā* refers to different realms of the cosmos that emerge from the pure level to the impure level and which contain various other sub-divisions within them including different worlds of experience. There are five such divisions of the cosmos that contain other categories. Thus, the passage indicates that the level at which the soul is incarnate controls or constrains its level of consciousness. As the commentator says, this is a limiting factor on the soul. Furthermore, the soul is constrained through its connection with sense organs and its modes of interacting with the world through the senses and inner instrument of the intellect (*buddhi*), mind, and so on (see below). In other words, the soul is embodied in a particular world of experience, and this embodiment is the result of a vast cosmological process of the unfolding or manifestation of matter that entraps the soul. This restriction of the soul is stained by passion, says the text, but also can be made known or revealed through wisdom or *mantra* (*vidyā*); the situation is not hopeless, however, as the soul can become free. This passion binds the soul, causing its attachment to objects of the senses (*viṣaya*), but such passion or attachment is not a property of the sense

41 *Kiraṇa Tantra* 1.16c–17. Goodall's translation pp. 201–202.

objects themselves, but only occurs internally within the soul (*adhyātma*).[42]

Furthermore, we cannot account for our experience of pleasure and pain other than through the operation of impurity on the soul, especially the impurity of past action or the accumulated traces that continue to affect the soul. There is a quality of binding fate (*niyati*) that links the soul to its *karma*, according to which the soul experiences the sphere (*gocara*) of its senses or world.[43] Rāmakaṇṭha introduces another classification set to explain the soul's limitation in its embodiment, namely impurity (*mala*), action (*karma*), and illusion/material substrate (*māyā*);[44] these cover the soul as it is entrapped within the impure universe created by Ananta. In a way not dissimilar to the Jain conception, *karma* is a substance (*dravya*) that needs to be cleaned from the soul to enable it to be free. This cleaning is done through action, through ritual action, but also achieved by the grace of God. As might be expected given this doctrine, there are different classes of souls depending upon their degree of impurity and bondage; more precisely, the soul has three conditions of isolation (*kaivalya*), being bound within the cosmos (*sakala*), and being pure.[45] To understand this, to understand the ways in which the soul is tied to the universe, we need to understand the structure of the universe itself and then how to escape from it.

---

42 *Kiraṇa Tantra* com, pp. 205–206.

43 *Kiraṇa Tantra* 1.20ab.

44 *Kiraṇa Tantra* com, p. 185. Later *mala* became a generic term for three impurities, namely of individuality (*āṇava-mala*), action (*kārma-mala*), and illusion (*māyīya-mala*) that are more dominant in later sources. Goodall, 'Introduction', *Kiraṇa Tantra*, p. xxxix, note 90.

45 *Kiraṇa Tantra* 1.23ab.

Pāśa/World

For the Śaiva Siddhānta the world we experience is part of a much larger cosmos, just one of very many worlds into which souls are born in a variety of bodies. The Śaiva cosmology became very elaborate with layers of added complexity. It is best to approach this historically, beginning with the ancient Indian system of Sāṃkhya, the school of philosophy that enumerated the categories that exist in the universe. These ontic categories were called *tattvas*, of which there are twenty-five. *Tattva* is not an easy term to translate; perhaps 'ontic category' is the best, because it designates both levels of the universe and constituents of the universe arranged in a hierarchical sequence. The word itself is simply the word 'this' (*tat*) plus the suffix designating 'ness' (*tva*), so the word literally means 'this-ness'.

Sāṃkhya was a dualist system of Indian thought maintaining a fundamental distinction between spirit or soul (*puruṣa*) and matter or nature (*prakṛti*). These are the first two ontic categories. The soul is passive consciousness that observes *prakṛti* from which the universe evolves or develops. Thus, *prakṛti* has an unmanifest state (*avyakta*) in which it is pure potential and a manifest state (*vyakta*) in which the different levels have evolved. Within *prakṛti* there are three qualities (*guṇa*) comprising lightness (*sattva*), passion (*rajas*), and darkness (*tamas*), and the evolutes from *prakṛti* depend upon the variation of the balance between these three – a preponderance of light, passion, or darkness. Indeed, this typology of *guṇas* became important in other fields of Indian thought, such as Āyurveda.

From *prakṛti*, the first evolute or category to emerge is *buddhi*. *Buddhi* is usually translated as 'intellect'; while this is not wrong, it is actually more than this since it denotes a higher level of mind: the emergence of cosmic, higher mind from primal matter – an idea perhaps not dissimilar to that of *nous* in Neo-Platonism. *Buddhi* functions, on the one hand, in an individual sense to mean the intellect of the person and, on the other hand, in a cosmological sense to mean higher mind as the first evolute of *prakṛti*. From *buddhi* – which is also called 'the great one' (*mahat*) – emerges the sense of limited self, the ego or 'I-maker' (*ahaṃkāra*); from this comes the mind (*manas*) along with the five senses (seeing, hearing, smelling, tasting, touching) and their objects, called the subtle elements or *tanmātras* (namely the objects of sight, sound, smells, taste, touch). Along with these there are the five organs of action (eye, voice, nose, ear, organs of excretion and reproduction). From the *ahaṃkāra* there also emerge the five gross elements (space, air, fire, water, and earth). These can be represented diagrammatically, as in Diagram 2.2: this is an analysis of a human being and the ways in which he or she interacts with the world.

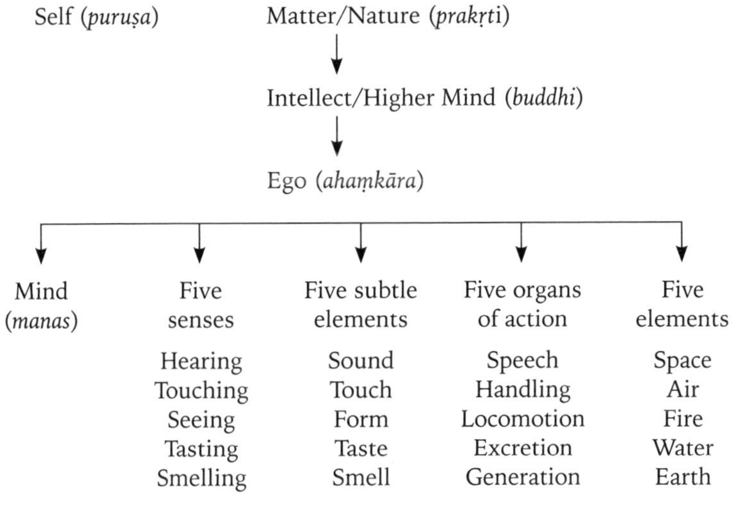

Diagram 2.2. The Twenty-Five Sāṃkhya Tattvas.

The Śaivas accepted this but thought it to be limited because it does not take account of even higher levels of the universe, including God himself. Sāṃkhya is an atheistic system: the Śaivas added a theistic dimension and further levels. Indeed, they added eleven further categories making a total of thirty-six, which became foundational in the Śaiva Siddhānta scheme, not only as an account of the universe and human life within it, but also of importance in ritual and eschatological anticipation of liberation.

Through his energy or Śakti, Śiva acts upon quiescent matter. The lower the universe unfolds or becomes manifest, the greater God is concealed; conversely, the more the universe retracts to its source, the more God is revealed. This is a cosmological process but is recapitulated in the practitioner in the symbolic action of creating and destroying the universe within the body (see below). The first emanation is the Śiva *tattva*, which is also called 'the drop' (*bindu*) or 'Great Illusion' (*mahā-māyā*). From the drop the pure creation emerges. Then the impure creation emerges from the pure creation, impelled or created by the demiurge or regent Ananta. *Prakṛti* becomes a lower manifestation of *māyā* which in turn reflects *bindu* or *mahā-māyā*. *Māyā* produces five 'coverings' around the soul, which then experiences the world through the even lower categories of *buddhi*, *ahaṃkāra*, and *manas* (these three called the 'inner instrument') along with the senses and organs of action (i.e. the human body). Diagram 2.3 presents a simple list of the thirty-six *tattvas*.

This whole process emerges in order for souls to experience the results of their actions and in order that they can gain liberation. These *tattvas* are both constituents of a person that describe the cosmological forces limiting the individual soul and also regarded as levels of the universe. The *śiva-tattva*, then, is not to be confused with Śiva as God, as the instigator of creation and deliverer of souls from suffering. The *śiva-tattva* is the

Transcendent Śiva

Pure Creation

1 Śiva
2 Śakti
3 Sadāśiva
4 Īśvara
5 Śuddha Vidyā

Impure Creation

6 Māyā [5 coverings (*kañcukas*)]
7 Limited authorship (*kalā*)
8 Limited knowledge (*vidyā*)
9 Passion (*rāga*)
10 Limited time (*kāla*)
11 Spatial constraint or Fate (*niyati*)
12 Limited self (*puruṣa*)
13 Nature, matter (*prakṛti*)
14 Intellect, higher mind (*buddhi*) }
15 Ego (*ahaṃkāra*) } inner instrument
16 Mind (*manas*) }

17	Hearing	22	Speech	27	Sound	32	Space
18	Touching	23	Handling	28	Touch	33	Air
19	Seeing	24	Locomotion	29	Form	34	Fire
20	Tasting	25	Excretion	30	Taste	35	Water
21	Smelling	26	Generation	31	Smell	36	Earth

Diagram 2.3. The Thirty-Six Śaiva Tattvas.

purest point of the universe from which all the rest unfolds. God (Śiva) impels the universe to evolve from a single point or drop (*bindu*) connected with the *śakti-tattva*.

Other Cosmological Systems

Apart from the *tattva* scheme, the Śaiva Siddhānta incorporated other cosmological systems. They all share the same basic idea that the universe is a hierarchy of levels with the pure, most immaterial, at the top, and the impure, most material, at the bottom. The journey of the soul back to God is a journey through these levels, from the bottom, most material level, to the top. The *tattva* hierarchy was incorporated into a scheme called the Six Paths (*ṣaḍ-adhvan*), which it divided into the three paths of sound (*vācaka*) and the three paths of objects (*vācya*); these are also related to time and space respectively. The scheme is as shown in Diagram 2.4.

Path of Sound	**Path of Objects**
Phoneme (*varṇa*)	Power (*kalā*)
Mantra	*Tattva*
Word (*pada*)	World (*bhuvana*)

Diagram 2.4. The Six Paths.

While the scheme can be laid out in this fashion, it also functions in parallel, so for example, the thirty-six *tattvas*, described above, are located within five levels of Power (*kalā*), and within the *tattvas* innumerable worlds are located. These paths are used in ritual, especially initiation, as we will see in a moment. Or the phonemes of the Sanskrit alphabet (*a, ā, i, ī, u, ū... ka, kha, ga, gha, ṅa* ... and so on) correspond to different *mantras*, which correspond with words, which correspond to the levels in the path of objects.[46] This can all get very complicated, but one of the most interesting features of these cosmologies is the Path of Worlds. Different texts add worlds

46 On the six ways, see Hélène Brunner, *Somaśambhu-paddhati*, vol. 3 (Pondichéry: Institut Français, 1977), Introduction, xiii–xxii. There are extremely useful diagrams laying out the correspondences, especially plate 5. See also André Padoux, *Vāc: The Concept of the Word in Selected Hindu Tantras*, trans. Jacques Gontier (Albany: SUNY Press, 1990), 330–371.

to the list, so we can do a kind of textual archaeology, with the lower worlds representing earlier traditions. Let us take an example from the *Parākhya Tantra*.

Chapter 5 of the *Parākhya Tantra* presents an account of the different worlds in the cosmos.[47] The cosmos is conceptualised as a gigantic egg (*aṇḍa*) which is divided into levels. So, in the *Parākhya* scheme, at the base, or to be more precise, some way above the base ('a hundred crores of *yojanas*'),[48] is the world of Kālāgnirudra, the Rudra of the Fire of Time.[49] His body, says the text, is ten million times as bright as the sun (5.8). Above this world are hell realms, which the text names, at the top of which is the world of Kūṣmāṇḍa who presides over the hells (34c–40b). The hells are vividly named – Needle Mouth, Sword, Razorblade, Heated-coals, Flesh-eater, Full of Sighs, Iron Pillar, Full of Worms, Full of Excrement, and so on (5.12–15). These are terrible places where souls suffer – Tāla is a hell where their bodies are cut open by bark garments, another hell comprises only flaming fire, another a mass of very cold snow (5.19–22), and Iron Pillar is where souls are scorched on iron plates (5.28).

Above the hells are the subterranean paradises (*pātālas*) at the top of which is the world of Hāṭaka who presides over them (40c–52). In contrast to the ferocious Rudras below him, he is kind, generous, and peaceful, and surrounded by lovely women (5.56–57). Above him and his world is the earth, our own world, comprising seven oceans and seven continents

47 Usefully summarized by Goodall, *Parākhya-tantra* 'Introduction', xxi–lxxii.

48 *Parākhya Tantra* 5.5–10.

49 The fire of time (*kālāgni*) is the fire that consumes the world at the end of a cycle of creation. This explains why it is situated at the very bottom, even below the hells.

(61–63b not known to modern Geography). This is the same as the cosmology in the Purāṇas, with the great mount Meru rising from the continent where we live, Jambudvīpa (63c–93). The text describes the worlds existing up to the edge of the cosmic egg. Above the earth is the world called *bhuvar-loka*, 'a place which causes amazement', in which are located the sun, the planets of the weekdays, and Rahu and Ketu, with the stars above them, the sages (*ṛṣis*) above those, and then the pole star (*dhruva-loka*). Above that is the sky world, *svar-loka*, and above that, further worlds up to *satya-loka* where the deity Brahmā lives (130–138b). Way above him is the world of Viṣṇu and way above that is the world of Śaṅkara. Above him is the shell of the cosmic egg (138c–140). The text then gives a slightly different scheme of the pure universe situated above the *māyā-tattva*: the levels of Pure Knowledge (*śuddha-vidyā*), Ananta in the *īśvara-tattva*, and Brahmā at the level of Sadāśiva (forgetting that it has previously described him as being in the *satya-loka*). People who are devoted to these gods are born in their heavens at death and remain there until the dissolution of the universe. Upon the re-creation of the universe, they will be born into good families in the human realm (5.138c–140b).

This account of the universe within the cosmic egg contains vivid descriptions of the hell realms worthy of Dante and presents a vivid picture of a vast but finite universe. Beings are born within it according to their actions and reap the fruits of those actions in these different worlds. Yogis through practice can achieve pleasure in the realms just below the earth (*pātāla*) with the beautiful women living there, and devotees of Viṣṇu, Śiva, and Brahmā can be reborn in their heavens. But the Śaiva Siddhānta offers not rebirth in the heaven of Śiva – which is for followers of the Purāṇas and Śivadharma texts – but total liberation and freedom from the cosmic egg, freedom from reincarnation. It is the process of gaining such freedom to which we now turn.

Figure 2.4. A mid-nineteenth-century depiction of Śiva breaking the cosmic egg.

Śaiva Siddhānta Practice

The goal of liberation is achieved through ritual together with the grace of Śiva. Having undergone initiation by the guru who embodies Śiva, the disciple then undertakes a regime of daily ritual until death, at which time he achieves liberation. Thus, there is no liberation in life (*jīvan-mukti*) for the Śaiva Siddhāntin, but only at death (*videha-mukti*). Initiation (*dīkṣā*) is the necessary condition for liberation. At liberation, the soul is taken from the human condition (*puṃs-bhāva*) to the liberated condition, through purifying the six paths within the body. This initiation imposes the Tantric vision on the body and supersedes the Vedic initiation, even such that Śaiva initiation eradicates or supersedes caste. Indeed, at least one text, the *Rauravāgama,* says that simply following the path of the Śaiva is enough and equivalent to initiation. The text says:

> From ashes and rosary beads and from binding [the body] through the ritual process of Śiva, wearing the topknot and the sacred thread, one is said to be initiated. A living being should devote himself entirely to the pure Śaiva [path] taught in this Tantra. By giving himself over to the teaching he is said to be initiated into it. Having matted hair or a shaved head, the teacher of Śiva makes entrance to an immoveable image (*liṅga*). He is said to be a living Maheśvara, [so] entering the condition of the Maheśvara he abides, possessing the mark of Śiva. Brahmin or outcaste, with good or bad qualities, using ash and the rosary beads, without doubt [he becomes] a Śiva. After becoming Śiva in this way [through ritual] he should act as a Śaiva.[50]

Following the Śaiva path ensures liberation.

The *Somaśambhu-paddhati*, an eleventh-century text described in detail by Hélène Brunner, prescribes three initiations: the general (*samaya-dīkṣā*) and the particular (*viśeṣa-dīkṣā*), allowing entry into the cult, and the liberating initiation (*nirvāṇa-dīkṣā*).[51] The main distinction here is between the general and the liberating; those who have undergone the former are called *samayin* and those who have undergone the latter are called *putraka* (Son of Śiva) and are guaranteed liberation at death. Two further consecrations can take place after this, for someone who wishes to become a teacher (*ācāryābhiṣeka*), which means he has the authority to initiate disciples, and for someone wishing to experience power and pleasure in higher worlds before liberation, called the *sādhaka* consecration (*sādhakābhiṣeka*). This distinction reflects that between one who seeks liberation (*mumukṣu*) and

50 *Rauravāgama*, ed. N. R. Bhatt (Pondichéry: Institut Français de Pondichéry, 1985), vol. III, 63.24–28.

51 She summarises the process in *Somaśambhu-paddhati*, Vol. 3, xxxviii–xliii.

one who seeks power and pleasure in higher worlds before final liberation (*bubhukṣu*).[52] Having undergone initiation, the disciple would undergo a regime of daily ritual practice until his death.

Generally, initiation was a precondition for liberation in the Śaiva Siddhānta. This was understood not only as a shift in social condition or status but also an ontological shift, in so far as the soul of the practitioner is guaranteed liberation through grace, mediated through the master called *guru, ācārya,* or *deśika*. The general (*samaya*) and particular (*viśeṣa*) initiations are part of a single rite; this involves preparing a ritual diagram (*maṇḍala*) onto which the deities of the Śaiva pantheon are installed, paying homage to the door guardians of the diagram, and preparing the fire ritual (*homa*). The master symbolically places Śiva and his throne in the disciple's body and initiates him by placing his hand, which is Śiva's hand (*śiva-hasta*), on his head, thereby completing the general part. The particular initiation then involves the master transporting the soul (*ātman*) of the disciple to the womb of the Goddess of Speech, Vāgīśvarī, who has been installed in the fire. The disciple is born from her womb, in a sense, as a son of Śiva (her consort) although at this stage he is called a *samayin*.[53]

The second initiation, the *nirvāṇa-dīkṣā,* ensures liberation. This is the most important Śaiva Siddhānta ritual and according to Somaśambhu takes two days under a ritual pavilion (*maṇḍapa*). After the first day of preliminary rites, the second day involves the master symbolically entering the disciple's body through the aperture in the crown of the head and travelling down to his heart. Here he takes the disciple's soul and leaves the body with the soul by the same route, leaving through the aperture

52 Hélène Brunner, 'Le Sādhaka, un personnage oublié du Śivaisme du Sud', *Journal Asiatique,* 1975: 411–416.

53 *Somaśambhu-paddhati,* Vol. 3, 4.93–104.

at the crown of the head and taking the soul into his own body, through the aperture in his own head, down to his own heart. He then emits the disciple's soul back through the crown of his head and establishes it in a cord the length of the body. This cord (*pāśa*) represents the universe which binds the soul as well as the central channel that is thought to pervade the body. The hierarchy of the universe (described above) is implanted on the cord through a practice of imposing mantras or *nyāsa*. Any of the six paths described above can be used on the cord, but Somaśambhu prefers the five *kalās* (see Diagram 2.5). Each *kalā* is 'purified' on the thread, which means that the disciple's soul is detached from it. Symbolically the cord is cut and that part, that *kalā*, burned in the fire. The rite takes a long time as the master must extract the *kalā* along with disciple's soul at each stage of the rite and attach them to the cord, and the disciple is symbolically born into the different worlds of the cosmos arranged along the cord. The initiand's soul is symbolically lifted through the hierarchy of the universe in this process, the master joining a soul with a particular world, letting him enjoy that world, then taking him to the next level. Thus, for example, first the disciple is symbolically born into the lowest world in the universe of Kālāgnirudra (see above) and from there rises up to higher worlds.[54] Initiation can therefore use any of the six ways as the path of purification. The purification of the five

54 For example, the *Mataṅga-parameśvarāgama, Kriyā-pāda* 7.17–18. 'The *mantra* master, with the appropriate ritual gesture of destruction and with the formula "*śarvaśarva*", should unite [the soul of the disciple] in the womb [of the world] to be grasped with [the form of Śiva] Sadyojāta. Having first imagined the world of the Rudra of the fire of time, he should visualize it [?]. In accordance with the rule of the soul, Śiva commands "come from the world of Rudra, *svāhā*".' *Mataṅgaparameśvarāgama,* ed. N. R. Bhatt (Pondichéry: Institut Français de Pondichéry, 1977).

kalās is in fact the purification of all the cosmic paths. The cord is thus 'the image of the disciple, with his *ātman* imprisoned by bonds (hence the name *pāśa-sūtra*, the "cord of bonds")'.[55] With the burning of the last *kalā* (called *śānty-atītā*, beyond tranquillity) on the last piece of cord, the disciple is purified, and his soul set free from the bond of the universe.

The *Kiraṇa Tantra* raises the pertinent question: if all bonds are destroyed in initiation, how is it that the body remains? The Lord answers this question by saying that as a potter makes a pot and once the pot is made, the wheel upon which it rests nevertheless continues to turn for a while, so it is with the body.[56] In more technical language, this means that the storehouse of *karma* (*sañcita-karma*) has been destroyed by the *mantras* at initiation, and future *karma* (*āgamin*) has been blocked, but *karma* to be used up in the present life (*prārabdha*) remains. Past karmic debt is all burned up and no future karma can be accrued.

Cord	Śāntyatītā	Śiva and Śakti *tattvas*
	Śānta	Sadāśiva, Īśvara, Śuddhavidyā *tattvas*
	Vidyā	Māyā to Rāga *tattvas*
	Pratiṣṭhā	Puruṣa to Water *tattvas*
	Nivṛtti	Earth *tattva*

Diagram 2.5. List of Kalās and Corresponding Tattvas Mapped onto a Cord Representing the Initiate.

Having been initiated, the disciple – the *putraka* – will

55 Brunner-Lachaux, *Somaśambhupaddhati*, Vol. 3, xxxix: 'La cordelette ainsi préparée est l'image du disciple, avec son ātman emprisonné de liens (d'ou son nom *pāśusūtra*, "cordelette des liens").'

56 *Kiraṇa Tantra*, 4.18–21.

then follow a regime of daily ritual (*nitya-karman*) until death, thereby burning up what remains of his *karma*. These are performed at the junctures of the day, dawn, dusk, and midday. The *Rauravāgama* says that rites are of two kinds, either for oneself (*ātmārtha-pūjā*) or for others (*parārtha-pūjā*) in public ritual before the icon of Śiva (*liṅga*) in a temple.[57] The text says that ritual requires purification of the self (*ātma-śuddhi*), purification of the place (*sthāna-śuddhi*), purification of ritual implements and substances (*dravya-śuddhi*), purification of the Śiva *liṅga*, and purification of *mantra*. The practitioner should worship Lord Sadāśiva in the heart first, followed by external offerings.[58] In the *Somaśambhu-paddhati*, a ritual manual somewhat like a recipe book of rites to be followed, we have morning ablutions, the evacuation of bodily impurities, bathing rites, followed by purification of the body, creating a divine body through *mantras*, mental worship, followed by external worship.[59] There are many ritual details given in the text: pilgrimage sites or 'crossing points' (*tīrtha*) are to be established on the hands, with the ancestors on the index finger, the deity Prajāpati on the little finger, Brahman on the thumb, and other gods on the remaining fingers.[60] Offerings of holy water are made to Śiva, to the gods, to the ancestors of one's family lineage (*gotra*), from father to paternal grandfather, up to the father of the father of the paternal grandfather, as well as on

57 *Rauravāgama*, Vol. 3, supplement 59.3–7b. On the distinction, see Brunner 'Ātmārthapūjā versus Parārthapūjā in the Śaiva Tradition', in *Sanskrit Tradition and Tantrism*, ed. T. Goudriaan (Leiden: Brill 1990), 1–23. Brunner observes that ritual for self or other does not map directly onto the private/public distinction because it makes no difference in temple worship whether there are witnesses or not (p. 7).

58 *Rauravāgama, Vidyā-pāda* 12.1–5.

59 *Somaśambhu-paddhati*, Vol. 1, chapter 1.

60 *Somaśambhu-paddhati*, Vol. 1, 1.65.

the Mother's side.[61] This shows how the *putraka* sees himself within the continuity of a family lineage, within a cosmos – we are not so very far here from Vedic rites.

As an example of the process involved, the purification of the body (*deha-śuddhi, bhūta-śuddi*) means visualising the body as pervaded by the cosmic hierarchy. The body is then purified by imagining the elements from feet to knees (earth), from knees to thighs (water), from thighs to navel (fire), from navel to throat (air), and from throat to crown (ether). Each is systematically 'destroyed' through *mantra* repetition. Finally the practitioner images a fire burning from the big toe – the fire of time, Kālāgni – rendering the physical body to a pile of ashes, which is then swept away by a flood from *mantra* repetition (I think released from the crown of the head, the abode of the nectar of immortality).[62] Here is an example of the injunction from another ritual manual, that of Īśānaśivagurudeva of Kerala, slightly later than that of Somaśambhu:

> The image of the earth (*bhū-maṇḍala*), which is a yellow square, marked with the sign of thunder (*vajra*), whose quality is smell, [associated with] the Sadya *mantra* and the sense organ of smell, with the cosmic region (*kalā*) of Nivṛtti, and with the divine four faced one (Brahmā). By means of the seed syllable *hlāṃ* [the body] is pervaded with the filling and holding breaths from the head to the soles of the feet. There

---

61 *Somaśambhu-paddhati,* Vol. 1, 3.8. On the place of ancestors, see Alexis Sanderson, 'Meaning in Tantric Ritual', in *Essais sur le Rituel III: Colloque du Centenaire de la Section des Sciences religieuses de l'École Pratique des Hautes Études*, ed. A.-M. Blondeau and K. Schipper (Louvain/ Paris: Peeters, Bibliothèque de l'École des Hautes Études, Sciences Religieuses, Volume CII, 1995), 15–95.

62 See Gavin Flood, 'The Purification of the Body in Tantric Ritual Representation', *Indo-Iranian Journal* 45 (2002): 25–43.

> is purification from repeating it [the seed syllable] five times and he should then visualize it as entering into the air [i.e. he exhales the earth element into the air element].[63]

This is a pan-Tantric practice, with each of the elements in turn being purified and merged into their subtle equivalent. Thus here, the earth element (the thirty-sixth *tattva*) is dissolved into the air element (thirty-fifth *tattva*). So, the lowest level of the body is associated with the lowest layer of the cosmos, the Nivṛtti *kalā*, governed by the deity Brahmā, which is symbolically dissolved. The dissolution of the universe is recapitulated in the dissolution of the body. Thus, daily ritual reflects the periodic dissolution of the cosmos and the vertical ascent of the soul to liberation. This process occurs with each of the elements mapped onto the body.

Once the purification of the body is complete, the practitioner can create a divine body (*divya-deha*) though placing *mantras* on it (*nyāsa*), for only a god can worship a god, followed by inner or mental worship, which is visualising the deity at the crown of the head and brought down into the heart, seated on a lion throne and worshipped there. External worship is making external offerings to the image of Śiva, and this is followed by a fire oblation.

The goal of this regime of daily practice is liberation (*mokṣa*) attained at death. Although the regime of regular practice is necessary, in the end it is through Śiva's grace that the soul is set free. In the Śaiva Siddhānta, this is understood not as the disciple merging with Śiva but as becoming equal to Śiva (*śiva-tulya*). This equality with Śiva means that one has all the qualities of Śiva – omniscience, omnipresence, omnipotence –

63 *Īśānaśivagurudeva-paddhati, Sāmānya-pāda* 10.14–15. *Īśānaśivagurudeva-paddhati*, ed. Unni, 4 vols. (Delhi: Srisatguru Publications, 1988).

except that one does not perform the acts of creation, maintenance, and destruction. There is numerical distinction from Śiva and hence this is an ontologically dualistic theology. This view is defended by the theologian Sadyojyotis (675–725 CE) in his *Para-mokṣa-nirāsa-kārikā,* an inquiry into the nature of liberation, which refutes twenty other concepts of liberation from the Buddhists to the Advaitins.[64]

In all of this we see the importance of the teacher. The *Mataṅga-pārameśvarāgama* describes the roles of master and disciple. Indeed, the *samayin* must serve the master almost as a slave, while the *putraka* should practice the general principles (*sāmānyācāra*) of Śaivism, especially honouring the master, the deity, and the fire, while remaining calm; the *sādhaka* should focus on his own *mantra*. The teacher similarly has duties and obligations towards his disciples, to initiate and teach them and so facilitate the descent of Śiva's grace (*śakti-pāta*) upon them.[65]

From these texts we can construct a picture of life in the medieval period, with clear distinctions between types of practitioner and levels of attainment. While the chapters on comportment (*caryā*) in the Tantras present a view of the householder, and his obligations to master and family, there is also room for the solitary Yogi, the *sādhaka* seeking power before final liberation. The Śaiva Siddhāntin conformed to Vedic orthodoxy and practice of *varṇāśrama-dharma,* although other Tantric traditions did not, as we will see in Chapter 3.

---

64 Watson, Alex, Dominic Goodall, and S.L.P. Anjaneya Sharma, *An Enquiry into the Nature of Liberation: Bhaṭṭa Rāmakaṇṭha's Paramokṣanirāsakārikāvṛtti, a commentary on Sadyojyotiḥ's refutation of twenty conceptions of the liberated state (mokṣa)* (Pondichéry: Institut Français de Pondichéry, 2013).

65 *Mataṅga-pārameśvarāgama, Caryā-pāda* 4.14–17.

But not everybody was welcome to practice Śaiva Siddhānta and the tradition adhered to Vedic social values and differentiation between social groups. The *Mṛgendrāgama*, for example, divides Śaivas into four groups: masters; *mantra* specialists or *sādhakas*; initiated Śaivas or *putrakas*; and ordinary initiates or *samayins*. These Śaivas may wear matted locks or shave the head, bearing the marks of the Śaiva such as covering the body in ash and wearing Śaiva markings on the body. But the lowest caste was excluded, along with the ignorant, the mad, women, the old, those with missing limbs, and so on.[66]

Temple Ritual

Apart from this elaborate process of daily rites, which can be performed more quickly with practice, there is worship of Śiva in the temple. Devotion (*bhakti*) is not a feature of Tantric traditions because it has 'no soteriological value'.[67] For Śaiva Siddhānta theologians such as Rāmakaṇṭha, *bhakti* was appropriate for women[68] and *bhakti* as an attitude was expected towards one's teacher.[69] But temple worship became an important feature of Śaiva Siddhānta. Texts of the Śaiva Siddhānta canon such as the *Dīptāgama* and *Sūkṣmāgama* are devoted to

66 *Mṛgendrāgama* 4.1.4. The commentary glosses the list as *śūdra-mūrkha-pramatta-strī-vṛddhāmayāvivikalāṅgair vā jaṭā na dhāraṇīyāḥ*, 'Those who may not bear matted locks are those of the lowest caste, the foolish, the insane, women, the old, the sick, or those with insufficient limbs'.

67 Dominic Goodall, 'Tantric Śaivism & Bhakti: how are they related?' Paper given at the International Workshop-cum-Conference 'Archaeology of Bhakti: Royal Bhakti, Local Bhakti', organised by Emmanuel Francis, Valérie Gillet, and Charlotte Schmid at the EFEO Centre in Pondichéry from 31 July to 13 August 2013.

68 *Parākhya Tantra* 6.11–12.

69 Sanderson, 'Meaning in Tantric Ritual', 26.

temple construction, the installation of images, and temple practices. There are accounts of temple construction and elaborate festivals. Thus, the Śaiva tradition came to appeal to all levels of society, from esoteric practitioners wishing to gain magical power, to kings and the royal family, to temple priests. Indeed, in the South, the Śaiva Siddhānta absorbed Tamil devotionalism, with the Tamil poetry of the Nāyanmārs becoming part of the Śaiva textual corpus. The *Tēvāram*, a collection of Tamil devotional poetry compiled by Nampi Antar Nampi in the tenth century, eventually came to be part of the canon.

The eleventh century witnessed the creation of the great regional temples focused on Śiva. The Cola kings were supporters of Śaivism and the Śaiva Siddhānta became a pan-Indic tradition. Chidambaram became a great temple city focused on Śiva (where the image is of Śiva Naṭarāja) and the Cola kings built Tanjavur and the marvelous Gangaikondacolapuram. The image in the temples is the Śiva *liṅga*. If the Śaiva Siddhānta is Tantric religion par excellence, these are Tantric temples.

Figure 2.5. The Naṭarāja temple in Chidambaram.

Figure 2.6. An early nineteenth-century gouache painting of Śiva Naṭarāja associated with Chidambaram.

Concluding Comments

With the Śaiva Siddhānta we have a highly successful religion that, along with more popular Śaivism, dominated India from the early medieval period to the thirteenth century. It was adopted by kings – in particular one thinks of the Colas in the South and the marvellous artwork produced – as well as by ordinary householders. It also became very influential on other religions. Based on a new revelation from a theistic reality, it considered itself as going beyond the earlier Vedic revelation; it guaranteed liberation and, not only this, but power and pleasure in higher worlds. It was certainly a soteriology, but it was also a religion of this world, with practical dimensions of protection from supernatural forces and empowerment of kings in their quest for power and territory. It succeeded even in penetrating the courts of Khmer kings in south-east Asia. The Śaiva Siddhānta became aligned with Brahmanical orthodoxy to some extent, but it succeeded in taking over much of the role of the Vaidika practitioner. It is the core Tantric tradition and it is in relation to this that other Tantric traditions need to be understood.

Discussion Topic: The Śaiva Siddhānta

- Why did the Śaiva Siddhānta have such appeal in the early medieval period?
- What could be an explanation as to why its cosmology is so complex?
- What are the goals of Śaiva Siddhānta?
- What was the religious situation from the seventh to eleventh centuries and who was the Śaiva Siddānta competing against?

Further Reading

R. Davis. *Ritual in an Oscillating Universe: Worshipping Śiva in Medieval India*. Princeton: Princeton University Press, 1991.

Dominic Goodall. 'Introduction'. *Bhaṭṭa Rāmakaṇṭha's Commentary on the Kiraṇatantra*, Vol. 1, Chapters 1–6. Pondichéry: Institut Français de Pondichéry, 1998.

Alexis Sanderson. 'Śaiva Literature'. *Journal of Indological Studies* 24/25 (2012/2013): 13–32.

III
Extreme Tantra

Tantrism in the modern world became famous – or infamous – for its use of sex in ritual and yoga. Sexual rituals were certainly a feature of some Tantric traditions, along with other antinomian practices such as consumption of polluting products of the body and making offerings of blood and alcohol to ferocious Goddesses. These were regarded as non-dualistic practices (*advaitācāra*) because the extreme traditions did not distinguish between pure and impure substances used as ritual offerings. You will recall from Chapter 2 that the Mantra Mārga (the more technical name for Tantric Śaivism) was made up of two groups, the Śaiva Siddhānta and the non-Siddhānta (or Saiddhāntika can also be used, denoting those who follow the Siddhānta) religions. The Śaiva Siddhānta revered Sadāśiva, had their own canon of scriptures (Tantras), and were aligned with Vedic or Brahmanical orthopraxy. The non-Saiddhāntika scriptures revered the ferocious form of Śiva, Bhairava, and rejected Vedic orthopraxy. These traditions comprised a number of groups, as we will see, but all rejected the idea of maintaining ritual purity, at least privately. So, the antinomian dimension of Tantra is within the Bhairava scriptures of the non-Saiddhāntika religions of the Mantra Mārga. These traditions revered a different set of Tantras, 'non-dualist' Tantras, and while usually accepting normative Śaiva practices, considered their own practices and revelation to go beyond even

Figure 3.1. Sculpture depicting Bhairava, Hoysala period (tenth–fourteenth century CE). Chhatrapati Shivaji Maharaj Vastu Sangrahalaya.

the Saiddhāntika scriptures. These non-Saiddhāntika religions were focused not on the calm and consortless Sadāśiva, but on Bhairava, the ferocious form of Śiva, and sometimes on his consort worshipped alone as the supreme Goddess. These traditions can be designated as Śākta-Śaiva, but there was also an independent tradition focused on the Goddess, a distinct Śākta tradition called the Kula Mārga.

Although the term 'Kashmir Śaivism' has become standard to denote the non-Saiddhāntika traditions, this is somewhat of a misnomer, as Sanderson shows, for these traditions also existed beyond the borders of Kashmir,[1] so I will use the more accurate 'non-Saiddhāntika' traditions. But having said that, there was indeed a strong non-Saiddhāntika current within Kashmir and a tradition of Tantric revelation and commentary. To understand these traditions, we must go back to the Ati Mārga introduced in Chapter 2.

The Kāpālika Ati Mārga (Ati Mārga III)

As we have seen in Chapter 2, the Ati Mārga was ascetic Śaivism initially comprising a sect known as the Pāśupatas. This became a highly successful tradition, owning land and monasteries and seeing itself as the fulfilment of the Vedic tradition. It was not anti-Vedic per se but regarded itself as going beyond the Veda. As you will recall, the tradition's founder was Lakulīśa, who was regarded as an incarnation of Śiva. Śiva incarnated into the body of the Brahmin and conveyed the Pāśupata teachings, as we have seen. There was a further, second layer to this tradition (Ati Mārga II) called the Lākula, also known as the Kālāmukha sect, and a third layer (Ati Mārga III)

1 Alexis Sanderson, 'Śaivism and the Tantric Traditions', in *The World's Religions*, ed. S. Sutherland, L. Houlden, P. Clarke, and F. Hardy, 660–704 (London: Routledge, 1988), 663.

called the Kāpālika, or Mahāvratin, or Somasiddhānta. It is this third layer of the Ati Mārga that we need to describe.

The Kāpālikas have a bad reputation in the history of Sanskrit literature. They were ascetics who rejected the Veda and were often lampooned as being monstrous and hypocritical characters in plays.[2] The Kāpālika ascetic was somewhat like a Pāśupata ascetic except that rather than cow dung ash, he covered himself in the ashes from the cremation ground, and so, rather than being pure in orthodox eyes, was polluted. The Kāpālika also carried a skull begging bowl and a skull-topped staff (*khatvāṅga*); hence the name 'Kāpālika', 'one who carries a skull (*kapāla*)'. The Kāpālika observance (*vrata*) resembled the 'great vow' (*mahā-vrata*) that was the punishment for killing a Brahmin. This penance, prescribed in Dharma literature, meant that the condemned had to wander with the skull of the Brahmin he had killed for twelve years, or some variant of this, such as living in a hermitage.[3] These ascetics are thereby imitating Śiva himself who, in one myth, decapitated one of Brahmā's five heads with his thumb nail. The head stuck to his hand and only freed itself after twelve years, falling at what is now the Kāpālamocana ghat in Benares.[4] Both the Lākula sect of Ati Mārga II and the Kāpālikas of Ati Mārga III followed this Kāpālika observance.

The Ati Mārga III, the Kāpālikas, had a canon of texts that taught propitiation of the ferocious Bhairava and the

---

2 David Lorenzen, *The Kāpālikas and Kālāmukhas: Two Lost Śaivite Sects* (Delhi: MLBD 1991 [1972]), 48–62.

3 *Manu Smṛti* 11.73: 'A man who has killed a Brahmin should construct a hut and live in the forest for twelve years, eating almsfood and making the head of a corpse his banner, in order to purify himself.' Patrick Olivelle, *The Laws of Manu* (Oxford: Oxford University Press, 2009).

4 Diana Eck, *Banaras: City of Light* (London: Routledge, 1984), 119.

terrifying Goddess Cāmuṇḍā. These texts also taught possession (*āveśa*), orgies, animal and human sacrifice, and offering meat and alcohol.[5] Sanderson describes how there is epigraphic record for this tradition from the seventh to twelfth centuries in inscriptions from various parts of India, from Tamilnadu, Andhra Pradesh, Karnataka, Gujarat, and Chhattisgarh. A Chinese text, the *Pusa chu tai jing* (*Bodhisattva Womb Sūtra*), translated by Zhu Fonian sometime between 384 and 417 CE, refers to ascetics, misguided ones, who dressed in bones and had food vessels made of bones. But this, Sanderson observes, could equally be evidence of Ati Mārga II as of Ati Mārga III.[6] This tradition influences the Mantra Mārga and the tradition of the Goddess, the Kula Mārga. Works of the Ati Mārga III tradition have not come down to us directly, but their ideas and perhaps even texts were brought over into the Mantra Mārga.[7] We will focus on the tradition's transformation into the non-Saiddhāntika religions of the Mantra Mārga and also the Kula Mārga.

Mapping the Texts and Traditions

As you may recall, the Tantras of the Mantra Mārga are classified by tradition according to which of the five mouths of Sadāśiva they came from. So, from the upward looking Īśāna face we have the scriptures of the Śaiva Siddhānta (divided into two sections of the ten *śiva-bhedas* and eighteen *rudra-bhedas*), and the non-Saiddhāntika scriptures coming

5 Alexis Sanderson, *Tantrāloka: Handout for Introductory Lecture*, OCHS, 26 January 2020, 2.

6 Sanderson, *Tantrāloka*, 6–7. On the dating of the Kāpālikas and Ati Mārga II, see Alexis Sanderson, 'Śaiva Literature', pp. 5-6, note 17.

7 Sanderson, 'Śaiva Literature', *Journal of Indological Studies* 24/25 (2012/2013): 1–113, 11–12.

out of the mouths of the remaining four heads facing the cardinal directions.[8]

A later classification speaks simply of Siddhānta Tantras and non-Siddhānta Tantras. The Siddhānta Tantras (such as the *Niḥśvāsa* and *Mṛgendra*) are non-transgressive and remain within the Vedic distinction between purity and impurity. While acknowledging that caste ultimately has no salvific value, the Siddhānta nevertheless abides by caste restrictions; when dining, for example, initiates sit in rows according to caste.[9] The non-Siddhānta Tantras or Bhairava Tantras, focused on the Bhairava form of Śiva, are transgressive, that is, they require transgressive ritual that goes against Brahmanical purity rules, making offerings of impure substances and so their practice is non-dualistic (*advaitācāra*) because they reject the Vedic distinction between pure and impure offerings. This branch of Śiva worship undermines caste, because all initiates belong to the caste of Bhairava (*bhairava-jāti*). These Bhairava Tantras are influenced by Goddess worship of the Kula Mārga, they are not interested in public worship, and are focused on ferocious Goddesses. As Alexis Sanderson observes: 'While the state looked to the Siddhānta for the dharmic aspects of Śaivism (the consecration of temples and monasteries, etc.,

8 Ibid., 32. The Vāma Tantras from the left or north-facing, gentle Vāma face, teach the cult of four Goddesses who are sisters along with their brother Tumburu; the Dakṣina Tantras from the right or south-facing, ferocious Aghora face, teach the cults of Bhairava and the Goddesses; the Garuḍa Tantras from the front or east-facing Tatpuruṣa face, teach cures for snake bites; and the Bhūta Tantras are from the rear, western-face of Sadyojāta that teach a cult of elemental spirits. Only some texts of the Garuḍa Tantras survive. See Michael Slouber, *Early Tantric Medicine* (Oxford: Oxford University Press, 2017).

9 Sanderson, *Tantrāloka*, 3.

and the empowerment and legitimation of the monarch), it looked to the non-Saiddhāntika Mantra Mārga for rituals of protection in times of peril and war.'[10]

The group of Bhairava Tantras is further classified into two parts: the Mantrapīṭha (seat of *mantra*) texts focused on Bhairava; and the Vidyāpīṭha (seat of 'female' *mantras*) texts focused on the Goddess (see Diagram 3.1).[11] The most important text of the Mantrapīṭha is the *Svacchanda Tantra* that has survived until today. It was evidently widespread in the medieval period as manuscripts of it are found in Kashmir, Nepal, and Tamilnadu, and it became the principle form of Śaivism in Kashmir.[12] The Vidyāpīṭha is again further subdivided into Vāma, Yāmala, and Śakti Tantras, each of which contained a number of scriptures. The only Vāma Tantra that has come down to us is the *Vīṇā-śikha Tantra*, which articulates the cult of the four sisters Jayā, Vijayā, Jayantī, and Aparājitā along with their brother Tumburu. The Yāmala Tantras are an important class that contains the *Brahma-yāmala* (also called the *Picu-mata*). This teaches the cult of Aghorī or Caṇḍā Kāpālinī. The Śakti Tantras contain the *Siddhayogeśvarī-mata* and the *Jayadratha-yāmala*.

The *Siddhayogeśvarī-mata* and the *Jayadratha-yāmala* each form the basis of two Tantric sects. The first teaches the cult of the goddesses Parā, Parāparā, and Aparā, and gave rise to the important scripture, the *Mālinī-vijayottara Tantra*, which is the scriptural revelation of the religion known as the Trika ('threefold' because it teaches the three Goddesses). The second (part of which survives) is the basis of the path focused on Kālī (Kālīkula) and the cult of the Goddess Kālasaṃkarṣinī, the focus of the Krama religion.

10 Ibid., 3.

11 Sanderson, Śaiva Literature', 35.

12 Ibid., 36.

Figure 3.2. A painting of Kālī from Jammu and Kashmir, c. 1660–70. Philadelphia Museum of Art.

The Trika is a Śākta system that forms the basis of Abhinavaguta's famous *Tantrāloka*, The Illumination of the Tantras. Within this tradition there is also the *Parā-triṃśikā*, teaching the cult of the Goddess Parā alone, and the meditation manual, the *Vijñāna-bhairava Tantra*. The Krama is based on a number of texts, one of them, the *Jayadratha-yāmala*, teaches the cult of the Goddess Kālī, also called Kālasaṃkarṣinī. This text and its religion are closely related to the Kula Mārga (treated on next page).

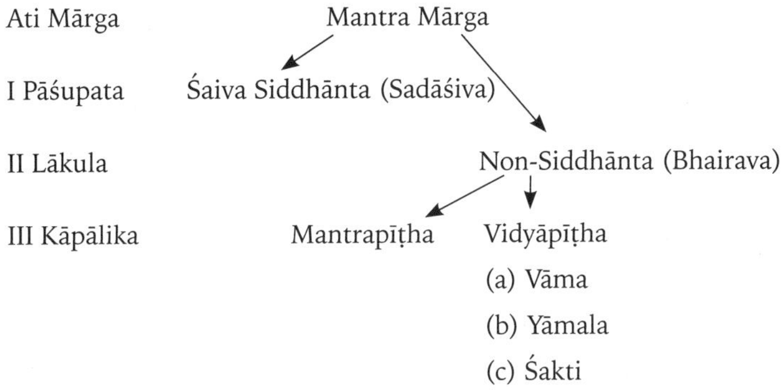

Diagram 3.1. Classification of the Early Tantric Textual Traditions.

Each class contains a number of texts, only some of which have survived. The Mantrapīṭha is Bhairava-centred, the Vidyāpīṭha is Goddess-centred. The most important texts of the Mantra- and Vidyā-pīṭhas are given in Diagram 3.2.

Mantrapīṭha		*Svacchanda Tantra*
Vidyāpīṭha	(a) Vāma Tantras	*Vīṇā-śikha Tantra*
	(b) Yāmala Tantras	*Brahma-yāmala Tantra*
	(c) Śakti Tantras	(i) *Siddhāyogeśvarī-mata Tantra*
		Mālinī-vijayottara Tantra
		Parā-triṃśikā, Vijñāna-bhairava Tantra
		(ii) *Jayadratha-yāmala (Ṣaṭka 1)*

Diagram 3.2. Important Surviving non-Saiddhāntika Tantras of the Mantra- and Vidyā-pīṭhas.

The Kāpālikas in the Mantra Mārga

The Kāpālikas were an important ascetic group (see pp. 105-106) who produced scriptures that became classified as being part of the Mantra Mārga. Sanderson describes the Kāpālika in the following way:

> Smeared with the ashes of funeral pyres, wearing ornaments of human bone, the initiate would carry in one hand a cranial begging-bowl and in the other a *khaṭvāṅga*, a trident-topped staff on which was fixed beneath the prongs a human skull adorned with a banner of blood-stained cloth. Having thus taken on the appearance of the ferocious deities of his cult, he roamed about seeking to call forth these gods and their retinues in apocalyptic vision thereby to assimilate their superhuman identities and powers.[13]

These were formidable ascetics who were in contrast with orthodox Brahmanism, the forerunners of the modern day Aghoris. This is the intentional and conscious adoption of pollution in the belief that this gives power as well as liberation. Although the scriptures of the Kāpālikas of Ati Mārga III have not come down to us, their doctrines and practices moved over into the Mantra Mārga and we have their practices and beliefs recorded in non-Saiddhāntika scriptures. Of particular importance is a text called the *Brahma-yāmala Tantra*, also known as the *Picu-mata Tantra*, the earliest manuscript of which is dated 1052,[14] although the text is attested from other sources as far back as 819 CE and also from the *Skanda Purāṇa* as early as the sixth or seventh century.[15]

The *Brahma-yāmala* is 'strongly Kāpālika in character'.[16] The practices it contains include sexual ritual that has become identified with Neo-Tantrism in the West, although here 'sacred sexuality' is quite different from the Westernised

13 Alexis Sanderson, 'Purity and Power Among the Brahmins of Kashmir', p. 201.

14 Sanderson, 'Śaiva Literature', 39.

15 Ibid., 40.

16 Ibid., 39.

version. It might first be informative to understand some background in terms of attitudes to sexuality. On the one hand, the Brahmanical tradition had a positive attitude to sex; *kāma*, pleasure and sexual desire, was one of the legitimate goals of life (*puruṣārtha*) to be pursued as a householder, along with duty (*dharma*) and wealth or prosperity (*artha*) (see Chapter 1). The enjoyment of sex for its own sake was generally thought to be a human good for the householder and it was the topic of the 'science of sexuality', the Kāmaśāstra, in which texts such as Vātsyāyana's *Kāma Sūtra* is the best and most famous exemplar.[17] Sex was also considered important within marriage for the generation of progeny: one of the three debts that every male Brahmin is born with, is sons to the ancestors (*pitṛ*) (the others being study to the sages and ritual to the gods (*deva*)). But, as probably in most cultures, there is ambivalence towards it. Within a yogic context, sexual desire is an enemy of concentration and spiritual attainment, so world renouncers were traditionally celibate. There was also the idea that semen was stored in the head as a reservoir of energy, so the letting go of semen meant the depletion of vital force. This is a common attitude even in contemporary times. So, in traditional Brahmanical discourse, sex was a legitimate goal of life in the realm of the householder, whereas the renunciation of sex was the realm of the renouncer.

There was a strong tradition of Sanskrit love poetry and a literature of love magic, ritual technologies for attracting a desired person (see below). One of the distinctive features of early Tantric sexual ritual is therefore that it employs sexuality in the service of spiritual attainment, liberation, and/or power, thus taking it out of the householder realm of pure pleasure

17 Alain Daniélou, *The Complete Kāmasūtra* (Rochester: Park Street Press, 1994).

or procreation.[18] Among the important sexual rites attested are ritualised sex for the production of sexual fluids to be offered to deities, particularly ferocious goddesses,[19] along with menstrual blood, blood from animal sacrifice, and alcohol. Another practice in the *Brahma-yāmala Tantra* is the *asi-dhārā-vrata*, the razor's edge observance, which refers to the male ascetic discipline of maintaining chastity while lying with a sexually available woman. This is attested in Tantras of the Śaiva Siddhānta, such as the *Mataṅga-parameśvara Tantra* and the *Niḥśvāsa-tattva Saṃhitā*.[20] According to Hatley, this is probably the first sexual ritual described in the Tantras (which is in fact a desisting from sexual activity). This practice has echoes in the modern world as a practice Mohandas Gandhi undertook as a test of celibacy.[21]

Linked to this in the *Brahma-yāmala* is sexual congress without ejaculation; should that occur, ritual fault would be incurred, and the Tantric practitioner (*sādhaka*) would have to perform expiation of repeating a *mantra* ten thousand times and start again.[22] In this ritual system, sexual congress is integral and central. Such ritual is male-orientated, and the female partner is the means to an end, or a ritual object, although there are indications in the text that both the *sādhaka* and his partner are initiates into the system. The partner in the rite is

---

18 See the description of different kinds of use of sex in early Tantra by Shaman Hatley, *The Brahmayāmalatantra or Picumata*, Vol. 1, Chapters 1–2, *Revelation, Ritual, and Material Culture in an Early Śaiva Tantra* (Pondichéry: Institut Français, 2018), 196–198.

19 David White has emphasised this aspect, see *The Kiss of the Yoginī: Tantric Sex in its South Asian Contexts* (Chicago: Chicago University Press, 2003).

20 Hatley, *Brahmayāmalatantra*, 200.

21 Ibid., 201.

22 Ibid., 40.8c–14b, 20–23.

called *śakti* (power) or *dūtī* (messenger) and should be attractive with the qualities described in poetry (*kāvya*).

But the third kind of sexual ritual in the *Brahma-yāmala* is sex without the reserve of non-ejaculation. The *Brahma-yāmala* uses the term *sādhaka* for the practitioner but does not know the later classification in the Śaiva Siddhānta of types of practitioner: the *samayin, putraka, sādhaka,* and *ācārya* (see Chapter 2).[23] Instead, here the *sādhaka* is divided into three types: the pure (*śuddha*), impure (*aśuddha*), and mixed (*śuddhāśuddha*). The pure type is also called a *tālaka*; he can perform transgressive rituals involving sex and offer meat and alcohol to the deity.[24] The impure and the mixed practices do not involve sexual congress. The central deity of the text is the Goddess Caṇḍā Kāpālinī, who with her retinue of nine circuits of deities transcends the orthodox Śaiva system.[25]

The *sādhaka* who is setting out on the transgressive spiritual path described in the *Brahma-yāmala Tantra* does so once he has met three conditions: having received initiation and performed purifying rituals; having received the command of the guru; and having acquired a beautiful partner (*dūtī*) for the rites who is brilliant, with auspicious qualities, who has mastered yogic postures (*āsana*) and dwells in non-duality (*advaitavāsitā*), and who knows how to attain higher awareness (*samādhi*).[26] The text describes the basic, daily ritual in some detail. It

---

23 *Brahmayāmalatantra or Picumata,* Vol. 2, Chapters 3, 21, and 45, ed. and trans. Csaba Kiss (Pondichéry: Institut Français, 2018), 35.

24 Ibid., Vol. 2, 36–37.

25 Alexis Sanderson, 'Maṇḍala and Āgamic Identity in the Trika of Kashmir', in *Maṇḍala et Diagrammes Rituel dans l'Hindouisme,* ed. André Padoux (Paris: CNRS, 1986), 672, quoted by Kiss, *Brahmayāmalatantra,* 22.

26 *Brahmayāmala,* ed. Kiss, 45.184–187.

Figure 3.3. Cāmuṇḍā, eleventh–twelfth century. National Museum of Delhi.

involves bathing (*snāna*), installation of *mantras* (*nyāsa*), going into the ritual site (*devāgāra*), and worship (*pūjā*). He should bathe three times a day and recall *mantras* mentally. In the sanctuary he should worship the two door-keepers, the two rivers and the bull, Vighneśa (i.e. Gaṇeśa), Kṣetrapāla (the protector) and the Cremation Grounds, along with the Heroes, the Yoginīs, Śiva, the Owl deities, and the lineage of gurus.[27] The main *mantra* to be repeated is that of the central deity Caṇḍā Kāpālinī, namely the nine-syllabled *oṃ caṇḍe kāpālini svāhā*.[28] This Goddess was typical of the emaciated, ferocious deities we find at this time, especially of note being Cāmuṇḍā, popular especially in Orissa (see Figure 3.3).

For the daily ritual, the *sādhaka* is naked, covered in ashes, hair dishevelled, and he worships the pantheon of gods (*yāga*) and performs fire ritual (*homa*). His partner is also naked with dishevelled hair, he worships her private parts, called the pilgrimage site (*pīṭha*), installing (*nyāsa*) the pantheon of deities there. They perform sexual congress, achieve orgasm (*kṣobha*), and ritually consume sexual fluids thereby generated. The fire ritual is then performed making offerings of transgressive substances such as meat from cows, which the *sādhaka* consumes, and further sexual congress is then carried out while uttering *mantras* a hundred thousand times and holding a conch or skull.[29] There are variants of this basic ritual and the text presents three levels of supreme, middling, and inferior. The supreme is described above, the middling entails non-ejaculation (*avagraha*), and the lowest simply aims at enjoyment (*bhoga*).[30] The purpose of all this is to achieve magical power (*siddhi*).

---

27 Ibid., 45.189–193ab.

28 Ibid., p. 257, note 191.

29 Ibid., 45.198–205.

30 Ibid., 45.263–305.

To prepare for this level of intense practice, the *sādhaka* undergoes a preparation in which he gradually loosens his connection with conventional behaviour. Thus, he tries to achieve a vision of a goddess or goddesses, the Yoginīs, who appear before him. This encounter (*melaka*) with the Yoginīs, in Kiss's words, is 'the turning point for the *sādhaka*, the moment in which he is assigned to one of the specialised paths by the Yoginīs'.[31] There are nine observances he needs to follow, including only eating at night, wandering around, and, like the Pāśupata ascetic, acting as if mad (*unmatta*).[32] As Kiss observes, the difference here is that whereas the Pāśupata ascetic wishes to accumulate good *karma* by being abused by the public, the *sādhaka* wishes to adopt non-conventional practices (*nirācāra*) in preparation for the rites involving sexual transgression.[33] These preliminary observances also involved imitating the deity Kapālīśa Bhairava by decorating himself with bone ornaments, imitating a child, and imitating a flesh-eating demon (*piśāca*). All these, in Kiss's words, 'aim at loosening the bonds of conventional behaviour'.[34]

It is, of course, difficult to assess the popularity of these practices and the numbers of people involved, but certainly the text of the *Brahma-yāmala Tantra* was popular and preserved through the generations. Kāpālika sects were widespread enough to cause concern to the orthodox, that they were undermining social mores and had a bad influence on society.

---

31 Ibid., p. 46.

32 Ibid., 21.5–46. The nine observances (*vrata*) are: being naked (*nagna-vrata*), being dressed in rags, wearing old garlands, acting as if mad, holding a skull-topped staff, wearing five bone ornaments, behaving like a child, behaving like a demon and eating raw flesh and human blood, and lastly holding a trident, carrying a skull, and howling like a jackal.

33 Ibid., p. 33.

34 Ibid., p. 33.

The erudite Vaiṣṇava satirist Kṣemendra was very concerned about this,[35] as was the ninth-century Bhaṭṭa Jayanta, as we have seen in the play *Much Ado About Religion*, in which the protagonist urges the King Śaṅkaravarman to ban a sect known as the Black or Blue Blanket (*nīlāmbara*) because they perform a sexual rite wrapped only in a blanket, in public and on public festivals.[36] The sect also existed in King Bhoja's kingdom, who ruled from Dhārā in Mālava (first half of eleventh century). There is a story told in a Jain text that Bhojadeva's daughter wished to join Blue Blankets. The king invited forty-nine couples of the sect to the court to hear their doctrine on the pretence that he wished to join them: he had all the men executed and the women banished;[37] a fine example of paternal care for

---

35 Kṣemendra, *Daśāvatāra-carita* 10.25–27, cited in Alexis Sanderson, 'Purity and Power among the Brahmans of Kashmir', in *The Category of the Person*, ed. Michael Carrithers, Steven Collins, and Steven Lukes (Cambridge: Cambridge University Press, 1985), 190–216, 103, note 112.

36 Jayanta Bhaṭṭa, *Nyāyamañjari of Jayanta Bhaṭṭa*, English trans. V. N. Jha (Delhi: Śrī Satguru Publications, 1995), 562; Csaba Dezső, *Much Ado About Religion* (New York: Clay Sanskrit Library, 2005). Alexis Sanderson cites Jayanta's text as follows (*Nyāyamañjarī*, vol. 1, p. 649, ll. 4–7): 'King Śaṅkaravarman, knowing the essentials of [brahmanical] religious law, prohibited the Nīlāmbaravrata on the grounds that with its many acts committed by licentious couples wrapped up in a single black blanket it was an observance without precedent reportedly invented by certain dissolute rogues; but he did not act in this way against the Jainas and other [non-brahmanical religious].' In Alexis Sanderson, 'Śaiva Exegesis of Kashmir', in *Mélanges tantriques à la mémoire d'Hélène Brunner/Tantric Studies in Memory of Hélène Brunner*, Collection Indologie 106, ed. D. Goodall and A. Padoux, 231–444 (Pondicherry: IFI / EFEO, 2007), 392, note 533.

37 Alexis Sanderson, 'Tolerance, Exclusivity, Inclusivity, and Persecution in Indian Religion during the Early Mediaeval Period', in *Honoris Causa: Essays in Honour of Aveek Sarkar*, ed. John Makinson, 155–224 (London: Allen Lane, 2015), 167, note 27.

his daughter! This was evidently a Kaula sect whose scriptures are no longer extant. These practices also influenced other traditions such as Buddhism, and texts of the Higher Yoga Tantra similarly convey transgressive rites, only perhaps even more extreme in attempting to erase the distinction between pleasure and disgust through the consumption of bodily products from the ritual partner.[38] The Kāpālika or Kāpālika-like *sādhaka* is an unconventional ascetic and the extreme observance that he followed as expressed in these transgressive Tantras was polluting to the orthodox Brahmin.

The Kula Mārga

Along with the Ati Mārga and the Mantra Mārga is the Kula Mārga, the path of the clans of Goddesses. It is non-dualistic in terms of ritual (*advaitācāra*), using impure substances as offerings. It uses 'three Ms' – (*madya* (wine), meat (*māṃsa*), and sex (*maithuna*) – as well as orgiastic worship (*cakra-yāga*) and stresses the role of the female practitioner as ritual partner (*dūtī*).[39]

The Kula Mārga presents worship that is counter to Brahmanical purity rules. The immediate source of inspiration is from the Kāpālika tradition of Ati Mārga III, as Sanderson has shown.[40] The distinguishing feature of this path is sexual ritual as in the *Brahma-yāmala Tantra* just described, making sanguinary offerings to ferocious deities, collective sexual rites with low caste women, drinking and offering alcohol, and

---

38 Christopher S. George, *The Caṇḍamahārośana-tantra: A Critical Edition and English Translation of Chapters I–VIII* (Harvard: American Oriental Society, 1974).

39 Sanderson, *Tantrāloka: Handout*, 4.

40 Sanderson, 'Śaiva Literature', 57.

possession (*āveśa*).[41] While this might sound like an Oxford undergraduate party, these traditions were highly polluting to the orthodox and were also kept secret by the practitioners.

The doctrine of the Kula Mārga called itself the Kula teachings (*kula-śāsana*), in parallel to the teachings of Śiva (*śiva-śāsana*) and the Buddha. The focus of this religion was the Goddess Kuleśvarī, sometimes with her consort Bhairava called Kuleśvara. She is surrounded by a retinue of eight goddesses called Mothers, attended by Gaṇeśa and Vaṭuka. There were a number of scriptural traditions, classified in an unedited early text called the *Ciñciṇī-matasāra-samuccaya* as four traditions (*āmnāya*) associated with the four directions: the east (Pūrvāmnāya), the north (Uttarāmnāya), the west (Paścimāmnāya), and the south (Dakṣiṇāmnāya) (see Chapter 1), each with its own pantheon.[42] The core cult of the Kula Mārga was that of the Pūrvāmnāya.[43] For convenience the classification is repeated here in Diagram 3.3.

Eastern transmission	Kula tradition of Kuleśvara and Kuleśvarī surrounded by eight mothers and ancillary deities
Northern transmission	Kālī cult (which comprises the Krama, also called Mata and Mahānaya.)
Western transmission	Cult of the hunchback Goddess Kubjikā
Southern transmission	Cult of the beautiful Goddess Tripurasundarī and love deities Kāmeśvara and Kāmeśvarī

Diagram 3.3. Kaula Classification of the Tantras.

41 Ibid., 57–58.

42 André Padoux, *The Hindu Tantric World: An Overview* (Chicago: Chicago University Press, 2017), 58–59.

43 Sanderson, Śaiva Literature', 58.

Eastern Transmission (Pūrvāmnāya)

The Eastern transmission is the core cult of Kuleśvarī, the Mothers, and also the Alphabet deity. It is also associated with the Trika and, in the form of the Kaula Trika, has a section in the *Mālinī-vijayottara Tantra*; we also know of the tradition through citations in other texts. But an example of the worship of the Eight (or Seven) Mothers is a text called the 'Hymn to the Circle of Deities Located in the Body' (*Deha-stha-devatā-cakra Stotra*). This text is a hymn of praise to the Eight Mothers who surround Ānandabhairava and Ānandabhairavī – almost the same as Kuleśvara and Kuleśvarī – in the calyx of a lotus that is imagined in the heart of the practitioner. Each of the Mothers is associated with one of the senses and with a particular direction (for translation and text of the hymn see Appendix 2). This is an interesting text that the *sādhaka* would recite while visualising a lotus in the heart associated with the goddesses on the petals, worshipping Ānandabhairava and

Figure 3.4. The Eight Mothers depicted in an early eighteenth-century Nepali manuscript. Los Angeles County Museum of Art.

Ānandabhairavī in the centre. Here we recognise the Sāṃkhya categories too: so, for example, the boar headed Vārāhī on the western petal offers flowers of sound, while Mahālakṣmī in the north-east, offers flowers of smell. There is reference to the thirty-six ontic categories in verse 14 and the text explicitly maps the totality of the cosmos onto the body. The body becomes a microcosm, with the entire pantheon of deities within it. This is another version of the Tantric theme of the divinisation of the body. Furthermore, the central deity is the essence of experience (*anubhava-sāra*), that all human experience is to be realised as divine.

The Northern Transmission (Uttarāmnāya)

In the Northern Transmission the main focus is the Goddess Kālī, so it is called the Kālīkula, where she takes the form of Kālasaṃkarṣinī in a religion known as the Krama, the Mata, or the Mahānaya. The scriptures of this branch that survive are the *Jayadratha-yāmala* sections 2-4, along with four other texts.[44] This Krama religion is the Gradation system, so-called because of its doctrine of Kālī having levels of realisation and a gradation of states of awareness.

One of the features of this tradition is that it describes encounters with supernatural Goddesses called Yoginīs. These generally wish to suck out the vital energy of the practitioner, but through a ritual process the *sādhaka* can use the encounter to gain power. The meeting with the Yoginī (*yoginī-melāpa/melaka*) occurs at the end of a process of practice; the Yoginī

44 All unedited and untranslated. These other tantras are: *Kālī-kula-krama-sadbhāva, Kālī-kula-pañca-śataka, Devīdvyardhaśatikā,* and the *Yoni-gahvara*. See Sanderson, 'Śaiva Literature', 64.

appears to the *sādhaka* and grants him supernatural powers.[45] The term *yoginī* is also used for human women who participate in Krama collective worship involving transgression. These extreme assemblies involve drinking, frenzied behaviour, and orgiastic worship by the group.[46] One passage in the *Kulārṇava Tantra* describes such a practice:

> When the heroic adepts have entered [the circle of their female counterparts], there is neither right nor wrong. Desire alone is Holy Scripture.... In that stage of bliss whatever actions of whatever sort are performed are lawful. But he who takes thought of right and wrong is a sinner.... Spontaneously they give free vent to their desires.... Putting the wind cup to their lips, they abide in bliss. One frenzied woman embraces another's man thinking him her husband... in his madness one man embraces a man instead of a girl. A crazy woman asks her husband, who are you? Who am I? and who are these? What have we come here to do? Why are we assembled here?... The female adepts of the Family dance with stumbling footsteps, singing songs in which the syllables fall indistinct – with hypnotizing rhythm. The Yogis, mad with liquor, fall upon the women's breasts: the Yoginis, confused with wine, fall upon the men. Together they enjoy the full pleasure of their desires.... But when the bliss holds sway, turning their minds, those bulls among Yogis participate in the Divine.[47]

---

45 Olga Serbaeva, 'The Jayadrathayāmala: Varieties of Melaka', in *Goddesses in Tantric Hinduism: History, practice and doctrine*, ed. Bjarne Wernicke-Olsen (London: Routledge, 2016), 51–73.

46 Sanderson, 'The Śaiva Age', in *Genesis and Development of Tantrism*, ed. Shingo Einoo (Tokyo: University of Tokyo, 2009), 41–250, 282–284.

47 *Kulārṇava Tantra* 8.57–75. Translation by Sanderson, modified by Zaehner, *Our Savage God* (London: Collins, 1974), 102.

Here licentious practice is described and advocated as not only rejecting Brahmanical purity rules, but the ecstatic state induced is believed to reflect the bliss of the divine.

The Krama religion also taught a doctrine of four categories or circles (*cakra*): creation, maintenance, destruction, and the Nameless (*anākhya*). The Nameless is worshipped in a cycle of thirteen Kālīs, where the thirteenth is identified with the Nameless. This tradition with its emphasis on immediate enlightenment experience has much in common with the Tibetan Buddhist tradition of the Great Perfection (Dzogchen) and the experience of the Great Primordial Purity (*gzhi ka dag chen po*), both regarding themselves as transcending lower revelation.[48] The Krama taught enlightenment as an experience of light as its highest goal. Thus, while it accepts that there are lower levels of practice – the other Śākta revelations – the ultimate goal of life is supreme awakening to the truth of the light of the Nameless reality. This is to shift from the theistic language of Kālī to an impersonal language of consciousness and light. This tradition became very influential on non-Saiddhāntika religion in Kashmir, particularly on Abhinavagupta who incorporates these teachings into his *Tantrāloka*.

In the cycle of the Nameless, Abhinavagupta describes the Krama meditation on twelve Kālīs, the thirteenth being the transcendent one. The idea is that the Kālīs emanate out from their source in the Nameless and contract back into it. This is a metaphor for the emanation and reabsorption of the cosmos, but also an understanding of the way in which consciousness projects out and contracts back to itself in human experience. In a meditation process described by Abhinavagupta, the mind moves out from itself and contracts back into itself, becoming

48 Sanderson, 'Śaiva Exegesis', 290.

absorbed in its own light. This Krama gradation of Kālī is incorporated into the system of three Goddesses: Parā, Aparā, and Parāparā. Here is a rendering of the difficult verses on the topic:

> These four powers [namely the supreme Śakti called Kālasaṃkarṣiṇī who emanates Parā, Parāparā and Aparā] due to their freedom, become manifested singly in three ways: in creation, in maintenance and in destruction and thus become twelve. 1. Consciousness projects existence at first only internally; 2. then expanding, it projects it externally; 3. then having grasped that [state of externality] made of the Goddess Rakti, it manifests existence by wishing to withdraw it internally; 4. then [consciousness] fastens onto and swallows the inhibition that has become an obstacle to reabsorption; 5. [next] with a portion of inhibition swallowed through withdrawing into the self, [consciousness] withdraws [even that] part of existence; 6. then [thinking] 'this withdrawal is my nature' [consciousness] withdraws even [this] essence; 7. then [consciousness] withdraws [even] what remains of any simple consciousness of any existence; this is established through the nature of being a destroyer, [which remains] as a trace. 8. then [consciousness] whose nature is manifested internally, withdraws the sphere of the senses; 9. then it reabsorbs even the Lord of the senses; 10. then it reabsorbs even the nature of being an experient constructed as illusion; 11. then it reabsorbs the object of experience even abandoning contraction and looking out to expansion, grasping, and tasting; 12. finally it reabsorbs even the nature of that expansion.[49]

49 *Tantra-sāra* 4, pp. 28–29 (my translation guided by Sanderson's description). See Sanderson, 'Purity and Power', 199–200; Sanderson 'Meaning in Tantric Ritual', 73–75.

Figure 3.5. Depiction of the cakras. *Wellcome Collection.*

We see here how the external cult of Kālī, her worship in images in ritual areas, is internalised by the *sādhaka* and Abhinavagupta identifies Kālī not so much as a Goddess but as a state of consciousness. This is a kind of psychologising of Śākta mythology.

Western Transmission

The Western Transmission is focused on the hunchback form of the Goddess, Kubjikā, the crooked one. The main text here is the *Kubjikā-mata Tantra* extant in the eleventh century, although there are others.[50] This teaching contains some esoteric *yoga* and the idea of the body with various focal points of power located along its axis, called wheels or circles (*cakra*). The famous six or seven *cakras* of later yogic tradition may have their first instantiation in this text, or perhaps in the *Netra-tantra*, depending on which is earlier. Kubjikā, the crooked Goddess, is identified with Kuṇḍalinī, the coiled 'serpent' Goddess.

Southern Transmission

Lastly in this classification we have the cult of the beautiful Goddess Tripurasundarī (see Śrīvidyā below). The origins of the Southern tradition are in love magic and the goal of powers in the world, but later the tradition developed into an important religion in its own right, especially in South India. The earliest scripture is the *Nitya-kaula*, of which only one damaged manuscript survives. This text teaches the magic of attraction, how to attract a partner through meditation techniques. The main deity worshipped is the beautiful Kāmeśvarī, who is sweet, holding an elephant goad, a noose, bow and arrows, sitting in a bower of Kadamba flowers. The idea is that with the goad she pulls the desired person, with the noose she holds her or him, and she shoots love with the bow and arrows (not dissimilar to Cupid). The text describes visualisation techniques to achieve this end, such as visualising the desired person or 'target' (*sādhya*) as red, immersed in nectar, to whom the practitioner should make offerings and

50 The other texts are: the *Kula-ratnoddyota, Ciñciṇī-mata-sāra-samuccaya, Manthāna-bhairava*. This latter is a vast text and has been translated by Mark S. G. Dyczkowski, *Manthānabhairavatantram, Kumārikākhaṇḍaḥ*, 12 vols. *The Section Concerning the Virgin Goddess* (Delhi: Indira Gandhi National Centre, 2009).

Figure 3.6. A mid-twentieth-century popular print of the Goddess Tripurasundarī.

repeat *mantras*. The purpose will be achieved in no time at all. Furthermore, if they should leave him, they will die! Different colours, such as red for attraction, grey for causing enemies to run, are associated with different magical purposes, so even the subjugation of enemies can be achieved through these meditation methods.[51]

Magical practices focused on the beautiful Goddess were attractive to the higher echelons of society and would have

51 *Nitya-kaula*, NGMPP Reel No. B26/21a. DSCN 6586. My understanding of the text is due to reading it in a class with Alexis Sanderson, Oxford, January 2014.

been current in the courts of kings. The general atmosphere and worldview within the royal palaces of the time would have been one in which belief in the efficacy of magical practices was the norm. Texts such as the *Nitya-kaula* would have been not out of the ordinary, although the orthodox Brahmin might reject any elements that went against caste normativity. But such magical practices in royal circles have come down to us even in recent times. For example, H. G. Querich Wales' account of life in the royal palace in Thailand shows how the palace women were protected by female guards and engaged in magical practices from protection to controlling the weather.[52]

The Threefold Religion (Trika)

In the third subdivision of the Vidyāpīṭha, the Śakti Tantras, is a tantra called the *Siddha-yogeśvarī-mata,* from which another emerges called the *Mālinī-vijayottara Tantra.* This text forms the scriptural basis of a religion called the Trika, or 'threefold', so named because it worships a triad of Goddesses: Parā, Parāparā, and Aparā. The Trika is an important religion because it is the tradition that the great polymath Abhinavagupta was initiated into and it is this tradition's scripture that forms the basis of his monumental work, the *Tantrāloka.* The Trika and its philosophical articulation in the Pratyabhijñā or Recognition school (see Chapter 5) became well established within mainstream householder Śaivism in Kashmir. I shall reserve an account of this philosophy and rather focus on the practices of this religion, especially as expressed by Abhinavagupta.

We might say that the Trika religion has its roots in the Kāpālika cremation ground asceticism but becomes domesti-

---

52 Horace Geoffrey Quaritch Wales, *Siamese State Ceremonies: Their History and Function* (London: Bernard Quaritch: 1931).

cated for the Śaiva householder seeking power and liberation in this life. To follow this religion required initiation into it. The tradition assumes the overarching ritual system of the Śaiva Siddhānta and uses the same cosmological categories, the difference being that the Trika initiate takes on extra ritual practices and adopts a distinct philosophy. Whereas the Śaiva Siddhānta is dualistic, maintaining an eternal ontological distinction between self, God, and world, the Trika is non-dualistic, claiming that these are in fact identical. Furthermore, this identity is constituted within consciousness. So, the ultimate reality that is spoken of in the Śaiva Siddhānta in theistic language as Śiva, is in fact pure consciousness. Philosophers such as Abhinavagupta speak of this reality in terms of identity, that the world simply is consciousness, and in terms of emanation, that the universe is an emanation or transformation of pure consciousness. The goal of the ritual and meditation practices is therefore to see oneself as identical with pure consciousness and this recognition is liberation from the cycle of reincarnation. Thus, liberation in life (*jīvan-mukti*) achieved through knowledge or cognition (*jñāna*) is the goal, in contrast to the Saiddhāntika liberation at death (*videha-mukti*) achieved through ritual action (*karma*). These were supererogatory practices taken on by the initiate while still maintaining his social role. Abhinavagupta says that one should follow the Vedas in one's social life, follow the teaching of Śiva in one's more limited social circle, but follow the teachings of the Goddess, the Kaula tradition, in one's inner life.[53]

53 Sanderson, 'Purity and Power among the Brahmins of Kashmir', p. 205: 'Thus one could be "internally a Kaula, externally a Śaiva [a worshipper of Svacchandabhairava in the Kashmirian context] while remaining Vedic in one's social practice".' Abhinavagupta/Jayaratha, *Tantrālokavivaraṇa*, Vol. 3, p. 27, 10–13; p. 277, 9; p. 278, 6.

To achieve the goal, there were two kinds of ritual system. One is the normative Tantric system called the *tantra-prakriyā*. To summarise Sanderson's account, this involved installing the Trika deities into two wine filled cups, making offerings to guardian deities around the place of worship, and performing the purification of the body (as in Śaiva Siddhānta) which the practitioner understands as the destruction of his public persona, so leaving him with awareness of his identity with pure, undifferentiated consciousness.[54] After the divinisation of the body through imposing *mantras* upon it (*nyāsa*), as in Śaiva Siddhānta, the adept visualises a trident (the *triśūlābja-maṇḍala*) pervading the body with the goddesses Aparā, Parā, and Parāparā at the prongs above the crown of the head. The practitioner identifies himself with Parā and symbolically moves up the trident, through the body, to Parā above the crown of the head. He then merges with pure consciousness understood as the invisible, unrepresentable Kālasaṃkarṣinī who we came across in the Krama tradition (see above).

The second ritual system is called the *kula-prakriyā*. This assumes the normative Tantric ritual of the *tantra-prakriyā*, but with the addition of the consumption of the 'three Ms': meat (*māṃsa*), alcohol (*madya*), and sexual ritual (*maithuna*).[55] This part of the religion was for the religious virtuosi and required

54 Sanderson, 'Maṇḍala and Āgamic Identity in the Trika of Kashmir', 169–214.

55 This system also contains a distinctive *yoga* on the subtle body that entails flooding the body with the nectar of immortality contained at the top of the head. This is what Wernicke-Olesen calls a 'Śākta Anthropology'. See Bjarne Wernicke-Olesen and Silje Lyngar Einarsen. 'Übungswissen in Yoga, Tantra und Asketismus', in *Übungswissen in Religion und Philosophie: Produktion, Weitergabe, Wandel*, ed. Almut-Barbara Renger and Alexandra Stellmacher (Berlin: Lit Verlag, 2018), 241–257.

initiation in which the adept displayed signs of possession by the Goddess, such as trembling. The rite is described by Abhinavagupta in Chapter 29 of the *Tantrāloka*.[56] As Sanderson observes, what is significant is that sexual experience itself is a reflection of the joy of Śiva and Śakti: the rite has become an aesthetic experience.[57] Sexual experience or orgasm (*kampa-kāla*) reflects the divine union, so human sexual experience reflects or recapitulates a cosmic sexuality. Abhinavagupta writes in his commentary on the *Parā-triṃśikā*:

> In the case of both sexes sustained by the buoyancy of their seminal energy, the inwardly felt joy of orgasm (*antaḥsparśa-sukham*) in the central channel induced by the excitement of the seminal energy intent on oozing out at the moment of thrill is a matter of personal experience to everyone. This joy is not simply dependent on the body which is merely a fabricated thing. If at such a moment it serves as a teaching of remembrance of the inherent delight of the divine self (*tadabhijñānopadeśadvāreṇa*), one's consciousness gets entry in to the eternal, unalterable state (*dhruvapade*) that is realised by means of the harmonious union with the expansive energy of the perfect I-consciousness which constitutes the venerable supreme divine Śakti (*parābhaṭṭārikārūpe*) who is an expression of the absolutely free manifestation of the bliss of the union of Śiva and Śakti denoting the supreme Brahman.[58]

Here the sexual rite is not for the production of fluids to be offered to the deity but is performed for the joy of the expe-

56 See John R. Dupuche, *Abhinavagupta: The Kula Ritual as Elaborated in Chapter 29 of the Tantrāloka* (Delhi: MLBD, 2003).

57 Sanderson, 'Śaivism and the Tantric Traditions', 681.

58 *Parā-triṃśikā-vivaraṇa* 1, pp. 44–45, Sanskrit text pp. 16–17. Translation by Jaideva Singh.

rience as a reflection of the joy of Śiva and Śakti. Here the Kāpālika type of transgressive rite has been absorbed into an esoteric householder practice.

There were practices prescribed for the Trika householder other than the *tantra-* and *kula-prakriyās*. From their origin in the *Mālinī-vijayottara Tantra*, Abhinavagupta describes three groups of practices called 'means' (*upāya*), based on the human faculties of willing, thinking, and acting. The first is the *śāṃbhavopāya*, the divine means, which is the intentional upsurge of emotion or instinct to shatter thought construction, as when we see a loved one unexpectedly, we experience an upsurge of emotion. The second is the *śāktopāya*, the energy means, which is thinking a true thought such as 'I am Śiva' and gradually there is a purification of the mind resulting in the existential realisation of its truth. Thirdly, there is the *āṇavopāya*, the individual means, which entails ritual, *mantra* repetition, and other actions. But this is not all. Abhinavagupta outlines a fourth 'non-means' (*anupāya*), which is the spontaneous realisation that all is consciousness; it is called the non-means because, if there is only one reality, there can be no means to attain it, for one is already it. This non-means ties in with a strict non-dualism, for if there is only the reality of consciousness, there cannot be a method to get there, which would imply a distinction between practitioner and goal.[59]

The Trika was the non-dualist religion that challenged the Śaiva Siddhānta, although a minority tradition and not well known other than through Abhinavagupta's exposition. This was largely a householder adaptation of a tradition whose origins are in the cremation ground, Kāpālika asceticism, and whose transgression has become secret. Perhaps the most

59 Gavin Flood, *Body and Cosmology in Kashmir Śaivism* (San Francisco: Mellen Research University Press, 1993), 245–255.

popular, householder-friendly Tantric tradition that developed, especially in South India, was the Śrīvidyā.

Śrīvidyā

We have seen the cult of the gentle Kāmeśvarī represented in early Kaula texts such as the *Nitya-kaula*. This tradition transformed into the cult of the beautiful Lalitā Tripurasundarī, or simply Tripurasundarī, a Tantric form of Śrī/Lakṣmī. This tradition became mainstream and popular. It is an example of highly orthodox Brahmins taking on a Tantric tradition and removing its transgression while leaving the *mantras* and ritual gestures (*mudrā*) and substituting impure substances used in ritual with pure ones. The Śaṅkara Brahmins absorbed the Śrīvidyā tradition and adopted it for the highly orthodox. There was a learned literature with this tradition until the nineteenth century, the most famous theologian being Bhāskararāya whose work is infused with the philosophy of Mīmāṃsā.

Tripurasundarī is worshipped in the form of a diagram or *yantra* of nine intersecting triangles called the Śrīcakra along with a fifteen-syllable *mantra* called the Śrīvidyā, from which the tradition takes its name. While the *Nitya-kaula* is an ancestor of the Śrīvidyā Tantras, the earliest texts used by the tradition are the *Nityā-ṣodaśikārṇava* ('The Ocean of the Sixteen Nityā Goddesses') and the *Yoginī-hṛdaya* ('The Heart/Inner Essence of the Yoginī'), which together form the *Vāmakeśvara Tantra*. The *Nityā-ṣodaśikārṇava* is about external rituals and their magical effects, while the *Yoginī-hṛdaya* is about the Śrīcakra as diagram of the cosmos. A later text, the *Tantra-rāja Tantra*, gives a detailed exposition. Even later texts, not Tantras, praise the Goddess Tripurasundarī, especially the *Saundarya-laharī* ('The Ocean of Beauty') and the *Lalitā-sahasra-nāma* ('The Thousand Names of Lalitā'). These latter

Figure 3.7. The Shringeri maṭha *in Karnataka, a historical centre of the Advaita Vedānta tradition.*

texts are traditionally said to have been composed by the Advaita philosopher Śaṅkara, but their content owes more to the Trika than to Advaita Vedānta. Indeed, the Trika Goddess Parā is said to be inner essence of Tripurasundarī in some texts.[60] The Śrīvidyā became distanced from its Tantric roots when it became adopted by the Daśanāmi monastic order of Advaita Vedānta at Shringeri and Kanchipuram. The tradition from here was adopted by the Smārta Brahmin community.

60 Alexis Sanderson, 'The Visualization of the deities of the Trika', in *L'Image Divine: culte et meditation dans l'Hindouisme,* ed. André Padoux (Paris: CNRS, 1990), 23–40.

Figure 3.8. The Śrī Yantra.

The theology of the tradition is that the supreme Goddess transcends the universe which is her manifestation and reabsorbs the cosmos back into herself in an endless cycle. This is understood as the manifestation and contraction of the primal word or sound (*śabda, nāda*), identified with energy (*śakti*), light (*prakāśa*), and consciousness (*saṃvit*). The *yantra* of the Śrīcakra is a representation of the emanation and contraction of the universe from its point of origin in the 'drop' (*bindu*). The upward pointing triangles represent Śiva, the downward pointing triangles represent Śakti. The interpenetration of the triangles represents the union of Śiva and Śakti. This cosmology occurs within the body and the tradition accepts the basic structure of the subtle body comprising various centres of wheels of power through which the Goddess in the form of Kuṇḍalinī ascends to freedom at the crown of the head. The Śrīvidyā became a mainstream, orthodox tradition, but it retains an echo of the earlier Tantric, transgressive Kaula worship.

LEFT-HAND TANTRA

With the left-hand Tantric traditions, we see a use of the cultural categories of purity and impurity and the recognition that a type of power lay within impurity. The Śrīvidyā distinguished between left- and right-hand Tantrism. Left-hand Tantric practices used 'the five Ms' (derived from the earlier 'Three Ms'): *madya* (wine), *māṃsa* (meat), and *maithuna* (sexual union), plus *matsya* (fish) and *mudrā* (parched grain). As these substances are prohibited in orthodox Brahmanism,[61] to use them is polluting. Right-hand Tantra uses symbolic substitutes (*pratinidhi*), milk for wine, sesamum for meat or fish, and flowers for sex or, in Nepal, egg. There was some controversy within the Śrīvidyā about the use of these prohibited substances; some theologians, such as Lakṣmīdhara (sixteenth century), rejected their use and followed the conventional way of worship (*samayācāra*), others, such as Bhāskararāya (1728–1750), insisted on the secret use of prohibited substances once a year,[62] revealing an echo of the hardcore transgressive Kaula rite.

Nor were these practices restricted to the Śaiva and Śākta traditions. They also became adopted by Vaiṣṇavas in Bengal in the tradition called Sahajiyā, in which men and women as embodiments of Kṛṣṇa and Rādhā achieved the bliss of their union through sexual ritual, and the Bauls of Bengal adopted the theology of the Sahajiyās along with their practices.[63]

---

61 *Manu* 10.88.

62 D. Brooks, *The Secret of the Three Cities* (Chicago: Chicago University Press, 1990), 28.

63 Rahul Peter Das, 'Problematic Aspects of Sexual Rituals of the Bauls of Bengal', *Journal of the American Oriental Society* 112, no. 3 (1992): 388–432.

Popular Tantric Worship of the Goddess

Aside from the specific traditions discussed above, there is popular worship of the Goddess in a Tantric form, in North and South India, such as the Virgin Goddess Kanya Kumarī at Cape Comorin, the Mīnākṣī temple at Madurai, and the Kālī temple in Calcutta. In some ways the whole of India is the Goddess who is identified with the Earth. But it is particularly in seats (*pīṭha*) at specific locations where the Goddess is worshipped which are important sites of pilgrimage. The *Devī-bhāgavata Purāṇa* and the *Kālikā Purāṇa* contain myths of the origin of these pilgrimage sites. In these Śiva's father-in-law Dakṣa does not invite him to a great sacrifice he is organising. His daughter Satī is so upset that she burns herself to death by the fire of her own yoga. On learning of this, Śiva becomes so angry and distraught that he takes on the ferocious form of Vīrabhadra and destroys Dakṣa's sacrifice. He picks up the burned corpse of his wife in the cremation ground and dances with it in a distraught state. The gods fear that the universe will be destroyed, so Viṣṇu hacks Satī's body, cutting it away in parts until Śiva becomes more composed. Where different parts of her body fell, there is a pilgrimage centre to the Goddess. There are four traditional sites listed (see p. 218), although the *Kubjikā-mata Tantra* says that all women's homes are pilgrimage sites.[64]

64 *Kubjikāmata Tantra,* ed. T. Goudriaan and J. A. Schoterman (Leiden: Brill, 1988), 24.

Figure 3.9. A lithograph of Śiva carrying the corpse of his wife, Satī, from late nineteenth-century Calcutta.

Apart from these important pilgrimage centres where the Goddess is worshipped, there are innumerable Goddess shrines throughout India; almost every village is protected by a local goddess. These goddesses (called *mātā*, 'mothers') are generally classified as 'hot' deities in contrast to 'cool' ones because they are associated with passion, hot diseases such as smallpox, pollution, and lower social levels. Cool deities are associated with cooling passion, purity, and higher social levels. The male 'high' gods of Śiva and Viṣṇu are 'cool' in contrast to the female, local goddesses who are 'hot'. The village deities (*grāma-devatās*) fall within the hot classification. The Tantric tradition has influenced these local cultures. The low-caste dance possession rituals in Kerala called *teyyam*,

Figure 3.10. A Goddess image from Kāmākhyā in Assam.

studied by Rich Freeman for example, are strongly influenced by Tantric traditions.[65]

A notable feature of these often low-caste (but not exclusively) Goddess cults is that they are sacrificial. The Goddess demands blood offerings. We see this in the Kālī temple in Calcutta and other places. The local *teyyam* goddesses (and some gods) are offered blood from sacrificed chickens and sometimes a buffalo is sacrificed to the Goddess Durgā. These traditions are only transgressive from the perspective of highly

65 Rich Freeman, 'The Teyyam Tradition of Kerala', in *The Blackwell Companion to Hinduism*, ed. Gavin Flood, 2nd ed. (Oxford: Blackwell, 2003), 307–326.

orthodox Brahmanism where blood and meat are impure ritual substances but simply normal practices from the perspective of those who perform them.

Distinctive Features

The Tantric traditions, as we have seen, have a complex history. To simplify this complex picture we might say that on the one hand there is mainstream, Brahmanical religion concerned with purity, making lacto-vegetarian offerings to mostly male deities (Viṣṇu, Śiva and their different forms), while on the other there is an unorthodox, Tantric religion that flouts Brahmanical purity, making offerings of impure substances to often ferocious deities (such as Bhairava and Kālī). The Brahmanical tradition is concerned with purity and gaining eventual liberation, the Tantric tradition is concerned with power, and gaining power and pleasure in higher worlds. Between the extremes of purity and power through pollution, we have respectable Tantric traditions such as the Śaiva Siddhānta that adheres to the new revelation of the Tantras but maintains caste purity and purity of offerings. The Tantras that taught antinomian practices were favoured by kings in times of crisis and war, while the Tantras of the Śaiva Siddhānta were for everyday protection and use.

Regarding the antinomian use of sex in ritual, we have seen how we need to understand this in relation to broader social mores. For the high-caste householder within the Brahmanical tradition, sex was regarded as one of the purposes of life (*puruṣārtha*) for pleasure and for procreation, especially of sons to fulfil one's debt to the ancestors. But for the orthodox Brahmanical renouncer, sex was regarded as a depletion of energy that took the ascetic away from his path towards liberation. Here celibacy is a high cultural value. For the Tantric householder, sexual ritual was allowed and even demanded in order to fulfil the practitioner's obligations to his practice and intention of gaining liberation and power. For the Tantric ascetic or *sādhaka*, such as the Kāpālika, sexual ritual was a means of attaining power, partly because it went against orthodox values in rejecting caste distinctions and partly because it embraced impure ritual substances and went against Brahmanical purity rules. On this view, both the Brahmin householder and renouncer are too restricted. The Tantric *sādhaka* has transcended Vedic inhibition (*śaṅkā*) to realise liberation and power. (These relationships are summarised in Diagram 3.4.)

	Dharmic sex as value	**Sex rejected**	**Sex as anti-orthodox value**
Brahmanical householder	/	x	x
Brahmanical renouncer	x	/	x
Tantric householder	/	x	/
Tantric *sādhaka*	x	x	/

Diagram 3.4. Orthodox and Tantric Attitudes to Sexual Cultural Values.

In the context of Tantric *sādhana* or practice, sexual ritual was used to go against orthodox or dharmic values in order to gain power, to produce impure substances to offer to ferocious deities, and as an end in itself, simply for pleasure.

Concluding Remarks

The history of antinomian Tantric practice is complex because of the diversity of scriptures and traditions. But it is important to note that such practices were embraced by much of medieval society and were especially attractive to kings. But, as we saw with Jayanta, there was concern among Brahmins that this new religion of the Tantras would corrupt social mores and lead to a degeneration – Jayanta successfully has the Black Blanket sect banned by the King. The Tantric traditions, including the antinomian ones, were attractive to royalty and had widespread appeal from India and Nepal to South-East Asia, especially among the Khmer kings. We must understand this history in terms of a spectrum of purity, from the highly orthodox Brahmin at one end, strictly adhering to the values of *dharma* (*varṇāśrama-dharma*), to the Tantric *sādhaka* at the other end, rejecting those values and wishing to gain power and pleasure in this and other worlds after death, eventually gaining liberation. The Tantric householder in the middle maintained varying degrees of conformity to Vedic values but performed transgressive rites secretly, wishing to be socially conformist but privately radical.

Discussion Topic: Extreme Tantra

- Does ritual non-dualism imply metaphysical non-dualism?
- Can we understand transgressive Tantric practice as social critique?
- Is an ethical worldview compatible with non-dualism?
- Does non-dualism privilege knowledge over ritual action?

Further Reading

André Padoux. *The Hindu Tantric World: An Overview*. Chicago: Chicago University Press, 2017.

Alexis Sanderson. 'Purity and Power among the Brahmans of Kashmir'. In *The Category of the Person,* edited by Michael Carrithers, Steven Collins, and Steven Lukes, 190–216 (Cambridge: Cambridge University Press, 1985).

IV
Tantra in the Land of Viṣṇu

Although Tantra originated in Śaiva religion, it came to be adopted by other traditions, partly because of its success in attracting patronage. As we have seen, the period from around the seventh through to the thirteenth century is characterised as the Śaiva age. During this time Tantric traditions became mainstream. There were antinomian Tantric traditions, the Kaula, which rejected purity rules and caste restrictions, but the traditions of the Mantra Mārga became aligned to Brahmanism. The religion of Viṣṇu which had tended to be more orthodox, adopted Tantrism; the Tantric worship of Viṣṇu developed in a tradition called the Pāñcarātra. Texts such as the *Jayākhya Saṃhitā* and the *Lakṣmī Tantra* were influenced by Śaiva philosophy and follow the same pattern of worship and *yoga*. In particular in this chapter, we will look at the divinisation of the body and the worship of God in the heart, as we find in this tradition. We will also look at how Tantra later influenced the worship of Kṛṣṇa in Sahajiyā religion where it becomes antinomian and rejecting of orthodoxy.

One might propose a hypothesis that from around the seventh, or at least the ninth, to the thirteenth century, Tantrism was the central religious tradition of India; after this time, we witness the decline of the medieval Tantric kingdoms in the north and the rise of the Delhi Sultanate. The Tantric-inspired kingdom of Vijayanagara continues, but from the fourteenth century to the beginnings of modernity, we have a different religious and cultural landscape. With the rise and establishment of Islam we also have *bhakti* or devotional Hinduism coming to the fore. Tantric traditions lose their power base and become minority traditions. When they do this, they become characterised by transgression and reversal of mainstream Brahmanism. Thus, the Sahajiyā cult reacts against Gauḍīya Vaiṣṇava tradition while adopting the same theology, and the descendants of the Kāpālikas, the Aghoris, offer worship to the Goddess reversing orthodox Brahmanical ritual procedures, substituting impure substances for pure ones, making obeisance with the feet rather than the hands, and so on. This is not dissimilar to devil worship in Christian societies which becomes parasitic on Christian ritual, reversing its procedures. So, from mainstream, institutional religion with Brahmanical sanction and aristocratic support, Tantrism becomes more esoteric and hidden from view, defining itself in reaction against orthodox Brahmanism and playing on the impurity/purity distinction. At no point does it become a political movement in support of the interests of caste equality. In one sense, the more recent history of Tantrism is a history of decline, from being the driver of a civilisation to being a negative reflection of it. But let us return to our topic, Tantrism in the land of Viṣṇu.

The Origins of the Pāñcarātra

There is an earlier and later tradition that goes by the name 'Pāñcarātra. The older tradition is found in relation to the worship of the god Nārāyaṇa, the 'support or resting place of human beings'. This god is found in the *Śatapatha Brāhmaṇa,* an ancient Vedic text, where he is identified with the cosmic man, the *puruṣa*. He also appears in the *Nārāyaṇīya* section of the *Mahābhārata* and in the *Mahānārayaṇa Upaniṣad,* probably from the early centuries CE, where he has become the

Figure 4.1. A sculpture of the Pāñcarātra-associated deity Vaikuṇṭha Caturmūrti from Jammu and Kashmir, c. 875–900. Los Angeles County Museum of Art.

supreme deity worshipped in the heart. This deity becomes identified with Viṣṇu and by the time of the eleventh-century CE *Kathā-sarit-sāgara,* he is depicted lying on the body of a cosmic snake Śeṣa, with Lakṣmī at his feet on an ocean of milk: he has become Viṣṇu. This deity is the focus of worship of the Pāñcarātra. The name means 'five nights' and may refer to the five-night sacrifice in the *Śatapatha Brāhmaṇa* (13.6.1), in which the god known as Puruṣa Nārāyaṇa has the idea of a sacrifice lasting five nights after which he would become the highest being. Having performed the five-night sacrifice he surpassed all beings (*atyatiṣṭhat sarvāṇi bhūtāni*). In the *Nārāyaṇīya* section of the epic, he is the focus of all religions and the preceptor of the Pāñcarātra tradition. The other name of God in the Pāñcarātra is Vāsudeva (a name for Kṛṣṇa, son of Vasudeva).

Thus, the origin of the Pāñcarātra may be in the five-night sacrifice – at least that is where it derives its name from – but the theology and worship of the religion may have its roots in

Figure 4.2. A mid nineteenth-century gouache painting of Viṣṇu resting on Śeṣa, served by his consort Lakṣmī. Wellcome Collection.

the Bhāgavata cult, an early form of Viṣṇu worship. Matsubara claims that both the Bhāgavatas and the Pāñcarātra were monotheists.[1] While it may be true that they became this, the focus of the early Bhāgavata cult could well have been the twin deities of Kṛṣṇa or Vāsudeva and his brother Baladeva. Twin deities were not uncommon in ancient times and there is ample attestation to their joint worship.[2] Eventually the Bhāgavatas came to worship the Lord (*bhagavān*), especially with *bhakti*, and became focused on Vāsudeva or Kṛṣṇa. It was this sect that produced the *Bhagavad-gītā*. By the time of the early medieval period, part of this religion had transformed into the Pāñcarātra which is Tantric Vaiṣṇavism. This religion has its own revelation, the Pāñcarātra Saṃhitās, which has an account of creation as emanation from more subtle to more solidified layers (as in Śaivism), a theology of a transcendent God who appears in different forms in the world to save devotees, and a doctrine of salvation through grace and through a pattern of devotional ritual (*bhakti* combined with strict ritual practice). The Tantric Pāñcarātra is in many ways a distinct religion from the earlier tradition that bears the same name. While worship of Viṣṇu as Nārāyaṇa is still present, the form of worship follows the pattern of the Śaiva Tantras.

Pāñcarātra Texts

Pāñcarātra texts develop from the seventh or eighth centuries CE as a revelation from the Lord. The term Pāñcarātra comes to refer to these texts and the revelation they contain. Many orthodox Brahmins rejected them. There are long lists of texts but three, known as 'the three gems' are most important:

---

1 M. Matsubara, *Pāñcarātra Saṃhitās and Early Vaiṣṇava Theology* (Delhi: MLDB, 1994), 140.

2 Charlotte Schmid, *Le Don de voir* (Pondichery: Institut Français, 2016).

the *Pauṣkara*, the *Sāttvata*, and the *Jayākhya Saṃhitās*. There are other important later texts within the tradition, the *Ahir-budhnya Saṃhitā* and the *Lakṣmī Tantra*. Dating is always difficult. Out of the large body of texts in the Pāñcarātra canon – there are lists of a couple of hundred texts – over twenty have been printed, and there are some translations into European languages of complete texts or parts of texts. There is only one translation of a complete text into English, the *Lakṣmī Tantra*, but sections of the *Jayākhya Saṃhitā* have been translated into German and English, as well as parts of the *Pādma Saṃhitā* into English.[3] The *Jayākhya Saṃhitā* is 'the compendium of verses of she whose name is Victory' and can be dated to no later than the Kashmiri Śaiva author Utpalācāra (*c.* 925–975 CE) who quotes it.

The Pāñcarātra provided the scriptural revelation for the Śrī Vaiṣṇava tradition; although the famous eleventh or twelfth century Vaiṣṇava theologian Rāmānuja does not usually cite these scriptures in his theological works, the liturgical life of the tradition assumes them. Although dating these texts is difficult, Matsubara optimistically places the earliest at around 400 CE.[4] This is probably too early because, as we have seen, the earliest Śaiva Tantra, the *Niḥśvāsa-tattva Saṃhitā*, is from

---

3 See References. Sanjukta Gupta translated the *Lakṣmī Tantra* and has written papers on the tradition. Otto Schrader translated sections of the *Ahir-budhnya Saṃhitā* as did M. Matsubara. Silvia Schwarz Linder has translated parts of the *Pādma Saṃhitā* and sections of Pāñcarātra texts have been translated into Polish by Marzenna Czerniak-Drożdżowicz who has also done a study of the *Parama Saṃhitā*. Daniel Smith has done a survey of literature and published a bibliography of printed texts. Sections of the important text, the *Jayākhya Saṃhitā* have been published by Rastelli, in German, and Flood in English. Diwakar Acharya has published editions of important early texts.

4 Matsubara, *Pāñcarātra Saṃhitās*, 34.

around the seventh century; the Pāñcarātra texts are modelled on the Śaiva Tantras and so must be later.

There is a parallel tradition called the Vaikhānasa, still active in South India. This tradition has its own scriptures and although it is close to the Pāñcarātra – the emanations of the *Jayākhya Saṃhitā* are Vaikhānasa deities, for example – the tradition distances itself from the Pāñcarātra. Indeed, because it aligns itself closely with Vedic revelation and the Brahmanical tradition, it regards the Tantric revelation of the Pāñcarātra as inferior. The Pāñcarātra canon is wide and various. Texts such as the *Jayākhya Saṃhitā* contain strong Śaiva influence. The cosmological hierarchy is structurally parallel, and the emanations of God are similar to the emanations of Śiva in the pure creation. The ritual structure described in the text and the mapping of the cosmos onto the body is virtually the same as that found in the Śaiva material. There is even a passage that describes ritual or yogic suicide in the *Jayākhya* (see below), showing that the text was incorporating teachings of Yogis and that the tradition was not originally focused on the temple. As with the Śaiva, the Pāñcarātra texts, particularly the *Jayākhya*, are concerned with the individual practitioner, the *sādhaka*, more than with temple worship and reflect a time from before the establishing of the religion as a mainstream temple cult.

A striking feature about these texts is that, while there are accounts of the cosmos and of God as the source of the cosmos, there is not much sustained theological argument. In Śaivism, the *Parākhya Tantra* and *Kiraṇa Tantra* have sustained philosophy in their doctrine or knowledge chapters, but the Pāñcarātra texts are restricted to statements of doctrine, to revealed truths, without positioning themselves in the context of other philosophies. This is arguably because the intellectual work of the tradition is being done within the Vedānta. We might regard the Pāñcarātra Saṃhitās as providing the ritual and meditative base (as well as temple construction in later texts), but as having little intellectual content; this is in contrast to the Vedānta literature that is devoid of ritual details but contains the theological reflection of the Vaiṣṇava tradition.

The Concept of God

The Pāñcarātra idea of God is that the supreme being is wholly transcendent, beyond the universe that he causes to become manifest. Although different texts describe the absolute reality (*brahman*) in different ways, they share a general conception that the supreme reality is:

> bliss, undifferentiated sound, unchangeable, unaffected by defects, free from change, actionless, self-conscious, spotless, beyond pairs of opposites, infinite, free from decay, light, tranquil, all-pervading, with eyes, feet and hands everywhere, the Lord of beings, the source, the object of enjoyment, the supreme person (*puruṣottama*), and without beginning.[5]

Although wholly transcendent, he yet bestows grace on devotees and grants all desires – this is still an elitist religion, however, in that he is not to be worshipped by untouchable castes. This list is fairly standard and shows a concept of God as the unchanging source of the eternal universe who is transcendent yet immanent, pervading the universe which is his body (with eyes and limbs everywhere) even though the six qualities are also said to be his body. This idea is developed in the later theology of Rāmānuja. The Lord is a mass

5 *Pādma Saṃhitā*, 35–37, in Sylvia Schwartz Linder, *The Philosophical and Theological Teachings of the Pādmasaṃhitā* (Vienna: Österrichische Akademie der Wissenschaften, 2014), 65.

Figure 4.3. Rāmānuja, the eleventh-century systematiser of Śrīvaiṣṇavism, who develops Pāñcarātra ideas.

of consciousness (*cid-ghana*) whose nature is consciousness (*cid-rūpa*), an idea that shows the influence of non-dualistic Śaivism on the tradition. He is all-pervading and as the wind flows through the world, so God pervades everything while remaining unchanging in himself. The Lord emits and withdraws the world as the sun emits and withdraws its light.[6] As oil is contained in the sesame seed, or clarified butter in milk, or sweetness in sugar, so the Lord pervades the world and the world is a transformation of the Lord in his aspect of the

6 Ibid., 74–75.

supreme self (*paramātman*).[7] The absolute Brahman becomes Vāsudeva, or rather that is simply another way of describing that reality. God is wholly transcendent and immanent power, abstract and impersonal, yet is also a personal God who takes form, such as Vāsudeva. The *Jayākhya Saṃhitā* describes God in the following way in a passage worth quoting in full:

> God is characterised by joy, bereft of everything that is to be avoided, known to itself, having no point of comparison, the highest limit, the highest abode. The Lord is the refuge of all, bereft of all action, as in the wish-fulfilling jewel everything embodied [and] attached is placed in order, so everything everywhere is known by the omnipresent one. Without beginning and without end, that one is not being and not called non-being; everywhere his hands, speech and feet, everywhere his eyes, head, and mouth. He stands everywhere possessing scripture, know [him to be] encompassing everything. He appears as having all senses and qualities but yet is bereft [of them]. That one is unattached being everywhere, without qualities and yet enjoying qualities, he is established outside and inside of everything. Know him to be moving and unmoving. He is not perceived on account of his subtlety. Standing far away, the Lord who is the supreme self, abides in the heart. Not distinct from all beings, he is perceived to be distinct from those beings. He is the support of all beings and objects and although he is the destroyer, he creates. Placed higher than ignorance he is the illumination of all lights. He is knowledge and object of knowledge; he is achieved by meditation on him. Bereft of all tastes and colours, yet possessing all smells and tastes, the Lord is the omniscient, all seeing one, the most eminent of all, the all, the Lord of all.

---

7 Ibid., 76.

> Made of all powers, autonomous, the supreme Lord is without beginning or end, bereft of all suffering. So, know the highest absolute through supreme knowledge. When a man [knows God] he is not born again in this cycle of rebirth.[8]

Concerning the relation of the Lord to the universe there is an ambiguity in that on the one hand the Lord is wholly transcendent as the creator of the world, while on the other the world is a transformation of the same substance as the Lord. This is a qualified theism in that the Lord, while remaining transcendent, becomes world through affecting material nature or *prakṛti* that the texts say is distinct from him. There is inconsistency here in that the Lord is distinct from material nature or *prakṛti* and yet the world is also the manifestation of the Lord as sweets are a coagulation of sugar cane. God is all of creation:

> I am the creator, protector, and destroyer again and again, through my gross form, O Nārada, by union with my own power. I dwell in the heart of all beings in a subtle form and I perform grace to devotees whose souls are developed. Through your pure form [which is] pure and pervading, I pervade all, O Brahmin, like sap in the tallest tree, watered at the root, having a top, branches, leaves, flowers and fruit.[9]

God in himself is unknowable, being beyond the range of speech and thought (*a-vāṅ-manasa-gocara*)[10] and yet he can liberate beings through his grace. Indeed, beings are immersed and trapped in the illusion created by material substrate (*māyā*) of the universe, but the Lord has the power to lift this veil of

---

8 *Jayākhya Saṃhitā* 4. 60cd–71 (my translation).

9 *Jayākhya Saṃhitā* 4.23–26ab.

10 Schwartz Linder, *Philosophical and Theological Teachings*, 77.

ignorance and liberate souls. To facilitate this, the Lord takes supreme, subtle, and gross forms that can be the object of meditation or visualisation (*dhyeya*). Such visualisation of the forms of God is also accompanied by *mantra* recitation, which is the sound-body of God: the Lord takes on forms both visual and aural, so that devotees can meditate upon him and so that through those forms he can bestow grace and ultimate salvation. The forms that God takes in the pure creation – the first emanation of the cosmos – are called the *vyūhas*. He takes these forms, but he is also present in all beings as their inner controller (*antaryāmin*), a term that is used later by Rāmānuja: 'He is the inner controller, whose nature is light and consciousness, who, having that form, is desireless, always arisen in that triad.'[11]

The Pāñcarātra is a theistic religion. God is transcendent as creator and the animating principle of the universe, or material energy (*māyā śakti*), retains some distinction from him. In his essence, God has no comparison (*anaupamya*): he is omniscient, omnipresent, beyond being (*sat*) and non-being (*asat*), possessing all qualities he is yet bereft of all qualities, being far away he is yet in the heart of all beings. This is typical language of theistic systems in which God is outside of creation, wholly transcendent, and so cannot be spoken about in language – or, rather, there is a limit to which language can express divinity. Our language can go so far, but because God is incomparable, no language can suitably capture his reality. The Pāñcarātra embraces both impersonal and personal descriptions of the divine. He is absolute consciousness (*cit*), desireless, all-pervading and so on yet he is also the supreme person who is dear to his devotees and perhaps – as in the *Bhagavad-gītā* – his devotees are dear to him.

---

11 *Jayākhya Saṃhitā* 4.14cd–15ab.

Pāñcarātra Cosmology

The Lord creates the universe in the sense of emanating it. He does not create the universe ex nihilo. First, he forms the pure creation, which is an emanation of himself, and secondly, he forms the impure creation by acting upon inactive and unconscious matter, a distinct substance which nevertheless depends upon God.

The lower layers of the universe, of which our world is one, are emanations of more subtle forms due to the action and will of a transcendent God. The *Jayākhya Saṃhitā* contains the earliest and most elaborate account of cosmology, as well as daily ritual practice and the mapping of the universe onto the body. It divides the universe into the pure creation and the impure creation, with an intermediate creation between. Within the pure creation are the manifestations of God known as *vyūhas*, emanations. This doctrine of the *vyūhas* is what the Pāñcarātra is most famous for. The text is a dialogue between the sage Nārada and the Lord (Bhagavān). The supreme absolute or Brahman is none other than the personal Lord Vāsudeva from whom the lower forms of the universe emanate. The *Jayākhya Saṃhitā* gives a good description of this that is worth quoting:

> [The ultimate reality] is non-distinct from Vāsudeva and other manifestations. Having a hundred-fold radiance of fire, sun and moon, Vāsudeva is the Lord, the truth of that [absolute], the supreme Lord. Agitating his own radiance through his own energy (*tejas*), the Lord whose form is light manifests the god Acyuta, like lightening, O Brahmin. [Then] that Acyuta of firm radiance spreads his own form, dependent on Vāsudeva as a wisp of cloud (depends) on the summer heat. Then shaking himself he [in turn] produced the god Satya, whose body is shining, as the ocean [produces] a bubble. He is called the light made of consciousness who produces himself by means

> of himself [as the god] called Puruṣa who is great, an unending stream of light. That supreme Lord is [in turn] the support of all the [lower] gods, their inner controller, as the sky [is the support] of the stars. As a fire with its fuel sends forth a mass of sparks, O twice-born one, so the Supreme Lord, who is yet desireless, [sends forth manifestation].[12]

This is a striking account of creation. Vāsudeva emanates the forms of Acyuta, Satya, and Puruṣa, who are named deities in the parallel tradition of the Vaikhānasa. Each emanation comes from the preceding, except the first. In other texts, these *vyūhas* have the names of Kṛṣṇa's relatives, namely his brother Saṃkarṣaṇa, his son Pradyumna, and his grandson Aniruddha. Each of these is an aspect of the supreme, transcendent deity. Vāsudeva, while being beyond qualities, can nevertheless be spoken about as possessing six qualities or *guṇas*: knowledge (*jñāna*), majesty (*aiśvarya*), power (*śakti*), strength (*bala*), energy (*vīrya*), and splendour (*tejas*). These six qualities actually make up the *vyūhas*; they exist before creation in a condition of inactivity but, once manifested, their totality is said to make up the body of Vāsudeva.[13] Each of the *vyūhas* is in essence the same as the others, abiding in Vāsudeva: 'And that triad whose nature is consciousness, Puruṣa, Satya and Acyuta, abides in Vāsudeva whose nature is pacified consciousness.'[14] Indeed, the emanations are ontologically non-distinct from Vāsudeva as sky seen through a crystal is essentially the same. This unity or identity is a secret doctrine:

12 Ibid. 4.3–9.

13 *Ahir-budhnya Saṃhitā* 6.25, cited in Otto Schrader, *Introduction to the Pāñcarātra* (Madras: Adyar Library, 1973 [1916]), 39.

14 *Jayākhya Saṃhitā* 4.13cd–14ab.

> On account of the very great purity, O Brahmin, of those who are attached [to each other], no division arises [between them]. As on account of light, there is unity of sky and crystal, O Brahmin, even so of them there is wholeness. This is the supreme secret revealed to you by me, the creation, beginning and end, the great soul of the endless.[15]

The term *vyūha* used in the Pāñcarātra is derived from *vy+ūh*, 'to shift or move apart'; the *Ahir-budhnya* says it refers to the six qualities shifting into three pairs, and the term is also used in Mahāyāna Buddhism where it denotes the manifestation of the pure land by the Buddha Amitābha, the Sukhāvatī-vyūha. That the term is used to indicate an emanated or displayed world from Amitābha has a parallel use here as the display or emanation of different aspects of the divine. These emanations were also depicted in stone sculptures with four faces, one emerging from the other (Fig. 4.4).

The *vyūhas* have a cosmological function to create the lower order of the universe and a moral function to help beings on their way to salvation. Saṃkarṣaṇa or Acyuta (in the *Jayākhya*) begins the process of manifestation; with him the universe is still in a state of potentiality and only beginning to emerge 'like a dark spot on the skin (*tilakālaka*)'.[16] Pradyumna or Satya produces the duality of Puruṣa and Prakṛti, the self and matter/nature, and Aniruddha or Puruṣa (not the same as the lower emanation) causes lower matter to manifest. The Lord is manifested not only in the *vyūhas* as cosmological entities, but also in manifestations (*vibhava*) or incarnations (*avatāra*) that comprise a series of lower gods including Kṛṣṇa, Rāma, and Kalkin, and also in temple images (*arcā*).

15 *Jayākhya Saṃhitā* 4.17cd–19.

16 Schrader, *Introduction to the Pāñcarātra*, 43.

Figure 4.4. Vāsudeva with the vyūhas *emanating from him. Mathura Museum.*

In this system the lower Puruṣa is the receptacle for all the souls who have returned in the periodic destruction of the universe. It is called the beehive (*kośa madhu-kṛta*) of the souls (*jīva*), from which they all fly out at a new creation. The *jīvas* are contaminated by the dust of beginningless *karma,* just as pollen is attached to bees. *Māyā* generates the lower order of the universe. She is a power (*śakti*) identified with the Goddess Mahā Lakṣmī, herself divided up into three goddesses, Mahā Śrī, Mahā Kālī, and Mahā Vidyā. From *māyā* emanates Prakṛti, the foundational substance of material creation. From this the lower order is manifested 'the great one' (*mahat*), also known as higher mind or intellect (*buddhi*); from this emerges the limited self or 'I-maker' (*ahaṃkāra*) and then the mind (*manas*), the five senses, five action capacities, five subtle elements, and five material elements. In other words, the twenty-five *tattvas* known from the Sāṃkhya system are incorporated in the scheme.

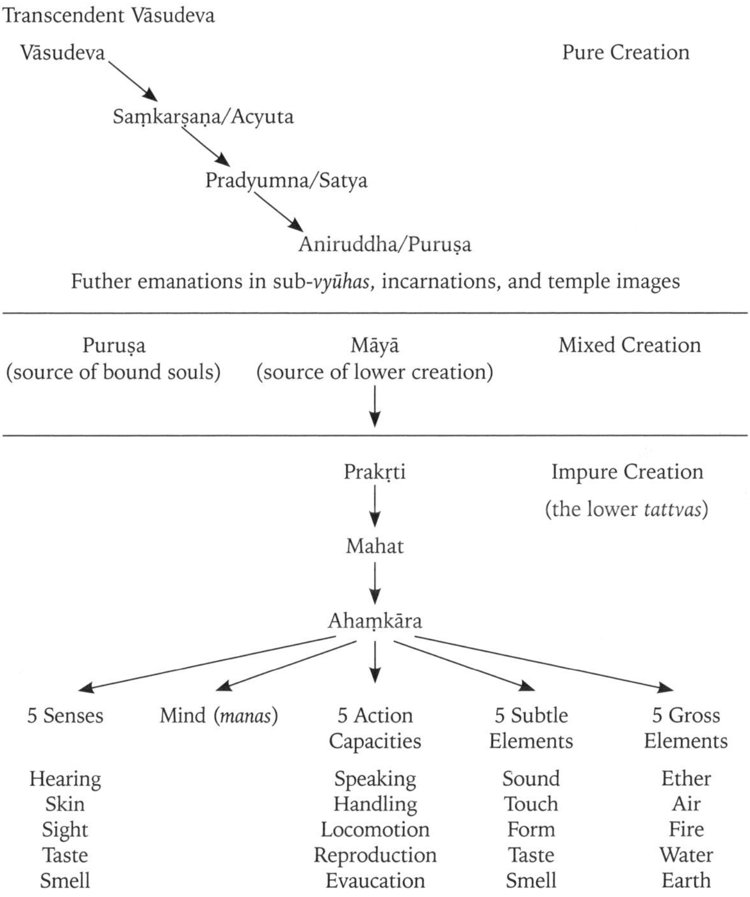

Diagram 4.1. Pāñcarātra Cosmology.

The Pāñcarātra speaks of the power of Vāsudeva as the Goddess and emanations of her. While the Lord is transcendent, he acts through the Goddess. Her actions express his wishes (although the texts also say that he is without desire!). The Lord is the efficient cause of the universe while the Goddess is the instrumental and material cause in her forms of *kriyā-śakti* (the power of action) and *bhūti-śakti* (the power of the earth or of existence).

The purpose of this whole complex scheme is the liberation of souls. The cosmos undergoes a process of emanation and contraction, creation and destruction, over and over again. The Lord out of compassion creates the universe so that souls can erase their karmic traces and gain liberation. The Lord by the energy of his *yoga* produces *mantras* that can liberate souls through material nature (*prakṛti*). The Lord says in the *Jayākhya Saṃhitā*:

> By the energy of *yoga*, O Brahmin, the ancient form of *mantra*, which is both without parts and with parts, is radiant and bestows pleasure and liberation. It is made by me, is radiant and bestows correct vision of the worlds. Through the gradual arising of *mantra*, [the *mantra*-form] is established with the soul which is most calm.[17]

Those beings that do not attain liberation go into a state of hibernation during a period of contraction – they go into the receptacle of the *puruṣa-tattva* – only to remerge again once the universe is manifested to go into the cycle of reincarnation. The Lord saves souls at death, although in life people need to undergo a process of ritual to erase karmic traces. The Pāñcarātra follows the usual Tantric ritual pattern of the

17 *Jayākhya Saṃhitā* 4.30–31.

purification of the elements within the body or the body's symbolic destruction; the creation of a divine body through the imposition of *mantras* upon it; mental worship or meditation; and external worship followed by offerings made into the fire pit. There is also the standard pattern of initiation.

Pāñcarātra Ritual

There are general qualities expected of the devotee. He should be kind and gentle, concerned for the welfare of all beings, and be focused on meditation practice. The *Jayākhya* says:

> [The practitioner should practice] purity, sacrifice, and austerity beginning with the recitation of the Veda, gentleness, not harshness, and constant patience, [speaking] truth and [concern for] the welfare of all beings, which is freedom from pain among beings. [He should practice] non-violence towards oneself and others, quelling the mind, O great one, non-desire for the pleasures of consumption by the senses. [The practitioner] should be non-attached, even on a path, a bed, a seat, and with food. He should not abandon meditation in the heart, which gives the fruit of joy. He should give as much as he is able, [speak] true, unharsh speech among enemies and friends, [treating them] evenly. [In this way] the mind truly rests.[18]

Pāñcarātra initiation follows the pattern of Śaiva initiation. The guru who initiates must be lenient towards the poor of intellect, well versed in the systems of Vedānta and Pāñcarātra, and capable of empathy for others. The student must belong to the top three castes (the twice born) and must have studied with application with the teacher for a number of years,

18 Ibid. 4.44cd–48 (my translation).

showing that he is free from greed and able to guard the secret tradition.[19] He is given the *mantra* by the guru at initiation. The *Jayākhya Saṃhitā* describes different kinds of practitioner, echoing the Śaiva scheme, namely the *samayajña* and *putraka*, followed by becoming a *sādhaka* and *ācārya*. The first two are grades of initiation into the tradition and the last two are different ablutions (*abhiṣeka*) that can be taken, the *sādhaka* being a path of power and pleasure in higher worlds, the *ācārya* (teacher) being a path that allows the initiate to become a teacher. After initiation, the adept will undergo a regime of daily practice: the purification of the body (*bhūta-śuddhi*), divinisation of the body (*nyāsa*), mental worship (*mānasa-yāga*), and external worship (*bāhya-yāga*), the standard Tantric practice.

The *Jayākhya Saṃhitā* gives a detailed description of this process, devoting a chapter to each, and showing how the structure of the cosmos is mapped onto the body. This is the earliest detailed description, and, after this text, others simplify the process. The purification of the body is described as visualising the cosmos mapped onto the body, with the earth element pervading from feet to knees, the water element from knees to thighs, the fire element from anus to navel, the air element from navel to throat, and the space element from the ears to the crown of the head. Each element is associated with a *mantra* and in the process the *mantra* of each element is breathed in from an imaginary point in front of the face, dissolved into its corresponding subtle element and breathed out before the next. This is accompanied by the symbolic destruction of the body, from feet to knees, from knees to thighs and so on until the body is completely destroyed. More specifically, a fire burns from the toe of the right foot, the fire of time (*kālāgni*), consuming the physical body to a pile of ashes,

19 Schrader, *Introduction to the Pāñcarātra*, 139.

which is then swept away by a milky ocean – the nectar of immortality from the crown of the head.

The origins of the *bhūta-śuddhi* may go back to Vedic and also to Buddhist sources. The *Bṛhadāraṇyaka Upaniṣad* describes offering ghee to the sacred fire to earth, atmosphere, and sky, and in early Buddhist meditation there are the *kasina* exercises described in Buddhaghosa's *Visuddhi-magga*. The *kasinas* are objects of meditation identified with the five elements and five colours. The earth *kasina*, for example, is a clay disc meditated upon which is then internalised in the mind's eye and so becomes a sign (*nimitta*) that leads into the first level of meditation (*jhāna/dhyāna*). There are echoes of such practices in the *bhūta-śuddhi*.

The practitioner should go to an unfrequented, charming place and offer obeisance to the Lord and the lineage of masters. With their mental command he is ready to perform the ritual. He first purifies his hands by reciting the weapon (*astra*) *mantra* and then he performs the purification of the body. Each element is associated with a *mantra* (thus the earth *mantra* is *oṃ ślāṃ pṛthivyai huṃ phaṭ*) which is visualised in a certain form – the earth is a yellow square – and each element in turn dissolved in the body. For example, the *Jayākhya* describes the purification of the earth element in the following way:

> [The practitioner] should visualize a quadrangular, yellow earth, marked with the sign of thunder, connected with the five, sound etc. [i.e. the five subtle elements *śabda, sparśa, rūpa, rasa,* and *gandha*] and filled with trees and mountains, adorned with oceans, islands, good rivers and walled towns. He should visualize [that earth] entering his own body from the outside with an inhaled breath, and uttering the *mantra* he should imagine it as tranquilized, pervading in due order from the knees to the soles of the feet by means of the retained breath, O best of twice born ones. Then, [the earth is]

> gradually dissolved in its own *mantra*-form, and this *mantra*-king [dissolved] in the energy of smell. After that he should emit the energy of smell with the exhaled breath.[20]

This process is repeated with each element until the universe is reabsorbed symbolically within the body back to its source and then the practitioner imagines a fire burning from the toe of the right foot, the deity Kālāgni, the fire of time, consuming the body to a pile of ashes, which are swept away by the nectar released through *mantra* repetition.

Having destroyed the physical body, a new body is created through placing mantras upon the body, as this procedure makes the practitioner equal to the god of gods (*deva-deva-sama*) with power over unexpected death.[21] The simple plank on the ground becomes the practitioner's throne (*āsana*). The pantheon of gods is imposed on the fingers. For example, the root *mantra* (*mūla-mantra*) with the form *mantra* (*mūrti-mantra*), *oṃ kṣīṃ kṣiḥ namaḥ, nārāyaṇāya viśvātmane hrīṃ svāhā*, is placed on the right thumb, the Vaiṣṇava goddesses Lakṣmī, Kīrti, Jayā, and Māyā on the fingers, and so on. Through this elaborate process the practitioner becomes identified with Viṣṇu-Nārāyaṇa, visualising himself as that deity, possessing the six divine qualities of the *vyūhas*, such that he can say 'I am the Lord Viṣṇu, I am Nārāyaṇa, Hari, and I am Vāsudeva.'[22] Once he has become the deity, he can worship the deity. This he does in his imagination in the inner or mental worship. Here Viṣṇu is imagined at or above the crown of the head and brought down through the central channel of the body to the heart where he is seated on a throne. The body is visualised as possessing the

---

20 *Jayākhya Saṃhitā* 10.

21 Ibid. 11.26–27.

22 *Jayākhya Saṃhitā* 11.

vertical axis of the central channel along which are located the centres (*cakra*) of power. Here is the visualisation as described by the *Jayākhya*, where we see the structure of the subtle body parallel to other Tantric texts.

> So having formerly become Viṣṇu [through the purification of the body previously described], the practitioner should then worship Viṣṇu with the mental sacrifice. Imagining [the area] between the penis and the navel filled with four parts, one should visualize the support energy (*ādhāra-śakti*), above that the fire of time [Kālāgni], above that Ananta, and then the Earth Goddess [Vasudhā Devī]. From the place of the 'bulb' (*kanda*) to the navel is divided into four parts. Visualizing the ocean of milk in the navel and then a lotus arising [out of it], extending as far as a thousand petals and whirling with a thousand rays [of light], having the appearance of a thousand rays, he should fix the throne on its back. The fourfold [dispositions] *dharma*, knowledge, detachment, and majesty, descend by means of their own *mantras* to the four [directions] of Fire [the south east] and so on [south west, north west, and north east], fixing those four up to the abode of the Lord Īśāna [the north east]. The four feet of the throne are white, with lion faces, but having the forms of men in their body, possessing exceeding strength. The parts from the eastern direction up to the northern abode are fixed with the opposites of *dharma*, knowledge, detachment, and majesty. These are of human form, blazing like the red *bandhuka* flower. The four [scriptures] the *Ṛg Veda* and so on have the form of a horse-man, are yellow, and [situated] in between the east and the direction of the Lord [north-east], between the east and the direction of Fire [the south east], between the south-west and Varuṇa [the west], and between the wind [north-west] and Varuṇa [the west]. The group of ages, namely Kṛta and so on, have the form of a bull-man, are black, and are

> located in the directions between Īśāna [north-east] and Soma [north], between Antaka [another name for Yama, the south] and Agni [south-east], between Yama [south] and the demon [Yakṣa, the south-west], and between the Moon [the north] and the wind [north-west]. They all have four arms; with two they support the throne and with two they make obeisance to the Lord of the universe. Above them he should fix first a white lotus [and then] threefold [forms, namely sun, moon, and fire], way above with those *mantras*, arising from himself and previously articulated, O Nārada. On the back of that he should establish both the King of Birds and the Boar. Having imagined [the area] from the navel to the heart pervaded by five equal sections, he should worship the *mantra*-throne.[23]

This complex visualisation shows how the hierarchy of the cosmos is mapped onto the hierarchy of the body. Kālāgni appears now at the navel, and the body is populated with Vaiṣṇava deities.

After worshipping the Lord in the imagination in this way, the practitioner should worship God in external reality. The outer worship is simply a standard Hindu ritual practice (*pūjā*). The *Jayākhya Saṃhitā* raises the question, why bother to perform external worship after the mental visualisation? It seems superfluous. This is because mental worship destroys mental *karma* or mental karmic traces (*vāsanā*) from internal causes, whereas external worship removes karmic traces from external causes. The ritual is performed by the practitioner drawing a ritual diagram (*maṇḍala*). He then installs Nārāyaṇa in the centre, with a host of surrounding deities through visualisation and *mantra* repetition. Incense and vegetarian food are offered along with the sound of a bell. *Mantra* repetition is

23 Ibid. 12.1–15.

performed with a rosary (*akṣa-mālā*) and the offerings (*homa*) are made into the fire pit (*kuṇḍa*). There are some concluding rites and the ritual is over, the text urging the practitioner not to forget the Lord (as in a Catholic mass).

This ritual procedure is fairly standard and shows the conservative character of the Tantric traditions in simply following procedures of Brahmanical practice, standard in the early medieval period. The followers of the Pāñcarātra, in contrast to the practitioners of the Kula tradition examined in the last chapter, are not disrupters of the Brahmanical system. The Pāñcarātrin practitioner saw his tradition as complementing the Vedic tradition, although his new revelation ensured final salvation.

Final salvation, the attaining of the highest self (*paramātman*) occurs at death. The Pāñcarātra also offers a practice of ritual death whereby the practitioner projects his self out of the body which dies: an act of ritual suicide. This practice of *utkrānti* is attested in Śaiva texts but is also found here in the Pāñcarātra.[24] The *Jayākhya Saṃhitā* describes a process in which the Yogi who is aware of the approach of his own death performs a meditation to expel his soul from the body in a process of conscious dying. Having meditated upon Viṣṇu as a figure possessing a body (*savigraha*), then as a form of sound (*śabda*), and then as space (*vyoma*), he then meditates himself leaving the body.

> Having established in this way [the meditations on Viṣṇu] he should abandon the restriction which is having a body. Knowing the full body which has the supreme characteristic

24 Schwartz Linder, *The Philosophical and Theological Teachings of the Pādmasaṃhitā*, 281–303. See Somadeva Vasudeva, *The Yoga of the Mālinīvijayottaratantra* (Pondichéry: Institut d'Indologie, 2004), 437–445.

> of being cooked [in the fire of ritual], having performed a contraction [of the self] on the twilight path, having freed the breath from the body after meditating by means of going out through the true hole of the absolute [at the crown of the head], he should thereby abandon the body if he is intent upon its constant practice. He goes to the imperishable, supreme absolute called Vāsudeva.[25]

Here the Yogi expels his vital breath out through the hole of the absolute believed to be at the crown of the head and goes to God, thereby killing the body. The text describes the impending signs of death that the Yogi becomes aware of and, with death knocking at the door, he resolves to leave the body in the way described.

The Pāñcarātra was a successful Vaiṣṇava religion, successful because it adopted the new Tantric mode of worship and had its own Tantric revelation. It is distinct from the other main Vaiṣṇava religion, the Bhāgavata cult, that produced the *Bhagavad-gītā*: it is less devotional, with more emphasis on ritual and meditation. The scriptures were regarded as revelation and Rāmānuja's teacher, Yāmuna, wrote a defence of those scriptures as revelation, distinct from the fraudulent Śaiva scriptures. It is curious that there is no commentary on the Pāñcarātra scriptures by any theologian, in sharp contrast to the Śaiva commentarial tradition. I think this is probably because the intellectual energy of the tradition went into the Vedānta: the Vedānta is really Vaiṣṇava theology and the Tantric revelation of the Saṃhitās was used only for ritual. Rāmānuja would have known the ritual procedures of the texts, but his intellectual interest lay in the scriptures of the Vedānta tradition not the ritual manuals of the Pāñcarātra.

25 *Jayākhya Saṃhitā* 33.57–59 (my translation).

After the decline of Śaivism around the thirteenth century, Vaiṣṇavism became predominant, but it was more a kind of *bhakti*-orientated religion rather than the Tantric form of the Pāñcarātra. The religion never completely died out, however, and Pāñcarātra rituals are still used in major temples today, as they would have been in Rāmānuja's day.

THE SAHAJIYĀS

The Tantric form of Vaiṣṇavism that bears closest resemblance to the Kaula Śaiva Tantric tradition is the religion of the Sahajiyās in Northeast India (Bengal, Assam, Orissa, Bihar). The Sahajiyās are the nemesis of the Hare Krishna tradition or Gauḍīya Vaiṣṇavism because they draw on the theology of Kṛṣṇa and Rādhā but interpret it in a Tantric way. There is a tradition of Sanskrit poetry which identifies married love as love in union, associated with lust (*kāma*), in contrast with love in separation, associated with longing (*viraha*) and the spiritual love (*prema*) of adultery. The relationship between Rādhā as an older married woman who becomes the beloved of Kṛṣṇa exemplifies this ideal. While Gauḍīya theology interpreted this symbolically to refer to the love of the soul for God, the Sahajiyās interpreted it literally and advocated sexual ritual outside of caste and family restrictions.

The origin of the Sahajiyās is in the seventeenth century. They thought the purpose of life is to realise one's innate divinity, *sahaja* (born within), a state of unity and joy. Ritual practice involved sex in order to awaken the experience of *sahaja*. So, they call their own religion the *sahaja-dharma*, a union of devotion (*bhakti*), passion (*rāga*), and divine love (*prema*). The ritual procedure of the Sahajiyās follows standard Vaiṣṇava devotion up to a point. *The Necklace of Immortality* (*Amṛta-ratnāvalī*) of Mukundadāsa (*c.* 1650 CE) describes Sahajiyā ritual.

Figure 4.5. Fourteenth-century fresco of Rādhā and Kṛṣṇa on interior wall of City Palace, Udaipur, Rajasthan.

First the text describes basic ideas and stages of the path from beginner to accomplished and perfected. The guru initiates the disciple and gives him the *mantra*. The adept then discovers the divine body (*divya-deha*) within himself through the process of ritual with a passionate female partner. She is like Rādhā; with her he realises the divine body and perceives the place of the hidden moon (the abode of *sahaja*) within.

The ritual involves sexual congress in order to realise the hidden moon of awakening and also to produce ritual substances regarded as cosmic substance, which is in fact the substance of the inner, divine body. The text reads:

> You must perform your practices with the physical body of your female partner. Through such practices you will attain your own Cosmic Substance. // The ponds are within the man, but the woman becomes conscious of them. A female partner suitable for such practices should be a desirable and joyful woman. // During sexual intercourse, the ponds and lotuses shimmer with erotic energies. The Pond of divine love, where divine love blossoms, is eternal. // The village of eternal bliss is located along the far shores of the crooked river. The crooked river flows in a northerly direction. //... The community of experienced ones dwells in the place of eternal bliss. The experienced ones are youthful; the experienced ones are numerous. // The people of the primordial place perform the rituals of the primordium (*sahaja*). The primordial being is the vessel of all divine essence.[26]

This is very esoteric material. The realisation of God within, the innate spontaneity of liberation, the *sahaja*, the place of the hidden moon, is realised through a meditation and ritual process. The text seems to be describing a journey within the self which is also a journey through the cosmos. But by the time of this text, we have a specific terminology and cosmic landscape described, with crooked rivers and specific locations. The mapping of the cosmos onto the body, which is prototypically Tantric, has become a rich landscape of the

---

26 Glen Hayes, 'The Necklace of Immortality', vv. 168–183, in *Tantra in Practice*, ed. David White (Princeton: Princeton University Press, 2000), 308–325.

inner journey. Moreover, this inner journey is not conducted alone, but with one's ritual partner, and the place of the hidden moon realised through an act of ritual intimacy. The Sahajiyās are still to be found today along with the tradition that developed from them, the Bauls of Bengal, famous for their music and particularly their singing.

Tantric Vaiṣṇavism in the form of the Pāñcarātra is not antinomian and the Saṃhitās are regarded as revelation from God by traditions such as the Śrī Vaiṣṇavas. The Pāñcarātra texts emerged in response to the Śaiva Tantric canon and success of those traditions. It became mainstream, normative tradition whose rituals form the basis of Śrī Vaiṣṇava tradition. The Pāñcarātra never completely died out, and there is still a strong community of the related tradition of Vaikhānasas in the South, and even the Swaminarayan tradition draws upon it. But Tantric Vaiṣṇavism became antinomian with the Sahajiyās, responding to Bengal Kṛṣṇa worship with their own version and believing in the innate divinity of all beings, a divinity that can be realised in spontaneous awakening to the truth of God within, in the union of man and woman in divine embrace.

Figure 4.6. Bauls in song in Santinekatan, Bengal.

Dicussion Topic: Vaiṣṇava Tantra

- What is Tantric about the Pāñcarātra?
- What is the Pāñcarātra attitude to other Tantric scriptures?
- Are the Pāñcarātra scriptures works of theology?
- Is it meaningful to put the Pāñcarātra and the Sahajiyā in the same category?
- What is the place of caste in the Pāñcarātra and the Sahajiyā traditions?

Further Reading

M. Matsubara. *Pāñcarātra Saṃhitās and Early Vaiṣṇava Theology*. Delhi: MLDB, 1994.

Otto Schrader. *Introduction to the Pāñcarātra*. Madras: Adyar Library, 1973 [1916].

V
Dualist and Non-dualist Philosophy of Tantra

While Tantra is largely about practice, in this chapter we will examine the philosophies of Tantra. On the one hand we have the dualist philosophy of the Śaiva Siddhānta that maintains an eternal distinction between self and God; for this tradition God is wholly transcendent. On the other hand, we have the non-dualist tradition of Kashmir Śaivism that maintains an identity between self and God.[1] We will examine, in particular, Abhinavagupta's arguments in support of non-dualism against the dualists and against the Buddhists. In the Recognition (Pratyabhijñā) school of philosophy, the goal of life is the realisation that 'I am Śiva' who is pure consciousness.

The philosophies of Śaivism were not included in the classical list of six orthodox systems, but a fourteenth-century philosopher, Mādhava, who wrote an interesting summary of many different philosophical systems called the *Compendium of All Philosophies* (*Sarva-darśana-saṃgraha*), describes Śaiva philosophies. But regardless of their non-inclusion in the famous

---

1 See Dyczkowski, Mark S. G., *The Doctrine of Vibration: An Analysis of the Doctrines and Practices of Kashmir Shaivism* (Albany: SUNY Press, 1987), 33–58.

list of orthodox philosophies, the Śaivas developed a rigorous discussion about metaphysics and the dualists of the Śaiva Siddhānta engaged in intellectual debate with the non-dualist Śaivas of the Recognition (Pratyabhijñā) school.

As you may recall from Chapters 1 and 2, the Śaiva Siddhānta was the main ritual system in medieval India and its theology was dualistic or, more accurately, pluralist in

Figure 5.1. The Bhairava form of Śiva, Durbar Square, Kathmandu, Nepal.

maintaining the eternal reality of three substances: God, self, and universe. By contrast another ritual and meditation tradition reacted against this and revered its own distinctive revelation that they believed came from the form of Śiva called Bhairava. Non-dualistic philosophy has its roots in this tradition. In the following we will discuss firstly the theology of the Śaiva Siddhānta, then that of the Recognition School.

Śaiva Siddhānta Theology

The cult of the form of Śiva called Sadāśiva, as we have seen, was the basis of the Śaiva Siddhānta. Theologians in the tradition wrote commentaries on the revealed scriptures, the dualist Tantras, and also some independent treatises. Their main protagonists were the Buddhists, and later their non-dualist co-religionists. There were a series of theologians in this tradition (see Appendix 1 for a list). One of the earliest to whom later writers refer was Sadyojotis (675–725 CE) in Kashmir. He wrote commentaries on scriptures and independent theological works, in particular the *Nareśvara-parīkṣā* ('An Examination of God and Man') and the *Paramokṣa-nirāsa-kārikā* ('Verses on the Refutation of Liberation according to Others'), in which is expressed the Siddhānta theology of God and the soul, although without it being tied to any specific scripture.[2] Two early theologians are of note: Bhaṭṭa Nārāyaṇakaṇṭha and his son Bhaṭṭa Rāmakaṇṭha (*c.* 950–1000 CE) both wrote commentaries on Śaiva Siddhānta scriptures. Bhojadeva (1000–1050 CE),a king in Mālava as well as a theologian, composed a summary of Śaiva Siddhānta doctrine, the *Tattva-prakāśa* ('Illumination of the Categories'). The opening

---

2 Alexis Sanderson, 'Śaiva Literature', 15, *Journal of Indological Studies* 24/25 (2012/2013): 1–113.

verse lays out the main topic: the three categories God (*pati*), bound soul or beast (*paśu*), and bond (*pāśa*). The soul is likened to a tethered cow that is freed by the Lord from its tether. Once freed, the soul realises itself as equal to Śiva (*śiva-tulya*), ontologically and numerically distinct but identical in terms of power and cognition. Indeed, the only difference is that Śiva has never been bound and Śiva, unlike freed souls, performs the five acts of creation, maintenance, destruction, revealing himself, and concealing himself. One of the last theologians of note in this tradition was Aghoraśiva (twelfth century) in the South who, like his forebears, wrote commentaries on the scriptures.

Figure 5.2. An early nineteenth-century Pahari painting of Sadāśiva. National Museum, New Delhi.

An early scripture of the Śaiva Siddhānta is the *Kiraṇa Tantra* ('Scripture of the Ray of Light from Śiva'), on which Rāmakaṇṭha wrote a learned commentary. This text and his commentary systematically deal with the main doctrines of the tradition, dividing these up into the categories of the bound soul, primal matter, *karma*, and the Lord.

The Soul

The term *paśu*, Rāmakaṇṭha reminds us, is used exclusively for those souls who are bound to the cycle of reincarnation by impurity. This is a complex doctrine in that different types and degrees of impurity produce different classes of bound soul. There are two broad divisions here: those souls that have a property of limiting power called *kalā* and those without that property. Those with *kalā* are in turn of two types: those souls with a subtle body and those with a gross body. The souls without *kalā* are also of two types: those who are devoid of *kalā* because of their knowledge or level of consciousness (*vijñānākala*) and those devoid of *kalā* because they have been reabsorbed into a higher level of the cosmic hierarchy.[3] These souls are covered by impurity, a substance that keeps them bound in the universe. This impurity itself is classified into different types: impurity derived from individuality (*āṇava-mala*), impurity derived from accumulated *karma* (*kārma-mala*), and that which is derived from material nature or *māyā* (i.e. *māyīya-mala*). Rāmakaṇṭha tells us that only a rare bound soul has simple impurity derived from individuality, having destroyed his *karma* through knowledge, *yoga*, asceticism, or simply through using it up. Likewise, the soul with

---

3 *Kiraṇa Tantra* commentary: Dominic Goodall, *Bhaṭṭa Rāmakaṇṭha's Commentary on the Kiraṇatantra* Vol. 1, Chapters 1–6 (Pondichéry: Institut Français, 1998), 184.

impurity derived from *māyā* remains in the body simply due to the residual traces of previous acts being used up 'as with the spinning of a wheel', which continues to spin even after that which set it in motion has stopped.[4] *Karma* too is a necessary force because of which souls undergo many experiences which are private or particular to each.

So, the soul is bound to reincarnation because of the force of impurity that is a cosmological category. Although not formally an ontic category or *tattva,* it nevertheless is a power that constrains each soul into what it is. Thus, ordinary souls, like human beings, undergo experience in gross bodies which accumulate further actions that control future reincarnations. Those souls with subtle bodies likewise undergo experience in subtle worlds that are generally invisible to this world. Indeed, there are countless other worlds into which souls can be reborn and in which they reap the fruits of their actions, and the texts give lists of these regions. This classification of types of soul is integrated into the cosmological hierarchy in a way that is characteristic of Śaiva Siddhānta theology.

In his commentary on Garuḍa's question about how the soul is bound, Rāmakaṇṭha describes doctrines of other schools in order to ascertain the degree to which they are favoured by the Lord, which thereby establishes his own doctrine. For the Buddhists, he tells us, the soul is nothing but a stream of cognitions which constantly perish; for those of the Vedānta versed in the Upaniṣads it is an effect of the cause which is God (Brahma). For the Nyāya school the soul is eternal consisting of nine qualities (cognition, happiness, unhappiness, desire, hatred, effort, virtue, non-virtue, latent traces), for the Materialists (Cārvāka) it is nothing but the

---

4 *Kiraṇa Tantra,* 185.

four elements, and for the Vaiśeṣika it is different from those elements. For the Sāṃkhya, the soul is inactive and without any qualities, whereas for the Mīmāṃsā it is active and an agent. For the Digamabara Jains the soul is not all pervasive and comes into being, whereas for others such as the Nyāya it is all-pervasive.[5]

So how are we to decide on all these diverse views, some of which are based on unfounded, bad arguments? Rāmakaṇṭha then cites the scripture to decide on these matters and to establish the settled doctrine (*siddhānta*). Śiva declares that the soul is eternal, it has no form, is without knowledge, is devoid of activity and qualities, and is impotent and all-pervasive.[6] Rāmakaṇṭha therefore reflects on how the Lord favours arguments of the Nyāya against the Buddhists. He is also against the Materialists in maintaining that the soul is without form and so is not a tactile object composed of the four elements. The Lord rejects the Nyāya school that the soul has qualities in favour of the view that it is without qualities, a view held by the Sāṃkhya, and that the soul is pervasive. Although specific arguments for the eternity of the soul are not presented here, Rāmakaṇṭha tells us that the soul is known through experience (*anubhava*) because it is an agent of perception and so is not established by argument. An experience such as 'this pot is round and made of iron' does not need an argument to establish it, likewise with the soul.[7] The soul is the subject of experience, the 'grasper' or agent of perception and the flow of changing external objects and is also all-pervading and eternal because it is not circumscribed by time or place.[8]

5 Ibid., 190–191.

6 Ibid. 1.15.

7 Ibid. 1.15.

8 Ibid., p. 198.

Rāmakaṇṭha then goes on to show how the soul is entangled in the world of experience. The world or universe (comprising all the ontic categories) is itself unconscious and only comes to consciousness by being united to a soul; this is done by Śiva who is the supreme agent. The soul is entangled with a cosmic power called *kalā*, which restricts it, and next it is limited by the sphere of the operation of the senses. Furthermore, the soul's engagement with the sphere of the senses and their objects entails other things coming into play, namely the instrument for consciousness that comprises the intellect (*buddhi*), including memories, creative imagination, and concepts, as well as the sense of self or ego (*ahaṃkāra*).[9] Finally, the soul is bound by passion (*rāga*) or attachment to the spheres of the senses.

The process of the soul's bondage is therefore quite complex. The pure, disembodied soul is all-pervading and yet numerically distinct from others and becomes constricted within the universe due to the power of cosmic restriction (*kalā*), along with restriction caused by the limited sense-spheres with which it interacts, which in turn are driven by interest or passion (*rāga*). On top of this we have *karma* built up over beginningless lives which also constrains a person into what or who they are, as well as time (*kāla*) itself which is a cause of experience.[10] *Karma* alone is insufficient to account for the embodied soul; we also need cosmological constraints that form a person into the particular outcome that they are.[11]

---

9 Ibid., p. 205.

10 Ibid.1.18, p. 210.

11 For those interested, the technical detail is that the *tattvas* that emanate from *māyā-tattva* are called the coverings (*kañcuka*). These are five: agential limitation (*kalā*), limited knowledge (*vidyā*), passion (*rāga*), time (*kāla*), fate (*niyati*). Goodall, *Kiraṇa Tantra*, 'Introduction', lii.

Through initiation the soul can become free of these bonds and, once freed, it becomes omniscient and omnipotent like Śiva. This can occur immediately or gradually, but either way, what counts is Śiva's grace and not *yoga* or knowledge:[12] grace along with the maturation of impurity. Thus, the class of souls called Vijñānakevala and Pralayakevala are liberated through the descent of Śiva's power but simply have to wait for the maturation of their impurity before final release.

While the constraints of beginningless impurity along with the other cosmological restrictions that produce the body are necessary conditions for the soul to undergo experience, they are not in themselves sufficient. For that we need *karma*, action. It is *karma* that determines the quality of experience, the soul's happiness and unhappiness. Commenting on a verse of the *Kiraṇa*, Rāmakaṇṭha writes:

> From impurity, termed 'bound-soul-ness' (*paśutva-*), results the soul's condition of being an experiencer; from primal matter his body, and his experience from *karma*, because it is past acts alone that are transformed into pleasure and unhappiness.[13]

This *karma* is without beginning, just like impurity, and is attached to the soul or covers the soul, preventing it from realising its innate omniscience and omnipresence. To become liberated means that all karmic residues have been erased. This occurs through initiation and the ritual regime that cleans the soul so that at death, when the final karmic residues are spent, the soul gains liberation. Death is the final destruction of the vestigial traces (*vāsanā*) that have been left

12 *Kiraṇa Tantra* commentary, pp. 220–221.

13 *Kiraṇa Tantra* 3.4c–5d commentary, p. 266.

behind after initiation. At death the soul understands itself as *a* Śiva, like Śiva in all respects except that it does not perform the five acts of creation, maintenance, destruction, revealing and concealing himself. The soul becomes equal to Śiva (*śiva-tulya*) but not identical.

God

So, the only essential difference between the Lord or God and soul, apart from the fact that they are numerically distinct, is that the bound soul has had beginningless contact with impurity, whereas God has not. Therefore, the soul's knowledge is limited whereas God is omniscient. To the question why this should be so, the *Kiraṇa Tantra* rhetorically asks, 'why is crystal clear? Why is copper tarnished? Just as there is no cause for this [pair of naturally given facts], so too there is none in the case of Śiva and the [bound] soul.'[14]

God is the creator of the universe in the sense that he acts upon pre-existing matter through his will. Rāmakaṇṭha attempts to refute views for the non-existence of God and offers proof (*pramāṇa*). The schools that disclaim the existence of God, says Rāmakaṇṭha, are the Sāṃkhya, the Buddhists, the Mīmāṃsā, the Jains, and the Materialists or Cārvāka. The first two schools, according to Rāmakaṇṭha, maintain that the world is an effect because it undergoes transformation (Sāṃkhya) or it just comes into being (Buddhists), while the remaining schools maintain that the universe has always been as it is, so is not an effect. Rāmakaṇṭha claims that we can prove that the universe is an effect because anything gross is an effect, as pots are. Although there is no direct experience of its creator, we must nevertheless infer a creator from the

14 *Kiraṇa Tantra* 2.4.

universe which is an effect. Furthermore, such a creator – as the creator of a pot – must have powers of knowledge and action.

In this way Rāmakaṇṭha refutes the schools that reject God through maintaining that the universe is not an effect, by arguing the opposite, that the universe is indeed an effect. But what about the Sāṃkhyas and the Buddhists who also accept that the universe is an effect but still deny a creator? Rāmakaṇṭha cites a Buddhist text (the *Pramāṇa-vārttika*) that says that we cannot necessarily establish an agent as a cause of an effect, as it is not logically coherent to infer fire from the presence of a pale substance called smoke.[15] But, says Rāmakaṇṭha, we can establish that every effect is invariably concomitant with an agent, as in the case of pots where the effect (the pot) is invariably concomitant with the pot maker. But do we need to infer that the cause of the effect of the universe is God? Why not say that the cause is *karma*, asks the Mīmāṃsaka? Rāmakaṇṭha refutes this by claiming that in the Siddhānta view, *karma* is insentient, and so cannot be the cause of the universe because something insentient cannot be an agent.[16] The agent who is the cause of the effect of the universe is God, who is not embodied but acts through will.

Initiation and Grace

The soul is liberated from the bonds of *karma* through initiation followed by a regime of ritual, because it is action that cleans the soul of impurity and ultimately the grace of God that frees it. Although initiation frees the soul, the initiated must continue to perform ritual because, says Rāmakaṇṭha,

---

15 Ibid. 3.12a–c commentary, p. 275. See also A. Watson, *The Self's Awareness of Itself: Bhaṭṭarāmakaṇṭha's Arguments against the Buddhist Doctrine of No-self* (Vienna: de Nobili, 2006).

16 *Kiraṇa Tantra* 3.12d, p. 278.

it is enjoined by scripture.[17] Grace descends upon the soul at initiation although if the person is alive, this is a weak descent of power that leaves sufficient karmic residues remaining to maintain the body until death. Initiation by which grace is manifested is understood as the descent of power. This descent of power (*śakti-pāta*), that all Śaiva traditions have, follows from such an act of grace. But, the *Kiraṇa Tantra* asks, how can there be a descent of power or God's grace if that power is all-pervading? If Śiva's power (*śakti*) is all-pervading, then it pervades the soul and so cannot 'descend' as it is already there.[18] The commentator Rāmakaṇṭha acknowledges the problem and states a further problem: if power has been beginninglessly there in all souls, then all souls should have been beginninglessly liberated through initiation, and so there would in fact be no transmigration.[19] Reflecting on this, Rāmakaṇṭha says that the descent of power is meant figuratively. As the soul, which is all-pervading, is said to move, so the idea of the descent of power can only be metaphorical. 'Passages of scripture', writes Rāmakaṇṭha, 'that refer to the "falling" of power express their meaning figuratively ... just as the inactivity of the bonds upon a soul who has been initiated ... [which] is spoken of as a "cutting" ... is not really a splitting in two.'[20]

While scripture is metaphorical in this regard, it is nevertheless not idealistic in the sense of denying the reality of soul and world. Even though God's power has always been in souls, it brings about liberation from worldly existence only at the time of the ripening of impurity in the soul.[21] Thus, the

17 Ibid. 3.12a–c commentary, p. 275.

18 Ibid. 5.1.

19 Ibid. 5.2ab commentary, p. 327.

20 Ibid. 5.2ab commentary, p. 328–329.

21 Ibid. 1.10 commentary, p. 176.

real impurity that covers the soul develops to a point where it can be cleansed through the 'descent' of power, even though that power is already innate within the soul.

Another way of describing this in the *Kiraṇa* and Rāmakaṇṭha's commentary is that the descent of power is also the equal balance of two simultaneously maturing actions.[22] That is, the vehemence of two equally strong actions from the past whose fruits mature at exactly the same time, creates a state of immovability in the soul; the soul is, as it were, frozen between two actions and so the results of neither can come to fruition, just as, says Rāmakaṇṭha, a lovesick woman does not experience either lover if equally attracted by two. These two blocking actions are rendered inoperative – they block each other – and so the descent of grace can occur at such a time, which is really the operation of the power that is already there within the soul and that comes out because the two actions are blocked. The descent of power is a way of talking about the maturing of actions and their release thereby, which is the illumination of the soul. Enlightenment or liberation is the ripening of impurity in which the soul's omniscience and omnipotence are revealed.[23]

Liberation

Liberation for the doctors of the Śaiva Siddhānta is therefore becoming free from the bonds of *karma* and impurity and understanding oneself to be omniscient and omnipotent, just like Śiva himself. The Saiddhāntikas regarded their view as truth and offered refutations of other schools. Sadyojotis wrote a refutation of twenty concepts of liberation, the

22 Ibid. 5.8.

23 Ibid. 5.9–10.

Para-mokṣa-nirāsa-kārikā, and Bhaṭṭa Rāmakaṇṭha wrote a commentary (*vṛtti*) on it. This is an interesting text in that it displays all the various view that were around at the time, including the Buddhists and different forms of Śaivism. Of the twenty views about liberation, there are three that teach liberation means that the soul becomes the same as God (*īśvara-samāna*). Sadyojotis says that all the other views are the product of deluded imagination[24] and Rāmakaṇṭha even describes those who hold that view as 'co-religionists' (*samāna-tāntrikas*).[25] These co-religionists seem to have been the Pāśupatas, Kālamukhas, and Kāpālika ascetics of the Ati Mārga (see Chapter 2): ascetics on the path distinct from the Mantra Mārga that the Śaiva Siddhānta belonged to (see Chapter 2 for this distinction). These three Ati Mārga sects taught that liberation is the arising of omniscience and omnipotence (the Kālamukhas), the transfer of omniscience and omnipotence from God (the Pāśupatas), and possession (*āveśa*) by omnipotence and omniscience (the Kāpālikas).[26] But the doctrine of the Siddhānta is superior, the theologians claim, because the scriptures teach equality with Śiva through its manifestation 'beyond the scriptures of the bound'.[27]

In the text, Rāmakaṇṭha and his predecessor Sadyojotis refute the other views of liberation going through each position systematically. While the three views of co-religionists are

24 Alex Watson, Dominic Goodall, and S. L. P. Anjaneya Sarma, *An Enquiry into the Nature of Liberation: Bhaṭṭa Rāmakaṇṭha's Paramokṣanirāsakārikāvṛtti: A Commentary on Sadyojyotiḥ's Refutation of Twenty Conceptions of the Liberated State (Mokṣa)*. Collection Indologie 122 (Pondichéry: IFP / EFEO, 2013), 2.17 p. 275.

25 Watson *et al.*, *An Inquiry into the Nature of Liberation*, 63.

26 See ibid., diagram, p. 16.

27 Ibid., 2.18.3, p. 281.

Figure 5.3. A fifth-century sandstone statue of the Buddha in Sarnath Museum.

close to their own, the other conceptions of liberation are far from their doctrine. The view of the Buddhists, for example, is that liberation is the cessation of everything. Rāmakaṇṭha develops an argument in the following way.

1. Firstly, the Saiddhāntika claims that an old man remembers things from childhood and so the soul is stable between birth and old age and so the self is permanent. If, as the Buddhists claim, the perceiver were different at each moment, then the old man would not remember his childhood. Because there is memory at a later time of things experienced at an earlier time, there must be a permanent self.

2. But the Buddhist might try to refute this by saying that there is a difference between memory and perception and experience is not the same as memory. The old man's memory now, whose content is of his earlier experience, is simply brought about by a trace left behind in the mind. So, there cannot be a permanent self, because such a self could not have modifications brought about by memory traces. A memory is due to the same mind-stream flowing from the past to the present. It is this that accounts for the old man's memory of his childhood, not a permanent self. There is no self separate from the stream of mental events.

3. Rāmakaṇṭha agrees that memory is not the same as experience but maintains that every person experiences themselves as undivided and that the stable self shines forth and is ever-present. The self does not sense a division in his own nature even though the objects of experience change.

4. The Buddhist response to this is that stability is superimposed. In reality there is just a stream of momentary perceptions which appear stable or unitary because of projection. Rāmakaṇṭha responds that this is an error because we experience the self's unity as distinct from the flow of objects and this unity

itself does not become an object of perception. If everything is momentary and there is no self, nothing could link up perceptions, but we do link up the flow of perceptions because we have or are a self.

So, the self for Rāmakaṇṭha is as follows:

> Thus in this [argument] it is the condition of being a rememberer – in the self, which is self-luminous, a witness to the arising and falling away of the activities of the mind, indeed stable, and a perceiver – which, having as its fruit the raising up again of awareness of the self as described above, because it (i.e. this condition) is self-cognized, is made the logical reason, since it sidesteps the group of arguments advanced by others that [attempt to] prove its non-existence.[28]

Both God and the self are established through reason necessitated by the truth of liberation and showing the contradictory nature of other positions.

The Pratyabhijñā

Although they were co-religionists in the sense of revering a body of Tantras as revelation and following a set of prescribed ritual acts, the Śaivas who were philosophical non-dualists were distinctive. As we have seen, they followed a set of observances that were transgressive of ritual and social norms (see Chapter 3). Philosophically the Recognition school, as it came to be known, became the intellectual articulation of the traditions rooted in the Bhairava and Kālī Tantras. The philosophical school traces its origin to Somānanda (*c.* 900–950 CE), Utpaladeva (*c.* 925–975 CE), Abhinavagupta (*c.* 975–

---

28 Ibid., 370.

1025 CE), and Kṣemarāja (*c.* 1000–1050 CE). It was idealist in claiming that the external world exists only as consciousness. The self has to recognise itself as pure consciousness, which is a liberating cognition. This recognition is the realisation of the ontological identity of consciousness with its object: there is nothing which is impure. The school also speaks in terms of emanation. The universe is an emanation of the pure consciousness that is Śiva, a vibration (*spanda*) of that consciousness: the world and our experience are appearances (*ābhāsa*) of that pure consciousness.

There are a number of philosophical influences on the philosophy of the Pratyabhijñā. Somānanda is influenced by the Buddhist consciousness-only school, the Vijñānavāda, and particularly by the Buddhist philosopher Dharmakīrti, but he creates a distinctive school that Nemec characterises as pantheism. He also engages and criticises the non-dualistic theology of the Śaiva Siddhānta (see above) and the philosophy of Grammar by the Grammarian Bhartṛhari – the view that the world is an emanation of three levels of sound.[29]

While Somānanda advocates a kind of non-dualism, that the pure consciousness of Śiva constitutes the world, the doctrine is made into a rigorous philosophy by Utpaladeva and Abhinavagupta, whose last work comments on Utpaladeva's verses. The essence of this philosophy is that consciousness and its objects – what I am thinking and aware of – is all within a supreme consciousness of God. Indeed, there is no difference between the consciousness of God and my own consciousness and the flow of experience that I am aware of. In a complex argument in the last of his works, Abhinavagupta reasons in his commentary on Utpaladeva's verses that objects of conscious-

29 John Nemec, *The Ubiquitous Śiva: Somānanda's Śivadṛṣṭi and his Tantric Interlocutors* (Oxford: Oxford University Press, 2011), 76–77.

ness, although they appear to be distinct, cannot have their own self-illuminating nature, because if they did, there would be no relation between the subject and the object. That is, if the objects of consciousness were self-illuminating or manifesting themselves, then they could not connect with a conscious subject because they would be self-contained. The objects of consciousness must be within consciousness. The self-luminosity of consciousness (rather than its objects) remains constant, while the objects of consciousness are differentiated and different from each other. The objects of consciousness appear to be different from consciousness, but in fact they are not. The object of consciousness is 'mere appearance' and in the relationship between 'I', the subject of consciousness, and 'this', the object of consciousness, the 'this' only seems to be distinct. The object of consciousness, the 'this', appears to become external or facing out (*bahir-mukha*), but in reality, this is only the way in which consciousness appears to itself.[30] The apple that I imagine is constituted only within consciousness.[31] In technical philosophy this is to deny that there is any difference between a primary quality (such as H_2O of water) and a secondary quality (such as the colour of water).

This process of objectification or externalisation, the process of consciousness becoming apparently external to itself, takes place through the powers of memory, knowledge, and differentiation. Like Rāmakaṇṭha, Abhinavagupta maintains against the Buddhists that if the subject of experience were

30 Abhinavagupta, *Īśvara-pratyabhijñā-vimarśinī* 1.3.7, p. 141. *Īśvarapratyabhijñāvimarśinī* by Abhinavagupta. ed and trans. R. C. Dwiwedi, K. C. Pandey, and K. A. Subramania Iyer as *Bhāskarī*, Vol. 1 (Delhi: MLBD, 1986 [1938]).

31 Isabelle Ratié, *Le Soi et l'Autre: Identité, difference et altérité dans la philosophie de la Pratyabhijñā* (Leiden: Brill, 2011), 176.

changing at every moment, then memory would not be possible.[32] Because there is memory, so there must be a continuous, conscious subject. The Buddhist might claim that this memory is simply the residual trace of past experience; that the direct object of a previous experience has become the object of memory and so there is no need to posit a permanent self. But, says Abhinavagupta, memory is a quality (*guṇa*) and a quality cannot stand alone but must rest in something, must rest in a substratum (*āśraya*). This substratum is the permanent self (*ātman*), a self that is self-luminous.[33]

So far so good. The Śaiva Siddhānta theologian Rāmakaṇṭha would not fault this reasoning. But this is where Abhinavagupta differs from his older dualist contemporary. This self-luminous consciousness that pours out its 'objects' into an apparent externality through its spontaneous power of freedom is not mine alone. The self is not unique or distinct but is shared by all and is our common property. Indeed, the self that seems to be distinct from its objects, although in truth it is not, is only one self, which is pure consciousness (*saṃvit, cit, citi*), understood in theistic language to be God (Śiva).

So, if all is one, all is a single consciousness, why does our perception seem to be differentiated and how do we experience a variety of things in the world: other people, mats, and pots? Abhinavagupta answers that we experience differentiation because of the power of exclusion (*apohana-śakti*). This power separates perceptions and is a differentiation (*pariccheda*, literally a 'cutting') of one experience from another. This is the power that controls each appearance into its particularity, into what it is.

32 Abhinavagupta, *Īśvara-pratyabhijñā-vimarśinī* 1.3.7, p. 141.

33 Ibid. 1.2.5, p. 99.

At the level of ignorant or unenlightened awareness, there seems to be a flow of objects of experience or cognitions distinct from the self, but in reality this is not the case. We know from experience and from scriptural revelation of the non-dual Tantras, thinks Abhinavagupta, that there is only one consciousness with which person and world are identical. This is different to the non-dualism of Advaita Vedānta because in this philosophy, consciousness is a vibrant power emanating and destroying its emanations. It is not that the world is unreal: it is real but just made of consciousness. Consciousness is the substance of all appearance. This is a kind of radical panpsychism, that the mind is all. The self-luminosity of consciousness remains and never changes, although the objects – which are non-different from consciousness – appear to change. While the world appears to be external, this externality (*bahir-mukha*) is really an interiority (*antar-mukha*). The world is merely an appearance (*avabhāsa-mātra*) but is not unreal; rather the world is consciousness but no less real for that.

The apparent flow of appearances is the succession of time. The power of time (*kāla-śakti*) is the power of the Lord who manifests the variety of experiences, although from the perspective of the true nature of consciousness, there is no sequence, no time, because all is simultaneous from the perspective of pure consciousness. The same is true of space, space is simply a cognition of relation (*saṃbandha*) organised by the powers of knowledge, memory, and exclusion, but in reality, space, and time are simply pure consciousness falsely perceived.

The ultimate reality of pure consciousness, which is God, is I-consciousness (*ahantā*). This is pure in contrast to the limited 'I' which is in the grip of material power (*māyā*). But again, this is a limited way of speaking about that which has no boundaries in its spontaneous freedom. The objects of this I-consciousness, the flow of experience, seems to detract from the purity of the 'I', but this is mistaken because the absolute 'I-ness' is the only reality and all is identical with it, even though they appear to be differentiated. From the highest perspective Abhinavagupta sees all as identical with consciousness, there is no impurity or distinction. From a lower perspective there is the manifestation or appearance of consciousness through and as the levels of the hierarchical universe. Pure I-ness is the essence of pure consciousness which is God. Speaking in the voice of God in the *Paramārtha-sāra*, Abhinavagupta says that it is in 'me' that the universe appears, and that pure subjectivity takes the forms of the world:

> It is I who have taken on the form of all things, thus resembling the body, whose nature is to have hands, feet and the like. It is I who appear in each and every thing, just as the nature of light appears in all existent things./ Though devoid of corporeal sense-organs, it is I who am the one who sees, the one who hears, the one who smells. Though not an agent, it is I who compose the wonderfully varied Siddhāntas, Āgamas and Tarkas.[34]

This 'I' is God (*deva*), says Abhinavagupta, in all beings, an awareness that is one's own self. This is the pure reflexivity of consciousness in which all apparent externality is grounded. It is the I that has taken on the form of all thing and exists 'even in cowherds, children, women, etc.'.[35] Although bereft of sense organs and body, nevertheless this I is the one who sees and experiences.[36]

---

34 *Paramārtha-sāra* verses 49–50. Lyne Bansat-Boudon and Kamalesha Datta, *An Introduction to Tantric Philosophy: The Paramārthasāra of Abhinavagupta with the Commentary of Yogarāja* (London: Routledge, 2011), 211.

35 Abhinavagupta, *Īśvara-pratyabhijñā-vimarśinī*, p. 213.

36 Ibid., p. 214.

Although the highest truth is this I-ness, pure reflexive awareness, in another way of speaking the I becomes manifest in the hierarchical cosmos. Different kinds of philosophy reach up to particular levels of this hierarchy, although at the top is the truth of non-dual consciousness, according to the Pratyabhijñā.

While Abhinavagupta's later work focuses on detailed exposition and argument against rival schools, mostly the Buddhists, his student Kṣemarāja wrote more popular works to propagate the philosophy of non-dualism. He says that he wrote the *Essence of Recognition* (*Pratyabhijñā-hṛdaya*) for those devotees with weak intellects and worn out by the arguments of sharp logic. Kṣemarāja promotes the non-duality of self, world, and God, although the essence of pure consciousness is the Goddess. Also, his text presents more of an emanationist philosophy than a pure non-dualism in the sense that his opening verse claims that the universe is a manifestation or emanation of pure consciousness. In the opening aphorism he says:

> Sūtra 1: Consciousness, due to its own freedom, is the reason for the actualisation of the universe (*citiḥ svatantrā viśva-siddhi-hetuḥ*).

The universe is the realisation or actualisation of pure consciousness: the spontaneous expression of consciousness due to its own freedom. Kṣemarāja uses the term *citi* for consciousness. He offers an interesting auto-commentary on his own aphorisms. His comment on the opening *sūtra* lays out the Pratyabhijñā teachings about the universe and its structure. He writes:

> 'Of the universe' means from the level beginning with Sadāśiva to the earth [i.e. the entire cosmic hierarchy comprising the *tattvas*]. 'Actualisation' (*siddhi*) means the production, illumination, maintenance, and destruction [of

> the universe], which comes to rest in the highest experient. 'Consciousness' (*citi*) means the Goddess (*bhagavatī*) whose form is absolute power (*parā-śakti-rūpā*). 'Freedom' (*svatantrā*) refers to the one comprising highest awareness who is non-distinct from Lord Śiva, and 'reason for' (*hetuḥ*) means cause (*kāraṇam*). Thus, the universe opens out (*unmiṣati*) in its diversity, continues, and closes down (*nimiṣati*) with its destruction. One's own experience (*svānubhavaḥ*) is a witness (*sākṣī*) in this matter. Other [levels of the universe], such as material substrate, matter, and so on (*māyā-prakṛty-ādeḥ*), [appear] distinct from the light of absolute consciousness (*cit-prakāśa-*). Due to their lack of energy through not possessing their own illumination, they are not a cause, and so are not anything (*na eva kiṃcit*). Hence space, time, and form, created by that [consciousness], are animated by it and so they are not sufficient [in themselves] to penetrate its true nature. That nature is complete, eternally arisen, and all-pervading (*vyāpaka-nityoditaparipūrṇa-rūpā*). This alone is the meaning to be grasped.[37]

The entire philosophy of the Pratyabhijñā is contained in this concentrated passage. The word 'universe' refers to the entire hierarchy of ontic levels, which in the Śaiva Siddhānta are from Sadāśiva through to the impure universe and the earth where we dwell. Kṣemarāja has inherited this view of the cosmos from the Śaiva Siddhānta and accepts it, although with the additional view that this universe is an emanation of consciousness itself. The universe emanates out and is contracted back into consciousness and this is also the highest experient, namely the supreme reality which is conceptualised by Kṣemarāja as the Goddess (*bhagavatī*). The Goddess is pure

37 *Pratyabhijñā-hṛdaya* 2 commentary (my translation).

consciousness (*citi*). She is non-distinct from Śiva, from whom the universe emerges, opening out in its diversity and closing down with its destruction. The Goddess opens her eyes (*unmiṣati*) and closes them (*nimiṣati*), creating and destroying the universe which is, in fact, nothing other than herself as pure consciousness. We, as apparently distinct persons, can witness this in our own experience, which reveals to us that we are in fact the pure consciousness of the Goddess. We are the Goddess and we need to recognise that reality, which recognition is a saving grace. Pure consciousness animates the universe which is identical with its light.

This philosophy of non-dualism, in which pure consciousness is the Goddess, is the esoteric heart of the Pratyabhijñā. The second verse develops this theme; it reads:

> Sūtra 2: [Consciousness] manifests the universe on her own screen by her own will (*svecchayā svabhittau viśvam unmīlayati*)

The auto-commentary reads:

> 'By her own will' means just that; not by the will of another as is maintained in [the doctrine of] the absolute and others, and not with regard to a material cause and so on. With the loss of freedom [in the doctrine] previously spoken about, [the doctrine of] only consciousness would not be possible. 'On her own screen' means not elsewhere.

Here Kṣemarāja develops the idea of pure consciousness manifesting the universe from within itself. Here the Goddess projects the universe on her own screen; like a painting, it appears to be distinct but, in reality, is not and, like the reflection of a city in a mirror, the universe is a reflection of pure consciousness. All apparent diversity is in truth but a single light.

This is the fundamental idea that Kṣemarāja develops in his text although he introduces more sect-specific terminology from the Goddess-centred Krama cult, that refers to the Goddess as manifesting and tasting the universe. Somewhat like Sadyojyotis, he also describes other philosophies as being partial truths, approximating or rising to particular levels of the cosmic hierarchy and so only approximating to the truth. In aphorism 8 he says:

> Sūtra 8: All the systems of philosophy are states which are [different] levels/roles[38] of that [supreme self] (*tad-bhūmikāḥ sarva-darśana-sthitayaḥ*).

The Materialists or Cārvākas are the lowest, as for Rāmakaṇṭha: they hold that the self is the body. The Logicians or followers of Nyāya identify the self with the intellect (*buddhi*) and, once liberated, the self becomes identified with emptiness. Similarly, the Mīmāṃsā maintain that the self is only the intellect; and the Buddhists also only reach the level of *buddhi* (the temptation not to put them here would be too great). The Vedānta is above this level, believing that the self is the life force (*prāṇa*), while the Buddhists of the Madhyamaka school reach a level where the self is identified with emptiness. The Pāñcarātra tradition that worships Viṣṇu reaches the level of the material substrate of the universe (*prakṛti*), while the Sāṃkhya goes higher to the level of the consciousness-only souls (Vijñānakala). The Upaniṣads reach the first level of the pure creation where Īśvara dwells and the Grammarians go up the Sadāśiva. Beyond that are Tantric practitioners who claim that at the level of Śiva, the truth of the self is transcendent

38 Here Kṣemarāja presents a play on words. *Bhūmikā* refers to a world or region of the cosmos as well as a role or character in a play. Śiva manifests the different worlds as an actor plays different parts.

(*viśvottīrṇa*), while those of the Kula sect claim that it is immanent (*viśvātma*). The Pratyabhijñā is the truth beyond both.

Ranking the philosophies in this way allow him to show how non-dualism incorporates all systems of philosophy, showing precisely how they come up to a particular level but no further and how the teachings of non-dualism are the most opportune in incorporating all other teachings and layers of the universe. In truth it is the self who assumes all these different roles like an actor.

Social Philosophy

The issues that these philosophers were concerned with are metaphysical: what is the self? Does the external world exist? What is consciousness? What is the structure of the universe? How do beings attain liberation from suffering? There is little discussion of social and political realities, nor does a philosophy of history develop. There is a discourse of ethics, but less overtly in philosophy and more in narrative traditions such as the epics.[39] The question of the degree to which these new Tantric religions and their accompanying philosophies were supportive of the social structure, notably the caste system and hierarchical polities, is nuanced. On the one hand, the doctors of the Śaiva Siddhānta were socially conservative and wished to support the social structure and obligations enjoined by Vedic scriptures, the duty regarding stage of life and social group (*varṇāśrama-dharma*), while, on the other hand, the Śākta religions belonging to the non-Saiddhāntika traditions of the Mantra Mārga and the Kula Mārga rejected the importance of social conformity. Some of these extreme traditions were

39 See B. K. Matilal, ed., *Moral Dilemmas in the Mahābhārata* (Delhi: MLBD, 1989).

overtly antinomian, advocating, as Sanderson says, 'collective orgiastic worship, initiation through possession, the ritual consumption of meat and alcoholic liquor, and sexual contact with women regardless of caste'.[40] But generally Śaivism – especially the Śaiva Siddhānta – did not wish to disrupt the Brahmanical social order; indeed, its adherents desired to see the religion in the royal courts and Śaivism became central to the political order of kingly polities in medieval India.[41] The philosophers who commented upon texts generally wished to emphasise the importance of social conformity and the rejection of any low-caste entry into the religion.

Nevertheless, the non-dualist traditions did tend to undermine social norms and expectations. Non-dualism has moral implications. Indeed, if all is one, and the only reality is pure I-consciousness, then how do we account for evil? Abhinavagupta acknowledges the issue and implies that from the perspective of ultimate reality, if all is one, there is no morality. So, he can say in the *Paramārtha-sāra*:

> Whether he performs a hundred thousand horse sacrifices, or kills a hundred thousand brahmins, he who knows ultimate reality is not affected by merits or demerits. He is stainless.[42]

If all is one, then ethics can have no significant place because ethics implies difference. If there is a unity of God and world and all distinctions are unreal, then it is difficult to

---

40 Alexis Sanderson, 'How Public was Śaivism?' Keynote Lecture at the Symposium in Nina Mirnig, Marion Rastelli, and Vincent Eltschinger (eds.), *Tantric Communities in Context* (Vienna: Osterreichische Akademie der Wissenshcaften, 2019), pp. 1-48.

41 Ibid., 5–6.

42 Abhinavagupta, *Paramārtha-sāra*, Kārikā 70. Boudon and Tripathi, *Introduction to Tantric Philosophy*, 247.

claim that some actions are bad and others good, or even, more simply, that some actions are better than others. If there is one homogenous reality, it is hard to differentiate the quality or worth of one action over another because everything happens within pure consciousness. Kṣemarāja himself also says that if there is only one reality in truth, then there is no ontic category that is impure. In his commentary on the *Spanda Kārikās* he says that as the experiencer constitutes the universe as God, there is no state which is not God, for everything is God.[43] There is no state that is not God, whether waking, dreaming, or sleeping.[44] In disclaiming any ultimate substance to conventional morality, passages such as these underline the potentially subversive nature of such texts; in a way, the Śaiva dualists who support the Veda are right to be alarmed at the moral and social implications of such a doctrine. As we saw in Chapter 3, thinkers such as Jayanta Bhaṭṭa are aware of the social implications of groups who follow the new non-dualist philosophy. The ethical implications are also social implications and the philosophy of the unity of consciousness potentially undermines rigid social boundaries because it implies an equality to different social groups, whether high or low.

Some Tantras do say that the religion is for everyone, regardless of gender or caste, but the philosophers who comment on the texts tend to wish to distance themselves from such claims. Bhaṭṭa Rāmakaṇṭha, for example, comments on a passage from a Śaiva Siddhānta Tantra that says that even untouchables can be initiated, saying that it does not really mean this literally. The line reads that the teacher 'may even

---

43 Kṣemarāja, Commentary on the *Spanda Kārikās* 2.3–4. Jaideva Singh, *Spanda Kārikās: The Divine Creative Pulsation*, trans. Jaideva Singh (Delhi: Motilal Banarsidass Publishers, 1980), p. 117.

44 Ibid. 3.12, p. 151.

initiate untouchables' (*śvapacān api dīkṣayet*).[45] Rāmakaṇṭha says that this simply indicates the power of initiation but not that untouchables should be initiated. But in contrast to this, if one maintains a non-dualism that all is identical with God, then these social distinctions are of no consequence. The knower of Śiva who is thereby liberated has no concern where the body dies and so by implication worldly matters of status and purity are of no consequence. Abhinavagupta in the *Paramārtha-sāra* says:

> Whether he gives up his body in a place of pilgrimage or in the hut of an outcaste, be he conscious or not, he goes [thence] to a condition of transcendent isolation, his grieving at an end, for he was liberated at the very moment he acquired knowledge.[46]

This is not a socially revolutionary statement but simply affirms that in the light of liberation, all distinctions are of no consequence; even the house of an untouchable is by implication not polluting from the supreme perspective and is equal to a holy pilgrimage site.

So, although the Śākta tradition can be understood as the incursion of lower social groups into a higher register of discourse, the philosophers of Śaivism were generally not concerned with social issues – but then, in this period, few were across world civilisations.

---

45 *Kālottarāgama* 7, p. 73. Muktabodha Indological Library, Catalog number: M00248, Manuscript: IFP/EFEO transcript T0059. Copied from IFP/EFEO transcript T0059, which is from a MS belonging to the GOML, Madras, No. R 14343. This line is also quoted by Kṣemarāja in his commentary on the *Netra Tantra* 10.11.

46 Abhinavagupta, *Paramārtha-sāra* 83, p. 272.

Concluding Remarks

The Tantric philosophers were engaged in mainstream philosophical debate. They were part of the broader philosophical discourse in medieval India, engaging in a scholastic philosophy articulated mostly through commentaries on sacred scripture. The dualist theologians of the Śaiva Siddhānta commented on the dualist texts, while the non-dualists commented on the non-dualist Tantras. In some cases, both claimed Tantras for their own, as in the case of the *Mālinī-vijayottara Tantra* that Abhinavagupta writes a part commentary on. Indeed, commentators generally wished to comment on texts that did not clearly articulate the position they advocated.

We know little about practical matters and the institutional basis of philosophy. There must have been a support system of patronage for philosophers and their students, along with an infrastructure for the copying of texts – ink, pen, and palm leaf or birch bark preparation – the equivalent of manuscript libraries containing texts copied by scribes. Texts were disseminated and in time spread through the subcontinent. The *Netra Tantra*, for example, was copied for a King of Nepal in 1200 CE, although it may have been composed in Kashmir between the eighth and ninth centuries.[47] Philosophical debate tended to continue without reference to or regard of social issues at the time, being concerned with matters of ontology and epistemology that the traditions regarded as transcending worldly concerns.

---

47 See Gavin Flood, Bjarne Wernicke-Olesen, and Rajan Khatiwoda, *Tantra in Medieval India and Nepal: An Annotated Edition and Translation of the Tantra of the Eye, the Netra Tantra*, Volume 1 (London: Routledge, forthcoming); Bettina Bäumer, *The Yoga of the Netra Tantra: 'Third Eye' and 'Overcoming Death'* (Shimla: Indian Institute of Advanced Study, 2019).

Discussion Topic: Philosophies of Tantra

- What are main issues of contention between the Śaivas and Buddhists?
- What do the Śaiva dualists and non-dualists understand by God?
- Is the Recognition School a pure non-dualism or an emanationism?
- Is the Śaiva Siddhānta more ethical than the Recognition School?

Further Reading

Lyne Bansat-Boudon and Kamalesha Datta Tripathi. *Introduction to Tantric Philosophy: The Paramārthasāra of Abhinavagupta with the Commentary of Yogaraja*. London: Routledge, 2011.

Alexis Sanderson. 'The Śaiva Exegesis of Kashmir'. In *Mélange Tantrique: à la mémoire d'Hélène Brunner*, edited by Dominic Goodall and André Padoux, 231–444. Pondichéry: Institut Français de Pondichéry, 2007.

Isabelle Ratié. *Le Soi et l'Autre: Identité, différence et altérité dans la philosophie de la Pratyabhijñā*. Leiden: Brill, 2011.

VI
The Spread of Tantra

The heyday of Tantric civilisation was between the ninth and thirteenth centuries. After that, the most important political power in north India shifted to the Delhi Sultanate and then to the Mughals and then to the British. Tantric traditions still continued but often became marginalised. In Nepal, kings continued to be aligned with Tantric deities, particularly the Goddess Taleju, and Tantric traditions in other regions continued but without state support. In this chapter we will examine the development of Tantra in other regions, particularly Nepal, and East and South-East Asia, and then look briefly at the exportation of Tantric traditions to the West.

Nepal

Tantric deities became the tutelary gods of the kings of Nepal. While Śiva retains a place of transcendence, tutelary goddesses represent connections to land and powerful ruling families. In Nepal, three gods especially are important for royalty, from whom the king derived his power: Viṣṇu, the sovereign deity, Paśupati, the master of ascetics and of Nepal generally, and the secret Tantric goddess Taleju. The king's consecration is modelled on Tantric initiation and Taleju is the one who conveys power to him, indeed, the king is consecrated with Tantric *mantras*.[1] The transgressive violence of aggressive Tantric goddesses becomes trapped and controlled by the institution of kingship. Indeed, the palace is akin to the temple and the divine body of the king in the palace recapitulates the divine body of the deity in the temple, a structure that held sway in modernity until the eradication of the monarchy in Nepal in 2008.

Through the medieval period from about 800 to 1200 the kings of Nepal in the Kathmandu valley were mostly devoted to Śiva. The Licchavi kings of Nepal also supported Buddhism, and both Buddhism and Śaivism lived side by side in the valley. For example, an inscription of 608 shows that a king gave a cash allowance from the court to a number of religious institutions ranked in order, with the Paśupati temple at the top followed by the principal Viṣṇu temple of Nepal, followed by three Buddhist monasteries plus two others, all of which were to receive the same allowance.[2] After the Licchavi kings came the Ṭhākurī kings (737–1200 CE), followed by the Malla kings (1200–1768). The Malla kings patronised Tantric deities and we know that the *Netra Tantra* was copied for Abhayamalla and/or his son in 1200. Śākta-Śaiva and Buddhist Tantric deities were worshipped and Taleju became the official deity of royalty, a form of the goddess Kubjikā and/or Guhyakālī. The famous Kumārī in Nepal, the young girl chosen to be the Goddess, is regarded as an incarnation of Taleju. In contemporary times, Tantrism remains an important part of religious life in Nepal. There are Tantric ascetics

---

1 Gérard Tofflin, *Le Palais et le Temple: La fonction royale dans la vallée du Nepal* (Paris: CNRS, 1993), 220–222.

2 Alexis Sanderson, 'The Śaiva Age', in *Genesis and Development of Tantrism*, ed. Shingo Einoo, 41–250 (Tokyo: University of Tokyo, 2009), 76.

Figure 6.1. Temple to the goddess Taleju in Durbar Square, Kathmandu, built in 1564.

representing a still extant Aghori sect who practice 'negative' rites which are the reversal of orthodox Brahmanical rites – performed at night, with offerings made by ascetics upside-down, and so on.[3]

3 These have been studied by Wernicke-Olesen and Prema Goet. See Prema Goet, *Against the Grain* (London: Utkranti Press, n.d.). See also the fine study by Jonathan Parry in *Death in Banares* (Cambridge: Cambridge University Press, 1993).

Figure 6.2. The Kumārī of Patan during a procession in 2011.

Bengal and Assam

The Nepalese child Goddess is a famous example of a Tantric Goddess, but there are other important locations of Goddess worship throughout India. Kanyakumari at the southern tip of the subcontinent has a shrine to the Virgin Goddess and there are other sites of pilgrimage to shrines of the Goddess, for example the Mīnākṣī temple at Madurai and the Kālī temple in Calcutta. Tantric literature refers to 'seats' (*pīṭha*) of the Goddess, distinct from other centres. The origin of these is traditionally located in mythology. In the Śaiva scriptures, in the Purāṇas and in the *Mahābhārata,* we have a myth of Dakṣa, which we encountered in Chapter 3. To briefly recap: Dakṣa is the son of Brahmā; his daughter Satī, who is both beautiful and powerful due to practising austerities, marries Śiva. At the wedding Śiva and his father-in-law do not get on well and Śiva with his wife retire to Mount Kailāsa. In the meantime, Dakṣa organises a horse sacrifice, but he does not invite his son in law, Śiva. Śiva is not concerned, but Satī is furious at the snub and goes to her father's sacrifice but is rejected. In her rage she kills herself through bursting into flames from her yogic power.

Śiva, on hearing this news, is enraged and attacks Dakṣa's sacrifice in the ferocious form of Vīrabhadra with hordes of demonic beings. Śiva destroys the sacrifice and kills Dakṣa who thereby becomes the sacrificial victim himself. In one version Śiva calms down, restores the sacrifice, and gives Dakṣa a goat's head. In another he is distraught with anger at the loss of Satī, so picks up her scorched body from the cremation ground and dances with it above his head. The other gods become concerned that Śiva will destroy the universe by this dance and so employ Viṣṇu to hack Satī's body with his discus, cutting it away until Śiva returns to a composed state of mind. Where different parts of her body fell, there is a pilgrimage site. These are the four great seats (*mahā-pīṭha*) at Jalandhāra (probably not Jullundur in the Punjab), Oḍḍiyāna or Uḍḍāyāna in the Swat valley, Pūrṇagiri (unknown), and Kāmarūpa or Kāmākhya in Assam. At these locations, the Goddess' tongue, nipples, and vulva fell. At Kāmākhya the Goddess is worshipped at her temple in the form of a vulva and her menstrual cycles celebrated. This was, and remains, the main Śākta pilgrimage site.

Figure 6.3. An iconic representation of Devī Kāmākhya in present-day Kolkata.

Bengal too is a place of Tantrism. Some Tantric groups in Bengal adopted the ritual use of the 'five Ms', transgressive substances used as offerings whose origin is in the extreme Kaula traditions (see Chapter 3). These are wine (*madya*), fish (*matsya*), meat (*māṃsa*), parched grain (*mudrā*), and sexual intercourse (*maithuna*), transgressive in contradistinction to Brahmanical worship. This became known as 'left-hand' Tantra in Bengal. In the later medieval period, a tradition arose with the religion of Viṣṇu called the Sahajiyās. These were groups who adopted the theology of orthodox Bengal (Gauḍīya) Vaiṣṇavism focused on Kṛṣṇa, especially in his form in the *Bhāgavata Purāṇa* in dalliance with the village cowgirls (*gopi*). These Sahajiyās were a later descendent of the Buddhist Sahajiyās; they simply adapted to the surrounding Vaiṣṇava tradition, adopting the theology. In this theology, a man and a woman reflect the divine forms of Rādhā, Kṛṣṇa's favourite girl, and Kṛṣṇa. This tradition practices left-hand Tantric ritual involving sexual congress regardless of caste. Although it has precursors, its particular form comes in the sixteenth century, long after the Tantric heyday of the Śaiva age. The sect takes its inspiration from poets such as Caṇḍīdāsa and Vidyāpati whose verses extolled the love of Kṛṣṇa and Rādhā.

Kerala

Kerala is a state where Tantric traditions still thrive and flourish. In Kerala, Tantric Hinduism is simply normative Hinduism, with Nambudiri Brahmins functioning as temple priests. The *Tantra-samuccaya* and the *Īśānaśivagurudeva-paddhati* function as ritual texts for the temples. The Nambudiris are traditional priests who follow the worship prescribed in these texts. Here Tantric forms of worship are integral to everyday practice. As we have seen, the Tantric tradition can be allocated generally as belonging to Śaiva, Śākta, or Vaiṣṇava traditions, but this is not the case in Kerala where worship incorporates a number of Brahmanical Śaiva and Vaiṣṇava deities such as Śiva, Viṣṇu, and Gaṇeśa, along with low-caste, regional goddesses that might be classed as Śākta. We are a long way here from the earlier, northern cremation ground traditions of the transgressive cults; Tantrism in Kerala is embedded with Vedic orthopraxy.

In Kerala, a Tantri is a temple priest: a Nambudiri Brahmin belonging to one of the families ranked high in a status hierarchy. These Tantris install icons in temples, but they do not perform daily rituals as that is the prerogative of different families of Pujaris. The Tantri can also function as a dispenser of *mantras*, or Mantri, to ward off misfortune, although this task is also performed by lower-caste priests. Thus, there is a tradition of offering cures for ailments through *mantra*, a *mantra-vāda* tradition, that accompanies the Tantric temple cult.

The precise origins of Tantrism in Kerala are unclear, although the tradition may have come directly from Kashmir, especially as many texts found in Kashmir are preserved in manuscripts in Malayalam script. Two key texts used in the temple ritual are the *Tantra-samuccaya* by Cēnnāsu Nārāyaṇam Nampū-tirippāṭu (fifteenth century CE) and the *Īśānaśiva-gurudeva-paddhati* from the twelfth century used by what are called Paddhati Brahmins.

Apart from mainstream religion, Tantrism in Kerala is found in lower-caste dance possession festivals, the *teyyam* festivals, which occur throughout Kerala in the dry season (Freeman 2003). In Kerala there is a broad distinction between social groups, one being classified as *savarṇa*, within the class/caste system, and the other classified as *avarṇa*, outside the class/caste system. The Nambudiri Brahmins are, naturally, *savarṇa*, all other groups being classified in the lower order, each having their own range of deities. While everyone

Figure 6.4. An early twentieth-century depiction of Gauḍīya Vaiṣṇavas performing kīrtana.

Figure 6.5. Nambudiri Brahmins in present-day Kerala.

reveres high-caste deities such as Aiyappan and Murukan, the low castes revere low-caste deities such as the local Goddess Māriyamman, the smallpox Goddess. The term *teyyam* may well be derived from the Sanskrit *deva* and refers to these ferocious deities, also associated with a class of gods called 'heroes' (*vīran*), protectors of the temples. These are 'hot' deities in contrast to the 'cool' gods of high-caste Hinduism (see Chapter 3, 'Popular Tantric Worship of the Goddess'). During the *teyyam* rite, the performer, dressed and adorned as the deity, will become possessed by the god and 'dance' around the shrine, giving her blessing to the community through being seen (giving her *darśanam*). This performance involves singing songs to the *teyyam* and reciting the story. These have been extensively studied by Rich Freeman and I refer the reader to his work.

For example, in Nīleśvaram there is a *teyyam* shrine owned by the weaver caste (Cāliya) and other groups perform the actual ritual, namely the washers,Vaṇṇān, who are professional sorcerers and the Malayans who practice Ayurvedic medicine. Each shrine also has a sacred grove attached to it with its own presiding deity. The festival lasts for about two days, with different deities being performed by the dancer chosen by the Cāliya community. The dancer moves from a shrine in front of the main houses of the gods, to the sacred surrounding area and even moves down the street to the local high-caste temple, where he symbolically knocks on the door but is barred entry. One deity is Viṣṇumūrti. He is a form of Viṣṇu and his story reflects that of Prahlāda. In the story, a wicked Nayar landlord forbade his servant from worshipping Viṣṇu, so Viṣṇu, in the form of Viṣṇumūrti, takes revenge on the landlord and kills him, reflecting how Narasiṃha kills the demon Hiraṇyakaśipu. Another example is Mūvāḷamkulī Cāmuṇḍī, a goddess who was protecting a Nambudiri against attack from a different Brahmin who ensnared her through the power of his *mantra*, imprisoned her in a copper vessel, and buried her in a hole. The goddess became furious, burst out of the pot, out of the hole, and chased the Brahmin up the road to the local Śiva temple for refuge. Here the goddess agreed

Figure 6.6. Viṣṇumūrti teyyam.

to calm down only if she would be installed beside Śiva in the shrine, which was duly accomplished as Freeman's definitive studies show.

There are other deities whose stories are performed, the last of whom is Guḷigan, the invisible planet who causes disasters. He is associated with Yama, the god of death, who in turn is associated with the planet Pluto. The dancer parades around the shrine, out to the temple of Śiva, and back to the shrine where offering of palm wine or toddy are made and a chicken sacrificed, the chicken's blood mixed with dyed water and that poured on the ground as a blood offering (*bali*) to the deity. With the offering, this particular *teyyam* performance ends.[4]

We see then that Tantric tradition pervades all levels of society in Kerala, from high-caste Nambudiri Brahmins to low-caste *teyyam* dance possession rites as Freeman shows. Indeed, there is even a Tantric school to teach young boys the craft of being a Tantri and Pujari, of being a temple priest. In Kerala there is no contradiction or tension between the Tantric tradition and the Vedic. The Nambudiri Brahmins are famous for their knowledge of the Vedas, specifically by its recitation off by heart, and the way they pass this knowledge on through the generations.[5] The traditions are distinguished through the different families who hand them down.

The Spread of Hindu Tantric Traditions to South-East Asia

Hinduism is in evidence in South-East Asia from around

4 On the *teyyam* tradition see the work of Rich Freeman. A good place to start is Rich Freeman, 'The Teyyam Tradition of Kerala', in *The Wiley-Blackwell Companion to Hinduism*, 2nd edition, ed. Gavin Flood, 307–322 (Oxford: Wiley-Blackwell, 2022).

5 See Frits Staal, *Nambudiri Veda Recitation* (The Hague: Mouton, 1961).

the sixth century CE but what we would recognise as Tantric forms of Hinduism begin to appear from the ninth century. The spread of Hinduism seems to have followed trade routes, along the Silk Road to China and by sea routes via South-East Asia, where local leaders adopted affiliation to Hindu deities who were linked to clans and ancestors such that kings became embodiments of those gods. In Khotan in North-West China Tantric Śaiva images have been found at the fortress of Dandean Oilik on the Silk Road, for example, an ithyphallic Maheśvara with three heads would have been a protector of the Buddhist monks.[6] The kingdoms in South-East Asia were also adherent to Tantric Śaivism. The Khmer kingdom in modern day Cambodia, the Cham kingdom in Indo-China, and the kingdoms of Java and Bali all worshipped the Tantric Śiva. The Khmer kingdom erected temples to Śiva and Viṣṇu, aligning state power to those deities. Angkor Wat was built in the twelfth century and, although it became a Buddhist temple, originally it was consecrated to Viṣṇu. Indeed, the Khmer kingdom adopted not only Śaivism but the Pāñcarātra form of Vaiṣṇavism, as well as Vajrayāna Buddhism from its rise in the eighth century to its demise in the thirteenth, after which time the dominant religion came to be Theravāda Buddhism. Śaivism was also the religion of the kingdom east of the Khmers, Champa, that occupied the coastal region and the highlands of Cochin-China through to the seventeenth century.[7] Śaivism entered the Khmer kingdom in two waves: first that of the Ati Mārga in around the sixth century and then that of the Mantra Mārga from the eleventh to fourteenth centuries.

There is an abundance of inscriptional evidence in Old

---

6 Imma Ramos, *Tantra: Enlightenment to Revolution* (London: British Museum, 2020), p. 117.

7 Sanderson, 'The Śaiva Age', 44.

Khmer and Khmer Sanskrit and scriptural evidence too, along with archaeological and architectural evidence. King Sūrya-varman I (*r.c.* 1002–1050), for example, wrote a manual of Śaiva ritual (a *paddhati*). When Śaivism was adopted by the Khmers it was not regarded as exclusive, in the sense of necessarily erasing any previous religion, but rather absorbed earlier traditions into itself. These were the tradition of local spirits (*neak ta*) that were relegated to a lower position in the hierarchy of deities, the higher – such as forms of Śiva – being adopted by the ruling elites. Sanderson mentions the possible names of these early deities, some of whom are referred to simply as 'my Venerable Lord/Lady'.[8]

Within the Khmer court and kingdom, orthodox Vedic Brahmanism was present in adherence to *śruti* (the Vedic revelation) and *smṛti* (secondary revelation of the law books); the Brahmins who followed these were the Śrautas and the Smārtas. The king – such as Rājendravarman (*r.* 944–968) – would employ such Brahmins to perform rites, especially the prestigious Soma sacrifice for which sixteen Śrauta priests needed to be present.[9] We know from Nepal that kings performed elaborate sacrifices with many Brahmins making offerings into many sacred fires for a period of forty-nine days. This seems also to have been done by the Khmer kings and inscriptions describe the sun being blocked out by the fires of these rites, which, as Sanderson observes, in the light of evidence from Nepal seems 'less like poetic exaggeration'.[10] This king also praises the two kings who founded the unified Angkor dynasty, Yaśovarman I (889–910) and Jayavarman II (802–835), for

8 Alexis Sanderson, 'The Śaiva Religion among the Khmers', 380, *Bulletin de l'Ecole française d'Extrême-Orient* 90–91 (2003): 349–462.

9 Ibid.

10 Ibid., 383.

their commitment to the sacred texts. There is also record of Brahmins conducting life-cycle ceremonies (*saṃskāra*).

We know that Brahmins from India went to the Khmer kingdom where they became integrated into the society and sometimes married into royalty. While the Brahmins and the rulers were the dominant social groups, there was no caste system, as we know it from India, in which there are untouchable castes who are polluting and must live outside of the boundary of the village. The Khmer was a slave society, as was India, but slaves were not polluting.[11] So, when Tantric Śaivism and the Pāñcarātra became embedded within Khmer society, it was a religion that impacted upon the elite ruling classes. We are a long way here from any cremation ground origins. The Khmer kings clearly performed straightforward Brahmanical, Vedic rites but employed Śaiva priests in addition, to perform Tantric Śaiva rites of initiation and empowerment, for which these priests were given land and slaves, golden palanquins, along with other royal insignia. There was also the gradual formation of the country itself as sacred to Śiva. Place names dedicated to Śiva in India are recapitulated in Khmer, for example Bhadreśvara is named after a place of the same name in northern India. There are also sacred places associated with Śiva, in particular the spontaneous phallic emblems of Śiva, the self-manifested *liṅga* (*svayambhū-liṅga*), which are identified with rocks and mountains. Mount Phu Kao in Khmer is one such symbol; it was given special status by King Jayavarman I, who decreed that no animal should be killed upon it, and prohibited riding about on it and extravagant behaviour, as well as the feeding of dogs or chickens. That is, this mountain is sacred and is to be set aside from normal activity; it is recorded as being the sustainer of the king. Sūryavarman

11 Ibid., 397–402.

I performed austerities in the vicinity of the mountain and installed *liṅgas* in temples after that, such austerity and vision of Śiva being the legitimising of furthering conquest. Indeed, this pattern of solitary asceticism by the king and the gaining of power thereby is attested throughout South-East Asia.[12] There also is a kind of economy here in that the Śaiva gurus who would initiate the king would receive lavish gifts as a donation. These gifts, they in turn would donate to the temple and *liṅga* at places like Bhadreśvara, building reservoirs, founding hermitages, and creating religious endowments. For example, Divākarapaṇḍita, the guru of King Sūryavarman II (*r.* 1115–1150), was given riches after initiating him, performing an annual Vedic sacrifice, and teaching him the Śaiva scriptures. The guru visited five sacred sites, giving gold palanquins to the deities installed in those temples, where he also had a reservoir excavated and founded a hermitage, giving it slaves and surrounding villages.[13]

Śaivism was evidently the dominant and royal religion of the Khmer kingdom. The kings adopted it, and it seems to have arrived in two waves, the first of the Ati Mārga and the second of the Mantra Mārga of the Śaiva Siddhānta with the *Niḥśvāsa-tattva-saṃhitā* and the *Parameśvara* (see Chapter 2) as the two key texts that were transmitted, but connection with India seems to have been lost outside of these impacts. There is no Bhairava cult in Khmer although that did exist in Java, and there were no Tantric Goddess cults. The Khmers adopted the religion but not some other Indian features such as caste and food restrictions. They were not prepared to adopt Brahmanical dietary restrictions, especially vegetarianism, and their traditional social structure, particularly inheritance and property

12 Ibid., 417–418.

13 Ibid., 420.

Figure 6.7. Kbal Spean, 'the valley of one-thousand ***liṅgas****', Ankor, Cambodia.*

rights, remained intact. They did adopt the Brahmin/non-Brahmin distinction but that is all. So, there is no caste in the Khmer kingdom but different lineages, and the term *varṇa* refers to professional groups rather than endogamous social segments.

While the religion of the court was initially Śaivism and Vaiṣṇavism, with Buddhism later adopted, the lower social levels worshipped local spirits. But there was also popular worship of Śiva by the sixth century, as we know from a Chinese monk visiting the region. He said the religion of the country was of Maheśvara, namely Śiva. There was also adherence to the Śivadharma corpus of literature, notably the *Śiva-dharmottara* whose manuscripts are dated between the ninth and eleventh centuries. There was devotion to these texts among the Khmer laity and Sūryavarman I was said to be skilled in the six-fold rite, a ritual of *liṅga* worship for the laity.[14] This rite the king would perform each day, but he would not need to perform further Tantric rites, even if initiated, because kings were exempt. The lay religion involved giving a third or a sixth of one's income to temples for which one would gain merit, in particular residence in heaven, such as *rudra-loka,* for oneself and one's family. The merit gained would be shared by one's dependents.

Śaivism also penetrated into Vaiṣṇavism. Evidence for this is seen at a Vaiṣṇava temple at Saṃkrāntapada with the use of Śaiva door guardians Nandin and Mahākāla instead of the Vaiṣṇava guardians Caṇḍa and Pracaṇḍa. Also, at Angkor Wat, the original temple was to Viṣṇu but we find a depiction of thirty-seven hells found in Śaiva texts depicted at the base of the temple. Even Mahāyāna Buddhism that is adopted later by the Khmer kings bears the influence of Śaivism in the personalisation of Buddhist images by incorporating the king's name on them, and Buddhism never completely erased Śaivism and observance of the Dharmaśāstras from the court.[15] Jayavarman VII replaced Śaivism with Vajrayāna Buddhism, but Śaivism did return until its eventual demise with the fall of the Angkor kingdom when Theravāda Buddhism became adopted as the religion . Although Jayavarman VII was an enthusiastic supporter of Buddhism, he is described on inscriptions as having Śiva in his heart.[16] Even though Buddhism replaced Śaivism as the main courtly religion, it continued to live alongside both Śaivism and Vaiṣṇavism. Indeed, there seems to have been tolerance of the different traditions with even kings having multiple allegiance, as we find elsewhere. Religion is not

14 Ibid., 383.

15 Ibid., 241–245.

16 Ibid., 429–430.

exclusive even though each king would follow a dominant system, the system that would in the end deliver salvation. Thus, kings of Khmer might have a name of the heaven to which they would go given to them after their death. The posthumous names of Jayavarman V and VII is Mahāparamasaugatapada,[17] the one who has gone to the place (*pada*) of the Great, supreme Buddha (Sugata). There is also the local practice of putting king's names on *liṅgas* and representing the king and his wives in likenesses of Śiva and Durgā after their demise. Sanderson regards this not as an apotheosis but the king as a clone of the deity in the god's paradise. The king and his wives become a Rudra; they become *sarūpya*, having the same appearance. We can see this because they remain as devotees, carrying a fly whisk, which is an attribute of devotees. Sacred fires are also named as a permanent installation, which is not practised in India. We see on the panels of Angkor Wat the king going to war with the sacred fire and the priest (*rāja-purohita*) in a palanquin.

So Tantric Śaivism was the dominant religion of the court of the kings of Khmer and the surrounding kingdoms before the arrival of Buddhism, Islam, and Christianity. It also existed in other regions of South-East Asia. Bali and Lombok bear witness to the spread of Śaivism, with ritual manuals for Śaiva Brahmin priests (*pēdanda siwa*) which display a form of the Śaiva Siddhānta.[18] There is also evidence of the older Ati Mārga in Java where in pre-Islamic times there was a cult of five Vedic sages (*ṛṣi*). This shows the adaptability of Tantrism to new contexts. From India, where there was a rigidly stratified society formed in the class/castes which were organised around a principle of purity and pollution, to Khmer where

17 Ibid., 429.

18 Ibid., 373.

there were certainly slaves, but where the notion of social pollution of the lower groups seems not have existed, Śaivism spread and adapted.

We have seen how Tantrism was deeply implicated in the societies and polities in which it emerged in South Asia, adapting to new contexts in South-East Asia. In particular it is associated with kingdoms and kings. Although some of the origins of transgressive Tantric practice may be found in cremation ground traditions supported by low castes and worship of low-caste deities, it became absorbed into mainstream Brahmanical tradition. In modern times, since the rise of Islam and since the emergence of modernity, Tantrism has undergone further transformation; it now has a presence, albeit in a very transformed way, in the modern, secularised West and now in what might be called global modernity. It is to this most recent stage of development that we must now turn.

Neo-Tantrism in the West

From the end of the nineteenth century, many Europeans and Americans reacted against the organised religion, mostly Christianity, of the West and sought spiritual wisdom in 'the East', going to India in particular to find teachers to impart this wisdom. What has become known as the Hindu Renaissance, a movement connected with Indian nationalism, linked Hinduism with ethics and the rejection of colonialism. Ram Mohan Roy (1772–1833) was particularly important in this, as was the later Swami Vivekananda (1863–1902), whose teacher was the interesting guru Ramakrishna (1836–1886). Ramakrishna was the priest of a Kālī temple at Dakshineshvar near Calcutta, who had intense religious experiences, going into trances akin to yogic absorption (*samādhi*). He is said to have had two teachers himself, an Advaitin, Totapuri, who taught him the non-duality of reality, and a female Tantric

Figure 6.8. Ramakrishna Paramahamsa (1836–1902).

Brahmin teacher, Bhairavī, who taught him to control the powers and desires in his body. From these teachers and from his own experience he is said to have discovered the unity of all religions in an experience of non-duality. For him, both Brahman and Kālī are different aspects of the same reality. Although Ramakrishna was Vivekananda's teacher, Vivekananda did not really take on board the Tantric side of Ramakrishna, although it was Vivekananda who paved the way for Tantric teachings to be brought to the West, through visiting the World Parliament of Religions and founding the Vedanta Society in 1895. The Theosophical Society founded in 1875 by the Russian psychic Madame Blavatsky and Colonel Olcott (1832–1907) sought to promote esoteric knowledge and was instrumental in transmitting Indian ideas to the West. But it was a British High Court judge, Sir John Woodroffe (1865–1936), who was very instrumental in transmitting Tantra to the West.[19] Under the name of Arthur Avalon he published editions of texts, translations, and books about Tantrism, most notably the *Serpent Power* and the *Garland of Letters*. These are scholarly works, especially given the paucity of knowledge about these traditions when he was writing.

Although Woodroffe's work was early scholarship of the tradition, with the explosion of interest in eastern spirituality and India during the 1960s, many Westerners became followers of Indian gurus and traditions. The Tantric traditions were not excluded and indeed became a fascination for young Westerners, attracted by their apparent rejection of normative ways of behaving and by the Kaula sexualised ritual. This tied in with the rejection of traditional mores and the celebration of unrestrained sexuality. There was a range in the teaching of gurus from India who appealed to Westerners. We have gurus who promoted non-dualism, such as Ramana Maharshi, Bhakti Vedanta Prabhupada promoting devotion to the theistic reality of Krishna and founding the Hare Krishna movement, and gurus promoting Tantric teachings. Of the latter, Swami Lakshmanjoo, a traditional Brahmin from Kashmir from a Śaiva family, was very learned and promoted the study through texts of the non-dual tradition of Śiva. Others were less scholarly, such as Swami Muktananda who went to the USA and started the Siddha Yoga Foundation. This was a Tantric tradition claiming

---

19 Kathleen Taylor, *Sir John Woodroffe, Tantra and Bengal: 'An Indian Soul in a European Body?'* (London: Taylor and Francis, 2001).

descent through a Kerala guru, Swami Nityananda. Cidvilas-ananda (a woman who was initially his translator) took over from Muktananda and runs the massive organisation based in Ganeshpuri, India and South Fallsburg, USA. Swami Nityananda also initiated a New York art dealer known as Rudi who was succeeded, after his death in a plane crash, by Swami Cetanananda who founded the Nityananda Institute and who had an ashram in Portland, Oregon. His teaching is based on his understanding of 'Kashmir Shaivism' although it absorbs elements from Buddhism as well. Cetanananda had met Swami Lakshmanjoo but we cannot really speak of a transmis-

Figure 6.9. Swami Lakshmanjoo (1907–1991).

Figure 6.10. Osho (1931–1990).

sion of Śaivism to the West. Lakshmanjoo was the last in a line of learned Brahmins who knew the texts and the teachings of his tradition that died with him in the sense of an initiatory lineage, although his tantric knowledge has influenced those who studied with him, including Alexis Sanderson, Bettina Bäumer, Lilian Silburn, and Mark Dyczkowski.

Osho (also known as Bhagwan Shree Rajneesh) presented his version of 'Tantra' as unrestrained sex on the catharsis model of psychoanalysis along with encounter groups in which members sometimes expressed violence as release of tension. Other Western gurus presented teachings indirectly linked to Tantra, such as Da Avabhasa Kalki (also known as

Figure 6.11. Da Avabhasa Kalki, also known as Da Free John (1939–2008).

Da Free John), Lee Lozowick, and Jean Klein.[20] These gurus have now passed away and that era of Western gurus is coming towards its close, although there are still advocates of Tantric sex workshops that can be found online in the spirit of Margo Anand, who was one of the first initiators of Western Tantra, as was Nik Douglas (1944–2012) whose book *Tantra Yoga* became famous in 1971. Alex Vartman, who founded the New Tantra, one of the largest Neo-Tantra schools, has also

20 Andrew Rawlinson, *The Book of Enlightened Masters* (Chicago: Open Court, 1997).

come under criticism for abuse.[21] In the context of contemporary sensibilities and issues of social justice, many of these gurus were exploitative of their disciples. It seems to have been the case that there were abuses of power, especially regarding female devotees, which in the light of the #MeToo movement would not be tolerated now and there have been exposures of such gurus and teachers. Much of these Tantric teachings have merged into a general New Age spirituality.[22]

There is an overlap between *haṭha* and Tantric *yoga* in the notion of the body and the *cakras* or centres of power located along its axis. But what seems to be unique to Neo-Tantra in the West is its association with sex and enhancing sexual pleasure in the belief that this is 'spiritual'. In eliding Tantric sex with pleasure, it thus fuses the traditions of Neo-Tantra and pleasure of which the *Kāma Sūtra* is the best example, although this confusion was not generally the case in traditional India where Tantric sex was in the service of power and/or salvation as we have seen. Clearly what is called 'Tantra' in the West bears some, but not much, resemblance to its traditional roots. While it has become a commodified product and consumerist option – advertisements for '*cakra* balancing' can be found easily online – this diminishes the important civilisational role Tantra played during the medieval period. Tantric traditions focused on Śiva were the dominant form of religious organisation, embedded within polities throughout South and South-East Asia. The Neo-Tantra that we are faced with now as a social reality is but a pale reflection of the important and rich tradition that Tantra once was.

---

21 B. Dominic, 'Behind the Scenes in the New Tantra', *Medium*, 10 December 2018, https://medium.com@beadominic/tnt-23fbd13b-ca3d.

22 Paul Heelas, *The New Age* (Oxford: Blackwell, 1996).

Figure 6.12. A Neo-Tantra workshop.

The Future

The heyday of Tantric civilisation, which spread from Kashmir to Cambodia and even further south to Indonesia, was in the post-Gupta period from around the seventh to thirteenth centuries. If we include the influence of Tantric Buddhism on Tibet, Mongolia, China, and Japan then the influence of Tantrism has been wide ranging. The differences between then and now are many but two in particular are important that have bearing on the question of the future of Tantric traditions.

First, the Tantric traditions were not obscure, esoteric, and minority religions, but mainstream traditions supported by the state. Tantric gurus were patronised by kings of Kashmir, Nepal, the Cola kings of the South, right the way through to the Khmer kings of what is now Cambodia. This was not a revolutionary movement from the social margins, even though some of the origins of Tantra might have been in lower-caste love magic along with possession and exorcism rites. Tantrism quite quickly became mainstream, within around eight generations, from its Śaiva origins in the ascetic and renouncer Ati Mārga to mainstream householder Śaiva Siddhānta. It declined with the rise of Islam, and arguably became more esoteric once it lost state support, although the kings of Nepal continued to be involved with Tantrism (Taleju was the Tantric Goddess who protected Nepal). That kings supported Tantric forms of religion we know through inscriptions recording land grants to monasteries and temples, as well as from the texts themselves, such as the *Netra Tantra* that describes rites for the protection of the royal family and the vanquishing of enemies. Tantrism is mostly an exoteric form of religion concerned with rituals, mostly supererogatory to Vedic or Smārta rites, and the protection of king and state. That there is an esoteric dimension is also true, as we see in the insistence on initiation and the subtle meditation practices it presents. The king was like a god and the king's realm like the sphere of a god's control.

Apart from the lack of state support, the second difference between contemporary Tantrism in the West and the traditional form is that the former was highly ritualistic. The Tantric practitioner took on extra rites on top of his householder ritual duties, in order to attain liberation at death – if a Śaiva Siddhāntin – or power and pleasure in higher worlds. The gnostic tradition of knowledge of Śiva through meditation and study could not thrive, or even survive, without the ritual system to support it. It is rituals – human action – that pass through the generations and Tantric knowledge is grounded in embodied, ritual practice. It is noteworthy that Lakshmanjoo was the last guru in the gnostic tradition of non-dualist Śaivism, the ritual tradition having died out probably towards the end of the nineteenth century, still being extant when the great Indologist Bühler visited the country.

Tantrism in Buddhism by contrast continues in a strong position. This is arguably because of the developed ritual system and institutional base in which it is grounded. Tibetan Buddhism is thriving, and in the West, in contrast to Hindu forms of Tantrism which lack the institutional and ritual support. Although Tantric traditions other than Tibetan Buddhism have transferred to the West – slowly at first with Arthur Avalon, then being taken up by Western esotericists such as Alistair Crowley and also theosophists – these have been generally of the gnostic variety. There has been some ritual transfer, and 'Tantric sex' has become aesthetic enhancement of pleasure through a ritual process. Whether these new forms of Tantrism have sustaining power through the generations (as the medieval Tantric traditions had) remains to be seen; but while some might be sceptical that they will, tantric traditions may continue to have significant impact on the human project into the future.

Discussion Topic: The Spread of Tantra

- What are the principal differences between Indian Tantrism in the medieval period and modern Neo-Tantrism in the West?

- Is caste relevant to understanding Hindu Tantra?

- Does Western Neo-Tantra have a coherent philosophy?

- Would Abhinavagupta recognize Tantric philosophy in Neo-Tantra?

Further Reading

Max Nihon. *Studies in Indian and Indo-Tibetan Tantrism.* Vienna: De Nobili Research Library 1994.

Jonathan Parry. *Death in Banares*. Cambridge: Cambridge University Press, 1993.

Andrew Rawlinson. *The Book of Enlightened Masters*. New York: Open Court, 1986.

APPENDIX 1

LIST OF MAJOR ŚAIVA SIDDHĀNTA THEOLOGIANS[1]

1. **Sadyojotis** (*c.* 675–725 CE) wrote commentaries on the *Svāyambhuva-sūtra-saṃgraha, Raurava-sūtra-saṃgraha,* both Siddhānta Tantras, and independent works the *Bhoga-kārikā,* the *Mokṣa-kārikā,* and the *Para-mokṣa-nirāsa-kārikā.* Also the *Tattva-traya-nirṇaya* and *Tattva-saṃgraha,* works based on the ontology of the *Svāyambhuva-*. In particular he wrote a notable independent treatise, the *Nareśvara-parīkṣā* on the doctrines of the soul and God.

2. **Bhaṭṭa Nārāyaṇakaṇṭha** (second half of tenth century) wrote a commentary on the *Mṛgendra* and a sub-commentary on Sadyojotis' *Svāyambhuva-vṛtti* and a long commentary on Sadyojotis' *Tattva-saṃgraha* (which is has not come down to us).

3. **Bhaṭṭa Rāmakaṇṭha** (second half of tenth century), the son of Nārāyaṇakaṇṭha, wrote commentaries on the doctrinal chapters of the *Kiraṇa, Sārdha-triśatika,* and the *Mataṅga-parameśvara.* He also wrote commentaries on four works of Sadyojotis, including the *Nareśvara-parīkṣā,* 'a work of rigorous philosophical

1 Based on Alexis Sanderson, 'Śaiva Literature', *Journal of Indological Studies* 24/25 (2012/2013): 1–113.

argument in which Rāmakaṇṭha attempts to establish Sadyojotis' Siddhānta against the positions of the Buddhists and others'.[2]

4. **Śrīkaṇṭha** (first half of the eleventh century), a Kashmirian who composed the *Ratna-traya-parīkṣā*.

5. **Bhojadeva, King Bhoja,** (first half of the eleventh century), a king in Mālava, wrote an independent treatise, the *Tattva-prakāśa* and a ritual exegesis, the *Siddhānta-sāra-paddhati*.

6. **Aghoraśiva** (mid twelfth century), in Cidambaram, the famous Śaiva temple in Tamilnadu, his works include a sub-commentary on Nārāyaṇakaṇṭha's commentary on the *Mṛgendra*, the *Mṛgendra-vṛtti-dīpikā*, commentaries on *Kālottara Tantra*, and on the doctrinal sections of Sadyojotis' works, the *Sarva-jñānottara*, the *Bhoga-kārikā*, and *Tattva-traya-nirṇaya*.

7. **Umāpatiśiva of Cidambaram** (mid–late twelfth century) who wrote commentaries on Tamil works that became incorporated into the Śaiva Siddhānta canon.

8. **Somaśambhu** (mid-eleventh century), abbot of the Golagī monastery in the kingdom of Kalacuris of Tripurī, who composed a ritual exegesis, the *Somaśambhu-paddhati*.

9. **Īśānaśivagurudeva** (eleventh century) in Kerala who composed the *Īśānaśivagurudeva-paddhati* used even today by Nambudiri Brahmins.

---

2 Sanderson, 'Śaiva Literature', 15–16.

Appendix 2

Hymn to the Circle of Deities Located in the Body (*Deha-stha-devatā-cakra-stotra*)

1. Oṃ homage to Gaṇeśa, Oṃ Holy, I praise Gaṇapati whose body is the exhaled breath, who is worshipped at the beginning of a hundred philosophical systems, who delights in the bestowal of desired wishes, and is praised by the circle of gods and anti-gods.

2. I praise Vaṭuka, known as the inhaled breath who removes people's pain; his feet are worshipped by the lineage of Perfected Ones, the hordes of Yoginīs, and the best heroes.

3. I always praise the pure, true master whose nature is attentiveness. By the power of his thought he reveals the universe as a path of Śiva for his devotees.

4. I praise Ānandabhairava, who is made of consciousness, whom the goddesses of the senses constantly worship in the lotus of the heart with the pleasures of their own sense-objects.

5. I praise Ānandabhairavī, whose nature is awareness, who continually performs the play of creation, manifestation, and tasting of the universe.

6. I constantly bow to her [the Goddess] as Brahmāṇī, whose nature is higher mind, situated on the petal of the Lord of gods (i.e. Indra in the east), who worships Bhairava with flowers of certainty.

7. I always praise the Mother Śāṃbhavī, whose nature is the ego. Seated on the petal of fire (Agni in the south-east), she performs worship to Bhairava with flowers of pride.

8. I always praise her as Kumārī, situated on the southern petal, whose essence is the mind, who gives offerings to Bhairava with flowers of discrimination.

9. I constantly bow down to her as Vaiṣṇavī, seated on the south-west petal, the power of whose nature is that which is heard, who makes offerings to Bhairava with flowers of sound.

10. I honour her as Vārāhī who possesses the sense of touch. Seated on the western petal she satisfies Bhairava with flowers of touch which captivate the heart.

11. I praise her as Indrāṇī whose body is sight, whose body is seated on the north-west petal, who worships Bhairava with the most beautiful and best of colours.

12. I bow to her as Cāmuṇḍā called the sense of taste, dwelling on the petal of Kubera (north); she constantly worships Bhairava with offerings of the varied six flavours.

13. I always bow down to her as Mahālakṣmī, known as the sense of smell who, seated on the petal of the Lord (Śiva in the north-east), praises Bhairava with varied fragrances.

14. I praise constantly the Lord of the body, who gives perfection known as the self, united with the thirty-six categories; he is worshipped as the Lord of the six systems of philosophy.

15. In this manner I praise the circle of deities innate within the body, always arising, continually present, the end of everything, vibrant, and the essence of experience. Thus, the sacred hymn to the circle of deities in the body is fully completed.

Glossary of Sanskrit Terms

antara/mānasa-yāga: Mental worship in the process of Tantric ritual.

āsana: Throne or seat of a deity visualised in meditation (*dhyāna*); *yoga* posture.

āveśa: Possession, especially by goddesses such as Yoginīs.

bāhya-yāga: Outer or external ritual.

bali: Blood offering, sacrifice.

bhakti: Devotion, love of God; not a quality emphasised in Tantra.

bhūta-śuddhi: Purification of the body through symbolically dissolving the elements (*bhūta*) within it in ritual meditation (*dhyāna*).

bīja: Seed syllable of a single phoneme in a mantra. Certain seed syllables are characteristic of Tantric mantras.

brahman: Absolute reality.

cakra: Location of significance within the body on a vertical axis. In Tantric *yoga*, the power of the Goddess rises through the body piercing these 'wheels' or 'circles'. The term also refers to cycles of realisation in the Krama system.

cit/citi: Absolute consciousness in non-dual Śaivism.

dhyāna: Meditation or visualisation in Tantric *yoga*, especially the visualisation of a deity.

dīkṣā: Initiation. In Tantra initiation by the master (*guru*) guarantees eventual liberation.

guru: Teacher who initiates the disciple. Tantric gurus are regarded as the embodiment of the deity and guarantee the disciple's liberation.

homa: Vedic fire ritual.

jīva: Soul bound in the process of reincarnation.

kāma: Desire, particularly sexual desire, a force that keeps beings bound in the cycle of reincarnation (*saṃsāra*). This is personified as a deity, burned to ashes by Śiva with his third eye.

karma: Action, particularly ritual action. In traditional Hinduism *karma* is the power that keeps beings bound in the cycle of reincarnation until liberation.

Krama: Tradition focused on the Goddess that advocates a metaphysics of the Nameless Goddess in the sky of consciousness (*cid-gagana*). The tradition also had a transgressive ritual dimension.

Kula: Tradition focused on the family of Goddesses expressed in particular Tantras.

Kuṇḍalinī: Power (*śakti*) located at the base of the trunk that once awakened through yoga or meditation practice, rises up through the body piercing the *cakras*, 'circles' or centres of significance. Once she reaches the crown of the head the body becomes filled with the nectar of immorality in one version.

maithuna: Sexual intercourse in Tantric ritual.

maṇḍala: Ritual diagram used in Tantric worship.

mantra: Sound formulas, often verses from scripture, the name of a deity, and seed syllables, used in Tantric ritual and meditation.

māyā: Material substrate of the perceived universe; a power occurring at the top of the impure cosmos in Tantric cosmology.

melaka: Meeting of transgressive Tantric practitioners involving group sex.

mokṣa: Liberation from the cycle of reincarnation; salvation.

mudrā: Ritual hand gesture; literally 'seal' expressed as a gesture in ritual.

nyāsa: Imposition of *mantras*, especially on the body thereby creating a divine body in ritual.

pāśa: Bond that binds the soul, namely the bond of the cosmos and reincarnation.

paśu: Soul, literally 'beast' or 'cow', in Śaivism.

pati: The absolute transcendent God, Lord Śiva.

pīṭha: Seats of power of the Goddess; pilgrimage centres such as Kāmākhya.

prāṇa: Breath, life-force.

pratyabhijñā: Recognition of one's identity with absolute consciousness in non-dualistic or 'Kashmir' Śaivism.

śakti: Power personified as the Goddess, in particular as the consort of Śiva.

śakti-pāta: Descent of power, grace, especially through initiation.

siddhi: Supernormal abilities attained through *yoga* and as gift from a deity.

śiva-tulya: Equality with Śiva, the goal of Śaiva Siddhānta.

Tāntrika: Follower of the Tantras.

tattva: Category in the hierarchical universe. In particular, the thirty-six tattvas in Śaivism.

utkrānti: Yogic suicide; transition of consciousness out from the physical body.

Vaidika: Follower of the orthodox Veda.

vyūha: Emanation of the supreme deity into further forms in the Pāñcarātra.

yajña: Sacrifice, making offerings to the fire.

yantra: Ritual diagram used in Tantric worship.

yoga: Practice. Within Tantra the word can refer to the classical Yoga of Patañjali, subtle Tantric yoga of Kuṇḍalinī, or erotic worship of transgressive Tantra.

References

Translations and Primary Sources

Abhinavagupta, *Tantrāloka,* 12 vols. Edited by M. S. Kaul. Srinagar: Kashmir Series of Texts and Studies, 1938 English translation by Mark Dyczkowski, 11 vols (Amazon, 2023).

Abhinavagupta, *Īśvarapratyabhijñāvimarśinī.* Edited and translated by R. C. Dwiwedi, K. C. Pandey, and K. A. Subramania Iyer, as *Bhāskarī,* Vol. 1 (Delhi: Motilal Banarsidass Publishers, 1986 [1938]).

Abhinavagupta, *Parā-triṃśikā-vivaraṇa.* Edition and translation by Jaideva Singh (Albany: SUNY Press, 1988).

Bakker, Hans and Peter Bisschop. 'Pāśupatasūtras 1.7–9 with the Commentary of Kauṇḍinya'. Unpublished, 2011.

Bansat-Boudon, Lyne and Kamalesha Datta Tripathi. *An Introduction to Tantric Philosophy: The Paramārthasāra of Abhinavagupta with the Commentary of Yogaraja.* London: Routledge, 2011.

Brahmayāmalatantra or Picumata, Vol. 2. *The Religious Obervance and Sexual Rituals of the Tantric Practitioner,* Chapters 3, 21, and 45. Edited and translated by Csaba Kiss. Pondichéry: Institut Français de Pondichéry, 2015.

Rauravāgama, Vols. 1–3. Edited by N. R. Bhatt. Pondichéry: Institut Français de Pondichéry, 1985.

Chakraborti, Haripada. *Pāśupata-sūtram with Pañcārtha-bhāṣya of Kauṇḍinya.*

Dehasthadevatācakrastotra, anon. H. Sri Ragunath Temple Manuscript Library, Jammu, pp. 205–206, 290–292. Copy courtesy of Alexis Sanderson. French translation by Lilian Silburn *Hymnes aux Kālī* (Paris: de Boccard, 1975). Text unattributed. Minor differences to the Jammu ms.

Dyczkowski, Mark S. G. *Manthānabhairavatantram, Kumārikākhaṇḍaḥ*, 12 vols. *The Section Concerning the Virgin Goddess*. Delhi: Indira Gandhi National Centre, 2009.

George, Christopher S. *The Caṇḍamahārośana-tantra: A Critical Edition and English Translation of Chapters I–VIII*. Harvard: American Oriental Society, 1974.

Goodall, Dominic. *Niḥśvāsatattva-saṃhitā: The Earliest Surviving Śaiva Tantra*, Vol. 1. *A Critical Edition and Annotated Translation of the Mūlasūtra, Uttarasūtra and Nayasūtra*. Pondichéry: Institut Français de Pondichéry, 2015.

Goodall, Dominic. *Bhaṭṭa Rāmakaṇṭha's Commentary on the Kiraṇatantra*, Vol. 1. Chapters 1–6. Pondichéry: Institut Français de Pondichéry, 1998.

Goodall, Dominic. *The Parākhyatantra: A Scripture of the Śaiva Siddhānta*. Pondichéry: Institut Français de Pondichéry, 2004.

Gupta, Sanjukta. *The Lakṣmī Tantra*. Leiden: Brill, 1972.

Hatley, Shaman. *The Brahmayāmalatantra or Picumata*, Vol. 1. Chapters 1–2, 39–40, and 83, *Revelation, Ritual, and Material Culture in an Early Śaiva Tantra*. Pondichéry: Institut Français de Pondichéry, 2018.

Īśānaśivagurudevapaddhati, 4 vols. Edited by Unni. Delhi: Srisatguru Publications, 1988.

Jayākhya Saṃhitā. Edited by Embar Krishnamacharya. Baroda: Gaekwad Sanskrit Series, 1967.

Jayanta Bhaṭṭa. *Nyāyamañjari of Jayanta Bhaṭṭa*. English translation by V. N. Jha. Delhi: Śrī Satguru Publications, 1995.

Jayantha Bhaṭṭa. *Āgamaḍambara*. Translated by Csaba Dezső, *Much Ado About Religion*. New York: Clay Sanskrit Library, 2005.

Kālottarāgama. Muktabodha Indological Library, Catalog number: M00248, Manuscript: IFP/EFEO transcript T0059. Copied from IFP/EFEO transcript T0059 which is from a MS belonging to the GOML, Madras, No. R 14343.

Krishnamacharya, E., ed. *Jayākhya-saṃhitā of the Pāñcarātra Āgama*. Baroda: Gaekwad Oriental Series, 1931.

Kṣemarāja, Commentary on the *Spanda Kārikās*. In *Spanda Kārikās: The Divine Creative Pulsation,* translated by Jaideva Singh. Delhi: Motilal Banarsidass Publishers, 1980.

Kṣemarāja. *Pratyabhijñāhṛdaya*. Translated by Jaydev Singh. Delhi: Motilal, 1980 and by Christopher D. Wallis, *The Recognition Sutras*, Mataayura Press, 2017.

Kubjikāmata-tantra. Critically edited by Teun Goudriaan and J. A. Schoterman. Leiden: Brill, 1988.

In Mataṅgaparameśvarāgama. Pondichéry: Institut Français de Pondichéry, 1977.

Nityakaula, NGMPP Reel No. B26/21a. DSCN 6586.

Rauravāgama. Vol. 1., edited by N. R. Bhatt. Pondichéry: Institut Français de Pondichéry, 1985.

Rocher, Ludo. *Jīmūtavāhana's Dāyabhāga: The Hindu Law of Inheritance in Bengal*. Oxford: Oxford University Press, 2001.

Secondary Sources

Acri, Andrea and Paolo E. Rosati (eds.), *Tantra, Magic, and Vernacular Religions in Monsoon Asia* (London: Routledge, 2023).

Bäumer, Bettina. *The Yoga of the Netra Tantra: 'Third Eye' and 'Overcoming Death'*. Shimla: Indian Institute of Advanced Study, 2019.

Bhatt, N. R. 'Introduction'. In *Mataṅgaparameśvarāgama*. Pondichéry: Institut Français de Pondichéry, 1977.

Bisschop, Peter. *Universal Śaivism: The Appeasement of All Gods and Powers in the Śāntyadhyāya of the Śivadharmaśāstra*. Leiden: Brill, 2018.

Bronkhorst, Johannes. *Greater Magadha: Studies in the Culture of Early India*. Leiden: Brill, 2007.

Brooks, D. *The Secret of the Three Cities*. Chicago: Chicago University Press, 1990.

Brunner, Hélène. *Somaśambhupaddhati*, Vol. 3 (Pondichéry: Institut Français, 1977), 'Introduction'.

Brunner, Hélène. 'Le Sādhaka, un personnage oublié du Śivaisme du Sud'. *Journal Asiatique*, 1975: 411–416.

Brunner, Hélène. 'Les Membres de Śiva'. *Études Asiatiques* 40, no. 2 (1986): 89–93.

Brunner, Hélène. 'Ātmārthapūjā versus Parārthapūjā in the Śaiva Tradition'. In *Sanskrit Tradition and Tantrism*, edited by T. Goudriaan, 1–23. Leiden: Brill, 1990.

Bühnemann, Gudrun. *Puja: A Study in Smarta Ritual*. Vienna: De Nobili Research Library, 1988.

Daniélou, Alain. *The Complete Kāmasūtra*. Rochester: Park Street Press, 1994.

Das, Rahul Peter. 'Problematic Aspects of Sexual Rituals of the Bauls of Bengal'. *Journal of the American Oriental Society* 112, no. 3 (1992): 388–432.

Davidson, Ronald M. *Indian Esoteric Buddhism: A Social History of the Tantric Movement*. New York: Columbia University Press, 2002.

Davis, R. *Ritual in an Oscillating Universe: Worshipping Śiva in Medieval India*. Princeton: Princeton University Press, 1991.

Derrett, Duncan M. 'A Juridical Fabrication of Early British India: The *Mahānirvāṇa Tantra*'. In *Essays in Classical and Modern Hindu Law*, Vol. 2. *Consequences of the Intellectual Exchange with Foreign Powers*, 197–242. Leiden: Brill, 1977.

Derrett, Duncan. *Studies in Hindu Law*. Turin: Indologica Taurensia, 1994.

Dimock, Edward. *The Place of the Hidden Moon*. Chicago: University of Chicago Press, 1966.

Dominic, B. 'Behind the Scenes in the New Tantra'. *Medium*, 10 December 2018. https://medium.com@beadominic/tnt-23fbd13bca3d.

Doniger, Wendy. 'The Body in Hindu Texts'. In *Religion and the Body*, edited by Sarah Coakley, 167–184. Cambridge: Cambridge University Press, 1989.

Dumont, Louis, 'World Renunciation in Indian Religions'. In *Homo Hierarchicus: The Caste System and its Implications*, 267–286. Chicago: University of Chicago Press, 1979.

Dupuche, John R. *Abhinavagupta: The Kula Ritual as Elaborated in Chapter 29 of the Tantrāloka*. Delhi: MLBD, 2003.

Dyczkowski, Mark S. G. *The Doctrine of Vibration: An Analysis of the Doctrines and Practices of Kashmir Shaivism*. Albany: SUNY Press, 1987.

Eck, Diana. *Banaras: City of Light*. London: Routledge, 1984.

Eliade, Mircea. *Shamanism: Archaic Techniques of Ecstasy*, translated by Willard. R. Trask. Princeton: Princeton University Press, 1964.

Filliozat, Jean. 'Introduction'. In *Rauravāgama*. Vol. 1. Edited by N. R. Bhatt. Pondichéry: Institut Français de Pondichéry, 1985.

Flood, Gavin. *Body and Cosmology in Kashmir Śaivism*. San Francisco: Mellen Research University Press, 1993.

Flood, Gavin. 'The Meaning and Context of the Puruṣārthas'. In *The Fruits of Our Desiring: An Enquiry into the Ethics of the Bhagavadgītā for Our Times*, edited by Julius Lipner, 11–27. Calgary: Bayeux, 1997.

Flood, Gavin. 'The Purification of the Body in Tantric Ritual Representation'. *Indo-Iranian Journal* 45 (2002): 25–43.

Flood, Gavin. *The Tantric Body*. London: Tauris Press, 2006.

Flood, Gavin. *Religion and the Philosophy of Life*. Oxford: Oxford University Press, 2019.

Flood, Gavin. *Hindu Monotheism*. Cambridge: Cambridge University Press, 2020.

Flood, Gavin, Bjarne Wernicke-Olesen, and Rajan Khatiwoda. *Tantra in Medieval India and Nepal: An Annotated Edition and Translation of the Tantra of the Eye, the Netra Tantra*, Vol. 1. London: Routledge, forthcoming.

Freeman, Rich. 'The Teyyam Tradition of Kerala'. In *The Wiley-Blackwell Companion to Hinduism*, 2nd edition. Edited by Gavin Flood, 307–326. Oxford: Blackwell, 2003.

Goet, Prema. *Against the Grain*. London: Utkranti Press, n.d.

Goodall, Dominic. 'Introduction'. In *Bhaṭṭa Rāmakaṇṭha's Commentary on the Kiraṇatantra*, Vol. 1, Chapters 1–6. Pondichéry: Institut Français de Pondichéry, 1998.

Goodall, Dominic. 'Tantric Śaivism and Bhakti: How are They Related?' Paper given at the International Workshop-cum-Conference, 'Archaeology of Bhakti: Royal Bhakti, Local Bhakti', organised by Emmanuel Francis, Valérie Gillet, and Charlotte Schmid at the EFEO Centre in Pondichéry from 31 July to 13 August 2013.

Goodall, Dominic. 'Introduction'. In *Śaiva Rites of Expiation: A First Edition and Translation of Trilocanaśiva's Twelfth-century Prāyaścittasamuccaya*, edited by R. Sathyanarayan, 15–63. Pondichéy: Institut Français de Pondichéry, 2015.

Gupta, Sanjukta, and Richard Gombrich. 'Kings, Power and the Goddess'. *South Asia Research* 6, no. 2 (1986): 123–138.

Halbfass, Wilhelm. *India and Europe: An Essay in Understanding*. Albany: SUNY Press, 1988.

Hanneder, Jürgen. *Abhinavagupta's Philosophy of Revelation: Mālinīślokavārttika I, 1–399*. Groningen: Egbert Forsten, 1998.

Hayes, Glen. 'The Necklace of Immortality'. In *Tantra in Practice*, edited by David White, 308–325. Princeton: Princeton University Press, 2000.

Heelas, Paul. *The New Age*. Oxford: Blackwell, 1996.

Kulke, Hermann and Dietmar Rothermund. *A History of India*. London: Routledge, 1990.

La Barre, Weston. *The Ghost Dance: Origins of Religion*. London: Allen and Unwin, 1972.

Leslie, Julia. *The Perfect Wife: The Orthodox Hindu Woman According to the Strīdharmapaddhati of Tryambakayajvan.* Oxford: Oxford University Press, 1989.

Linder, Sylvia Schwarz. *The Philosophical and Theological Teachings of the Pādmasaṃhitā.* Vienna: Österreichische Akademie der Wissenschaften, 2014.

Lorenzen, David. *The Kāpālikas and Kālāmukhas: Two Lost Śaivite Sects.* Delhi: Motilal Banarsidass, 1991 [1972].

Malamoud, Charles. 'On the Rhetoric and Semantics of the Puruṣārthas'. In *Way of Life: King, Householder, Renouncer*, edited by T. N. Madan. Delhi: Motilal Banarsidass, 1988.

Mallinson, James and Péter-Daniel Szántó. *The Amṛtasiddhi and Amṛtasiddhimūla: The Earliest Texts of the Haṭhayoga Tradition.* Pondichéry: Institut Français de Pondichéry, 2021.

Matilal, B. K., ed. *Moral Dilemmas in the Mahābhārata.* Delhi: MLBD, 1989.

Matsubara, M. *Pāñcarātra Saṃhitās and Early Vaiṣṇava Theology.* Delhi: MLDB, 1994.

Monier-Williams, Monier. *Hinduism.* London: Society for the Promotion of Christian Knowledge, 1880.

Nemec, John. *The Ubiquitous Śiva: Somānanda's Śivadṛṣṭi and his Tantric Interlocutors.* Oxford: Oxford University Press, 2011, volume II (Oxford: Oxford University Press, 2021).

Nihon, Max. *Studies in Indian and Indo-Tibetan Tantrism.* Vienna: De Nobili Research Library, 1994.

O'Connell, Joseph and Rembert Lutjeharms. *Caitanya Vaiṣṇavism in Bengal: Social Impact and Historical Implications.* London: Routledge, 2018.

Olivelle, Patrick. *The Āśrama System: The History and Hermeneutics of a Religious Institution.* Oxford: Oxford University Press, 1993.

Olivelle, Patrick. *The Laws of Manu*. Oxford: Oxford University Press, 2009.

Padoux, André. *Vāc: The Concept of the Word in Selected Hindu Tantras*, translated by Jacques Gontier. Albany: SUNY Press, 1990.

Padoux, André. *The Hindu Tantric World: An Overview*. Chicago: University of Chicago Press, 2017.

Pandey, Rajbali. *Hindu Saṃskāras: Socio-Religious Study of the Hindu Sacraments*. Delhi: Motilal Banarsidass, 1969.

Parry, Jonathan. *Death in Banares*. Cambridge: Cambridge University Press, 1993.

Pollock, Sheldon. 'The Sanskrit Cosmopolis, 300–1300 CE: Transculturation, Vernacularization, and the Question of Ideology'. In *Ideology and Status of Sanskrit: Contributions to the History of the Sanskrit Language*, edited by Jan E. M. Houben, 197–247. Leiden: Brill, 1996.

Rajneesh, Bhagwan Shree. *The Book of Secrets 1: Discourses on the Vigyan Bhairav Tantra*. Poona: Rejneesh Foundation, 1974.

Ramos, Imma. *Tantra: Enlightenment to Revolution*. London: British Museum, 2020.

Rastelli, Marion. *Philosophisch-theologische Grundanschaungen der Jayākhyasaṃhitā*. Vienna: Österrichischen Akademie der Wissenschaften, 1999.

Ratié, Isabelle. *Le Soi et l'Autre: Identité, difference et altérité dans la philosophie de la Pratyabhijñā*. Leiden: Brill, 2011.

Rawlinson, Andrew. *The Book of Enlightened Masters*. New York: Open Court, 1986.

Samuels, Geoffrey. *The Origins of Yoga and Tantra: Indic Religions to the Thirteenth Century*. Cambridge: Cambridge University Press, 2008.

Sanderson, Alexis. 'Purity and Power among the Brahmans of Kashmir'. In *The Category of the Person,* edited by Michael Carrithers, Steven Collins, and Steven Lukes, 190–216. Cambridge: Cambridge University Press, 1985.

Sanderson, Alexis. 'Śaivism and the Tantric Traditions'. In *The World's Religions,* edited by S. Sutherland, L. Houlden, P. Clarke, and F. Hardy, 660–704. London: Routledge, 1988.

Sanderson, Alexis. 'Maṇḍala and Āgamic Identity in the Trika of Kashmir'. In *Maṇḍala et Diagrammes Rituel dans l'Hindouisme,* edited by André Padoux. Paris: CNRS, 1986.

Sanderson, Alexis. 'The Visualization of the Deities of the Trika'. In *L'Image Divine: culte et meditation dans l'Hindouisme,* edited by André Padoux, 23–40. Paris: CNRS, 1990.

Sanderson, Alexis. 'The Doctrine of the Mālinīviyajottaratantra'. In *Ritual and Speculation in Early Tantrism,* edited by T. Goudriaan, 281–312. Albany: SUNY Press, 1992.

Sanderson, Alexis. 'Meaning in Tantric Ritual'. In *Essais sur le Rituel III: Colloque du Centenaire de la Section des Sciences religieuses de l'École Pratique des Hautes Études,* edited by A.-M. Blondeau and K. Schipper, 15–95. Louvain/Paris: Peeters, Bibliothèque de l'École des Hautes Études, Sciences Religieuses, Volume CII, 1995.

Sanderson, Alexis. 'The Śaiva Religion among the Khmers'. *Bulletin de l'Ecole française d'Extrême-Orient* 90–91 (2003): 349–462.

Sanderson, Alexis. 'Religion and the State: Śaiva Officiants in the Territory of the King's Brahmanical Chaplain'. *Indo-Iranian Journal* 47 (2004): 229–300.

Sanderson, Alexis. 'The Śaiva Exegesis of Kashmir'. In *Mélanges tantriques à la mémoire d'Hélène Brunne / Tantric Studies in Memory of Hélène Brunner*, Collection Indologie 106, edited by D. Goodall and A. Padoux, 231–444 (Pondicherry: IFI / EFEO, 2007).

Sanderson, Alexis. 'The Śaiva Age'. In *Genesis and Development of Tantrism*, edited by Shingo Einoo, 41–250. Tokyo: University of Tokyo, 2009.

Sanderson, Alexis. 'Śaiva Literature'. *Journal of Indological Studies* 24/25 (2012/2013): 1–113.

Sanderson, Alexis. 'Tolerance, Exclusivity, Inclusivity, and Persecution in Indian Religion during the Early Mediaeval Period'. In *In Honoris Causa: Essays in Honour of Aveek Sarkar*, edited by John Makinson, 155–224. London: Allen Lane, 2015.

Sanderson, Alexis. 'How Public was Śaivism?' Nina Mirnig, Marion Rastelli, and Vincent Eltschinger (eds.), *Tantric Communities in Context* (Vienna: Osterreichische Akademie der Wissenshcaften, 2019), pp. 1-48.

Sanderson, Alexis. *Tantrāloka: Handout for Introductory Lecture*, OCHS, 26 January 2020.

Schrader, Otto. *Introduction to the Pāñcarātra*. Madras: Adyar Library, 1973 [1916].

Schmid, Charlotte. *Le Don de voir*. Pondichéry: Institut Français, 2016.

Serbaeva, Olga. 'The Jayadrathayāmala: Varieties of Melaka'. In *Goddesses in Tantric Hinduism: History, Practice and Doctrine*, edited by Bjarne Wernicke-Olsen, 51–73. London: Routledge, 2016.

Slouber, Michael. *Early Tantric Medicine*. Oxford: Oxford University Press, 2017.

Smith, Daniel H. S. *Descriptive Bibliography of the Printed Texts of the Pāñcarātrāgama*. Baroda: Gaekwads Oriental Series, 1980.

Stein, B. *Peasant, State and Society in Medieval South India*. Delhi: Oxford University Press, 2002.

Taylor, Kathleen. *Sir John Woodroffe, Tantra and Bengal: 'An Indian Soul in a European Body?'* London: Taylor and Francis, 2001.

Thapar, Romila. *Somnath: The Many Voices of a History*. New Delhi: Viking, 2004.

Tofflin, Gérard. *Le Palais et le Temple: La fonction royale dans la vallée du Nepal*. Paris: CNRS, 1993.

Urban, Hugh B. *The Power of Tantra: Religion, Sexuality and the Politics of South Asian Studies*. London: Tauris Press, 2010.

Vasudeva, Somadeva. *The Yoga of the Mālinīvijayottaratantra*. Pondichéry: Institut d'Indologie, 2004.

Wales, Horace Geoffrey Quaritch. *Siamese State Ceremonies: Their History and Function*. London: Bernard Quaritch, 1931.

Wallis, Christopher D. *Tantra Illuminated: The Philosophy, History, and Practice of a Timeless Tradition*. Mattamayura Press, 2013.

Watson, A. *The Self's Awareness of Itself: Bhaṭṭarāmakaṇṭha's Arguments against the Buddhist Doctrine of No-self*. Vienna: de Nobili, 2006.

Watson, Alex, Dominic Goodall, and S. L. P. Anjaneya Sharma. *An Enquiry into the Nature of Liberation: Bhaṭṭa Rāmakaṇṭha's Parmokṣanirāsakārikāvṛtti: A Commentary on Sadyojyotiḥ's Refutation of Twenty Conceptions of the Liberated State (Mokṣa)*. Pondichéry: Institut Français de Pondichéry, 2013.

Wernicke-Olesen, Bjarne and Silje Lyngar Einarsen. 'Übungswissen in Yoga, Tantra und Asketismus'. In *Übungswissen in Religion und Philosophie: Produktion, Weitergabe, Wandel*, edited by Almut-Barbara Renger and Alexandra Stellmacher, 241–257. Berlin: Lit Verlag, 2018.

Wernicke-Olsen, Bjarne and Silje Lyngar Einarsen, eds. *Hovedvaeket om Haṭhayoga Svātmarāmas Haṭhapradīpikā*. Holberg: Narayana Press, 2022.

White, David, ed. *Tantra in Practice*. Princeton: Princeton University Press, 2000.

White, David. *The Kiss of the Yoginī: Tantric Sex in its South Asian Contexts*. Chicago: Chicago University Press, 2003.

INDEX

N

U

V

W

Y

MANDALA

An Imprint of MandalaEarth
PO Box 3088
San Rafael, CA 94912
www.MandalaEarth.com

Find us on Facebook:
www.facebook.com/MandalaEarth

Publisher Raoul Goff
Associate Publisher Phillip Jones
Publishing Director Katie Killebrew
Editorial Assistant Amanda Nelson
Creative Director Ashley Quackenbush
VP Manufacturing Alix Nicholaeff
Sr Production Manager Joshua Smith
Sr Production Manager, Subsidiary Rights Lina s Palma-Temena

Mandala Publishing would also like to thank Steve Turrington for copyediting this series.

ISBN: 979-8-88762-113-5
ISBN: 979-8-88762-142-5 (Export Edition)

Manufactured in India by Insight Editions
10 9 8 7 6 5 4 3 2 1

Library of Congress Cataloging-in-Publication Data

Names: Flood, Gavin D., 1954- author.
Title: Tantric knowledge : philosophy, history, practice / Gavin Flood.
Description: San Rafael, CA : Mandala Publishing, 2025. | Series: The Oxford Centre for Hindu Studies Mandala Publishing series | Includes bibliographical references and index. | Summary: "This book is intended as a general introduction to the history of Tantric traditions: what it is, where it fits into the history of South Asia and beyond, what its links are to Hinduism and Buddhism, and how contemporary Tantra transforms the older tradition."-- Provided by publisher.
Identifiers: LCCN 2024021505 (print) | LCCN 2024021506 (ebook) | ISBN 9798887621135 (hardcover) | ISBN 9798887621142 (ebook)
Subjects: LCSH: Tantrism. | Tantric Buddhism. | Hinduism. | South Asia--Religion,
Classification: LCC BL1283.84 .F55 2024 (print) | LCC BL1283.84 (ebook) | DDC 294.5/514--dc23/eng/20240627
LC record available at https://lccn.loc.gov/2024021505
LC ebook record available at https://lccn.loc.gov/2024021506

ROOTS of PEACE
REPLANTED PAPER

Mandala Publishing, in association with Roots of Peace, will plant two trees for each tree used in the manufacturing of this book. Roots of Peace is an internationally renowned humanitarian organization dedicated to eradicating land mines worldwide and converting war-torn lands into productive farms and wildlife habitats. Roots of Peace will plant two million fruit and nut trees in Afghanistan and provide farmers there with the skills and support necessary for sustainable land use.

FSC
www.fsc.org
MIX
Paper | Supporting responsible forestry
FSC® C016779